DOCU-FICTIONS OF WAR

DOCU-FICTIONS OF WAR

U.S. INTERVENTIONISM IN FILM AND LITERATURE

Tatiana Prorokova

UNIVERSITY OF NEBRASKA PRESS   LINCOLN

© 2019 by the Board of Regents of
the University of Nebraska

Library of Congress Cataloging-in-Publication Data
Names: Prorokova, Tatiana, author.
Title: Docu-fictions of war: U.S. interventionism
in film and literature / Tatiana Prorokova.
Description: Lincoln: University of Nebraska Press,
[2019] | Includes bibliographical references and index.
Identifiers: LCCN 2018048121
ISBN 9781496207746 (cloth: alk. paper)
ISBN 9781496214256 (paper: alk. paper)
ISBN 9781496214447 (epub)
ISBN 9781496214454 (mobi)
ISBN 9781496214461 (pdf)
Subjects: LCSH: American literature—History and
criticism. | War in literature. | War films—United
States—History and criticism. | United States—Foreign
relations—1989– | Intervention (International law)
Classification: LCC PS169.W27 P76 2019 |
DDC 810.9/358—dc23 LC record available
at https://lccn.loc.gov/2018048121

Set in Questa by Mikala R. Kolander.
Designed by N. Putens.

CONTENTS

ACKNOWLEDGMENTS

First and foremost, I want to express gratitude to Carmen Birkle, for her invaluable guidance and constant support. I also immensely appreciate her help with several grants I received, which facilitated my travel to conferences worldwide that contributed to the work on this project and also helped me grow professionally. I want to thank Philipp Gassert for his insightful comments.

A large contribution to the advance of this project was my stay in 2016 as a visiting scholar at the University of South Alabama, at the Center for the Study of War and Memory and the English Department, which was generously covered by the Marburg University Research Academy. I would like to thank Steven Trout and Susan McCready for inviting me to come, and also for their professional support throughout my stay. I thank the English Department and the Department of Foreign Languages at USA for their warm welcome. To Ekaterina Zakharova, Nick Gossett, Christine Rinne, Madeline Trout, and Hank Hodde, I say thank you all for making my stay in Mobile such a great experience!

I would also like to thank Georgiana Banita for offering the course "All Work and No Play? The Films of Stanley Kubrick," which I attended as a master's student at the University of Bamberg, Germany. The discussion of *Full Metal Jacket* in one of our sessions during the summer semester of 2013 was perhaps the moment I first became interested in war studies.

Last but not least, I say a big thank-you to my family, who have always had faith in me and have been supportive of what I have done.

DOCU-FICTIONS OF WAR

Introduction

Reconsidering the Status of Fictional and Documentary Narratives on War

Fiction and documentary are the two categories into which both film and literature can be broadly divided. One traditionally associates works with invented plots with fiction, and those that claim to reflect real events with documentary. Documentary is a genre that *documents* historical events. Therefore works of historical writing are the most illustrative in this regard. Yet the genre of documentary encompasses other media that record reality, historically and in the present. These media *might* include documentary film, memoir, autobiography, television news reporting, and written journalism. I use "might" to underscore the rather inconsistent nature of the documentary genre because texts of various media, including those listed above, might be *fiction that rhetorically claims to be nonfiction* and thus only purport to be documentary. It is believed that fiction, as opposed to documentary, is the genre that is primarily based on imagination and is thus disconnected from historical, everyday, or any future reality.[1] Hence, whereas documentary can be considered a "serious" genre, fiction is merely the expression of one's imagination that has been translated into a literary or cinematic work. In other words, the two modes, fiction and documentary, are

1

in a conventional sense dichotomous, and remain persistently so in particular subject areas.[2]

The main difference between historical writing and fiction has as much to do with the ways that these two modes of representation *ask to be read* as it does with their referential relationship to facts, reality, or truth. Each conveys different meanings through different means for different purposes; the two modes nonetheless might work in similar ways and may frequently borrow various techniques from each other. The ambivalent nature of the documentary genre has been widely investigated by scholars, who have singled out certain media—or particular examples from those media—that only claim to be documentary but in reality consist of multiple fictional aspects and elements; however, these scholars have overlooked the inconsistency within fiction itself. Fiction is firmly labeled the genre of imagination. Yet this study contends that fiction can adopt elements of documentary and, in its unique way, record reality too. Such works of fiction should be termed "docu-fiction."

Exactly how and in what sense do works of imagination document historical events? While not exaggerating fiction's ability to compete with historical writings in questions involving the authentic representation of true facts, I contend that fiction—and specifically war fiction, which is at the core of this analysis—can represent history, although, significantly, it can never conspicuously or even openly claim to do so. War fiction is unable to present its audience with the history of a given war in its traditional sense, yet it can interpret a war's events and re-create scenes of war via aesthetic means in order to appeal to the audience's emotional side. Frequently exaggerating, sometimes minimizing and even simplifying, and always dramatizing, war fiction aims to provoke a response from the audience. Intruding into the history of real wars, war fiction may focus on some of the most important, well-known, or controversial aspects of the war it addresses. But it always aims to present a multifaceted nature of war that includes the perspectives of soldiers, civilians, the enemy, and others. In doing so, war docu-fiction not only restages a portion of the history of a specific war but also interprets it imaginatively, providing a plausible viewpoint and thus frequently helping the audience understand, even if only in part, the complex story behind the war. Using specific attributes (e.g., uniforms and weapons), re-creating war geographies and environments, and including various documents, such as letters and videos, war docu-fiction, in perhaps a rather theatrical manner, stages and reanimates historical events. Its main goal is not so much to *document*, although it inevitably does that, as to *present* this part of history to its audience, thus providing a viable, valid reading of the war it is considering.

Some of the narratives analyzed in this book are based on soldiers' accounts of their military experiences, among them Sam Mendes's *Jarhead*, based on Anthony Swofford's memoir; the miniseries *Generation Kill*, based on the book by Evan Wright, an embedded reporter during the Iraq War; and Matt Gallagher's *Kaboom*, based on the author's military blog of his experience in Iraq. Some of the texts were written by authors who were involved with the military or participated in war. These include Gabe Hudson's *Dear Mr. President*, Jesse Goolsby's *I'd Walk with My Friends If I Could Find Them*, Kevin Powers's *The Yellow Birds*, and Phil Klay's *Redeployment*. Some of the authors, such as Tom Foley, the author of *This Way to Heaven*, and Douglas Cavanaugh, the author of *Into Hell's Fire*, lived in war-affected territories. Numerous other texts claim to be based on real events. Does this supposed basis in fact result in a more reliable and realistic finished product, thus imbuing some works of war fiction or film with more of a documentary dimension than others? It is doubtless true that fictional narratives that seem to be more tightly connected to reality—either through the author's background or through the real military events that they claim to have been based on—might borrow more of that reality and thus become more historically authentic portrayals of war. Yet just like any other fictional text, these narratives largely rely on the aesthetics determining the fictional mode and, just like any other fictional war narrative, they strive to dramatize and interpret the history that they attempt to present. Regardless of genre, then, works of fiction document war history, yet in this context it would be wrong to attempt to find some sort of optimal proportion and calculate their validity based on, say, the number of true facts they bring forth. The aim of docu-fictional texts is not to *compete* among one another in making use of more facts but, as stated above, to *re-create* and *interpret* history through the employment of certain parts drawn from historical episodes. The faith in humanitarian intervention manifested thematically in so many post-1990 American war narratives—which I substantively consider in my analyses of those narratives—helps illustrate the status of these texts as works of docu-fiction: through the discussion of the reasons for U.S. involvements in the conflicts since 1990, one finds that the narratives not only deal with the successes and failures that accompanied those interventions but also deconstruct the nature of the interventions, questioning the means by which liberation was brought, approving of certain tactics and largely censuring others. Through this multidimensional interpretation of the interventions as initially humanitarian wars, these war narratives not only present but also question history, which ultimately only reinforces their status as docu-fictions.

Before examining the peculiar nature of fiction that deals with history, let us define the genre of historical fiction. Richard Lee, for example, claims, "To be deemed historical . . . a novel must have been written at least fifty years after the events described, or have been written by someone who was not alive at the time of those events (who therefore approaches them only by research)."[3] In turn, Sarah Johnson, offering an "obvious" interpretation of historical fiction as "simply 'fiction set in the past,'" points out the highly controversial nature of the previous definition and asks: "How far back does a novel have to be set to make it 'historical'? A hundred years? Fifty years? Five years?"[4] These questions are indeed crucial, as they underline the problem of classifying historical fiction as fiction that necessarily comes from the distant past. Is it correct to call historical fiction only those works of fiction that describe events that took place decades or centuries ago? Are we not living history right now? Are not the episodes that are happening in the U.S.—including recent upheavals such as the 2016 presidential election, the Women's March on the weekend following Trump's inauguration, the rollout of new environmental policies (and withdrawal from existing agreements)—part of U.S. history too (or will eventually become so)? Or, speaking specifically about wars, is the work of fiction that deals with World War II properly called historical fiction, but not history that tells its readers about the recent war in Iraq? I find the attempt to connect historical fiction specifically to the distant past highly problematic and ultimately wrongheaded. I agree with Jill Paton Walsh, who argues that "a novel is a historical novel when it is wholly or partly about the public events and social conditions which are the material history, regardless of the time at which it is written."[5] Yet Johnson's speculation succinctly identifies the gist of the matter: "But the reality is, however, that almost everyone—and this includes readers, authors, publishers, agents, and the press—seems to have his or her own idea of what historical fiction is, and also what historical fiction should be."[6] Nonetheless, even if one agrees to call historical fiction only the fiction that deals with events that took place long ago, one clearly needs a term to define "soon-to-be-historical" fiction. Perhaps this term is "docu-fiction." Yet by proposing such usage I by no means want to narrow the focus of the term "docu-fiction" since, as this work will demonstrate, "docu-fiction" is a collective term that unites texts from (and about) the distant past with the most recent ones. Instead I suggest using it (among its other usages) to describe those works of fiction that are not yet "historical" fiction as traditionally conceived.

It is apparent that "the terms 'historical fiction' and 'history' are far from synonymous. Each has its own purpose: History is a disciplined method of enquiry of the past; historical fiction is a creative art, making extensive use of historical personages and events."[7] What is so special about historical fiction? Its very name combines what might seem to be two incompatible terms: "history" and "fiction." But are they so inconsistent? One might argue that history presents facts, whereas fiction is derived from imagination. Yet this project refutes this superficial view and draws on the extensive research of a number of scholars, among them Hayden White, to claim that history can adopt fictional elements and fiction can contain elements drawn from the study of history.

To start with history and to demonstrate that the historical or documentary mode does not necessarily lack a fictional dimension, I refer to White's explanation of the nature of history through the use of a "Fabian tactic." On the one hand, "history has never claimed the status of a pure science. . . . It depends as much upon intuitive as upon analytical methods, and . . . historical judgments should not therefore be evaluated by critical standards properly applied only in the mathematical and experimental disciplines." On the other hand, "history is after all a *semi*-science. . . . Historical data do not lend themselves to 'free' artistic manipulation, and . . . the form of [the historian's] narratives is not a matter of choice, but is required by the nature of historical materials themselves."[8] This sense of the nature of historical study does not undermine the status of history as a discipline, but it succinctly underlines one of its important characteristics—namely, that history is interpretive. Apparently when one considers purely historical accounts, one deals with, as a rule, a well-formulated text—a constructed story with facts and dates that are generally considered to be part of history. To put it differently, historical accounts are not just data—or, as White puts it, they are not "*mere* chronicles";[9] rather they are texts whose creation depends on these data. In historiography, historical events therefore turn into stories based only on real facts. This is what White dubs "emplotment," claiming that this technique is employed "to make of the events [a classic historical narrative] describes a comprehensible *dramatic* unity."[10] White elucidates the interpretive side of history with the observation that "the historical record is both too full and too sparse"; therefore the historian chooses what to include in the historical writing in the most "objective" way possible.[11] As White rightly pinpoints, "History does not consist of all of the events that ever happened, as the distinction between merely natural and specifically human events itself suggests. But neither do all human events belong to history, not even all human events that have been recorded and therefore can be known to a later consciousness."[12] Significantly the historian's interpretation is needed when looking over all human history as a stratum and selecting those events that will make up the construction of history. Interpretation in a more narrow sense, that is, the construal of specific events, is impossible here, for history is based not on one's personal thoughts and opinions but on facts. In this respect, White claims that in theoretical accounts, "explanation" is more important than "interpretation."[13] However, when one considers "metahistory," that is, the discipline that recognizes "the historical work as . . . a verbal structure in the form of a narrative prose discourse," each of these two elements plays an equally significant role, as, when combining the two, one creates a text that narrates the past event and elucidates the reason why it took place.[14] Finally, White underlines the significance of metahistory's role in the formation of historical accounts in general, thus foregrounding the pivotal role of interpretation.[15]

Creating historical texts, historians largely rely on "the choice of a plot structure" and "the choice of a paradigm of explanation."[16] As some scholars have pointed out, every historian is a "story teller."[17] A traditional historical text always has a plot. More than that, it has a title that indicates what the text is about. Therefore, structurally, the historical text is similar to the fictional one. But because it combines facts and interpretation, such a text provides no easy solution to the problem of how to "discriminat[e] within the discourse between the two."[18] The historical text is thus obnubilating, and despite its status as "history" it clearly contains parts of its author's thinking and wording. In this respect, White calls such texts "the fictions of factual representation," clearly underscoring their interpretative nature, and goes so far as to claim—anticipating skepticism from historians and literary scholars— that historiography itself is "a form of fiction-making."[19] White cites Erich Auerbach: "To write history is so difficult that most historians are forced to make concessions to the technique of legend."[20] History therefore is presented in texts that largely rely on facts but employ the techniques of fictional narrative, which by no means undermines its status as a serious discipline.

If there are elements of fiction in historical and documentary texts, can one, conversely, discover documentary elements in works of so-called historical fiction? Yes, according to the argument that follows. But before turning to the analysis of fiction, it is important to compare and draw parallels between historical and fictional texts; doing so will offer a foretaste of my approach and eventual argument on the existence of docu-fiction. White pinpoints the chameleon-like nature of history and fiction, claiming that "there are many histories that could pass for novels, and many novels that could pass for histories considered in purely formal . . . terms." And while a closer treatment of a given text usually allows one quite easily to understand whether one is dealing with documentary or fiction, one finds many similarities between these modes when considering such texts rather abstractly. In this regard, White provides a lengthy speculation:

> But the aim of the writer of a novel must be the same as that of the writer of a history. Both wish to provide a verbal image of "reality." The novelist may present his notion of this reality indirectly, that is to say, by figurative techniques, rather than directly, which is to say, by registering a series of propositions which are supposed to correspond point by point to some extra-textual domain of occurrence or happening, as the historian claims to do. But the image of reality which the novelist thus constructs is meant to correspond in its general outline to some domain of human experience which is no less "real" than that referred to by the historian.[21]

This is not to claim that fiction and history are the same thing, as there are several other crucial issues involved, including those of truth and authenticity, which will be thoroughly examined in chapter 1. Nonetheless, while constructing various realities, historians, writers, and directors of historical fiction alike must rely on specific data. Historians work with facts. What do creators of historical fiction consider their clay to be? They deal with both history and fiction. The proportion of fiction to documentary can vary from text to text, but it is undoubtedly true that such texts contain elements of both genres. Therefore I propose calling them docu-fictions. However, to claim as I do that fictional texts possess certain documentary elements does not necessarily mean that they contain specific facts or dates and locations. Indeed, many fictional texts lack them, especially the former. The viewer or reader is frequently informed about the time period when the action takes place, for example, specifying which war or battle is being represented, including information on when and where it took place. However, in its further narration, such texts do not always follow the historical line but instead interpret their histories in the service of dramatic purposes. On the other hand, a docu-fictional text can even attempt to present a real historical event (consider, for instance, the example of D-Day in Steven Spielberg's *Saving Private Ryan* [1998]), yet this will not be a history but rather a *reconstruction* of history. War docu-fiction does not *teach* history per se, yet it helps one *understand* history, interpreting it and presenting it in a more dramatic yet perhaps more memorable and approachable way than a straightforward historical account.

Barbie Zelizer pinpoints "the ability of popular culture to provide *both* entertainment and historical understanding, *both* fiction and fact."[22] Joshua Hirsch contends that along with documentary films, "fiction films carry with them this indexical aura, which can be used to create a sense of witnessing history," and adds, "Insofar as historical films—both documentary and fictional, though with different emphases—contain a tension between the witnessing of reality and the witnessing of fantasy, they both help construct historical consciousness and embody a contradiction within historical consciousness."[23] Vivian Sobchack underlines "the fiction film's intersections with documentary—and its quite common arousal (purposeful or not) of what we might call the viewer's 'documentary consciousness': a particular mode of embodied and ethical spectatorship that informs and transforms the space of the irreal into the space of the real." Thus Sobchack claims that there are cases when fictional films, or rather "fictional space," can be "charged with the real." This "charge of the real," which she also labels an "ethical charge," "moves us from fictional into documentary consciousness" and eventually "calls forth not only response but also responsibility—not only aesthetic valuation but also ethical judgment."[24] Scholars therefore underline the possibility of fiction to present history.

Nevertheless fiction that contains aspects of history is a rather equivocal phenomenon. And although I will claim that there are elements of truth in such fiction—hence it is plausible to call it docu-fiction—these texts remain *fiction*; that is, they largely rely on imaginative aspects. White makes an interesting observation in this regard: "Unless a historical story is presented as a literal representation of real events, we cannot criticize it as being either true or untrue to the facts of the matter. If it were presented as a figurative representation of real events, then the question of its truthfulness would fall under the principles governing our assessment of the truth of fictions."[25] It is crucial to realize that when dealing with historical fiction, or for that matter docu-fiction, one cannot take for granted everything that is written or shown; instead one should interpret the meaning and estimate the reliability of the text via notions of truth, authenticity, and falsity. These issues are of primary concern in chapter 1. Yet it is worth mentioning that any fictional treatment inevitably distorts real events, for if it did not, then one would be dealing with nonfiction. Analyzing Holocaust literature, White, for example, claims that such "distortions" are due to "the use of figurative language."[26] Yet considering fiction in general, one can claim that the distortions of history that can overtly be noticed in fiction are due to the aestheticization of the text, that is, the stylistic or visual embellishment that is necessary in fiction but arguably of no importance in documentary accounts. That is not to say that there is no "aesthetics of documentary texts"— quite the contrary. But this aesthetics differs in form and purpose from that of fictional texts.

It would be wrong to teach the history of key battles or other specific events through fictional filmic or literary treatments of war; these representations fail to provide an objective and authentic overview of history because they exaggerate or obscure certain events, providing only a partial and frequently a subjective viewpoint. However, this viewpoint is not necessarily wrong and does not always yield a misinterpretation. What it provides is one version, one reading of specific events that is disclosed to its audience. Viewing or reading a fictional war text, the audience is always aware that the story presented is not, strictly speaking, authentic; however, the audience does not consider it to be an abstract story but rather always relates it to specific political or military events that have, indeed, taken place. Moreover various novels and films are described as being *about* certain conflicts; the very use of this word points to the expectation of at least some kind of connection between the work of art and actual events. Therefore a fictional war story is positioned within a historical discourse, as the war it deals with is a real historical event—whether from the remote past or fresh in the minds of its audience. Yet while "a historical and critical account should attempt to provide a measure of distance toward events that is required in order to hold a degree of objectivity and self-critical perspective,"[27] in the case of a fictional narrative this distance is drastically reduced, and the created story gains the status of fiction because it is a subjective creation and the described event is no longer part of a larger historical narrative but is, rather, an individualized view of the matter. Berel Lang's view of the problem of "figurative discourse" in his discussion of "the limits of historical representation," which includes historical fiction, is salient here:

> Whatever else it does, figurative discourse and the elaboration of figurative space obtrudes the author's voice and a range of imaginative turns and decisions on the literary subject, irrespective of that subject's character and irrespective of—indeed defying—the "facts" of that subject which might otherwise have spoken for themselves and

which, at the very least, do not depend on the author's voice for their existence. The claim is entailed in imaginative representation that the facts *do not* speak for themselves, that figurative condensation and displacement and the authorial presence these articulate will turn or supplement the historical subject (whatever it is) in a way that represents the subject more compellingly or effectively—in the end, more truly—than would be the case without them.[28]

Nevertheless the works of fiction whose plots are derived from or inspired by various historical events, specifically wars, contain elements of the real. Such works are therefore neither pure fiction nor documentary. Still, in such texts there is a greater presence of fictional than documentary elements; hence I do not call them fictional documentaries but rather dub the genre docu-fiction, stressing its fiction constituent.

Intervention versus Humanitarian Intervention: Tracing Differences, Finding Similarities

Although I do not seek to analyze the history and policy of U.S. interventionism deeply and meticulously but focus instead primarily on an examination of certain fictional texts, some brief remarks on such notions as "intervention" and "humanitarian intervention" are necessary at the outset. In sending its soldiers into war, the U.S. government has followed a policy whose ultimate goal is to address economic, social, or political problems and conditions in the affected countries. Actions of this kind are examples of what is known as interventionism. However, the act of intervening, I argue, has changed over time; therefore I propose that interventionism is to be treated not as a fixed concept but rather as a reasonably flexible phenomenon, especially when it is applied in a historical context.

The policy of interventionism conspicuously dominates U.S. military history. The country itself would never have existed had it not been for the discovery of the New World and the intervention of European settlers in its territories, some of which became the United States.

Having started with a relatively innocent search, loaded with positive aims, for a place where people would be able to build a society free from corruption, oppression, and fear—a humanitarian goal—the settlement of the territory eventually became a forceful and hostile intrusion in a place already richly populated by indigenous peoples. Later, in the first half of the seventeenth century, the migration of the Puritans from England was significant to the formation of specific values in the soon-to-be-American consciousness, for the religion that the newcomers preached, through its sense of building a "city upon a hill" in their adopted land, ultimately gave birth to the ideology of American exceptionalism.[29]

Paul R. Viotti argues that the propensity of Americans to protect themselves, use arms, and be always on alert was already evident in the time of the early European settlements, since the people were supposed to protect their new homes from intrusion by others.[30] One can argue that the ideas behind such conduct represented the sort of exceptionalism that stimulated the violence so characteristic of the European settlers. Throughout history, like perhaps any other state, the U.S. could not avoid fighting wars, either to protect its own territory or to participate in conflicts abroad, defending in the process the core principles of the American nation.

However, one should be careful labeling the United States an endless (from the historical perspective) intruder. For a considerable time—up to the end of the nineteenth century—the United States adhered to a policy of isolationism based on its geographical location, which was not easily reached by would-be aggressors.[31]

Nevertheless, in the 1890s the believers in U.S. imperialism wanted to draw wider attention to their ideas. Among them was John Fiske, who claimed, "Now the 'manifest destiny' of America was to spread to other parts of the globe."[32] The American people were finally won over by imperialistic speeches only in 1898, when, with the start of the Spanish-American War, the American elite "discovered that the nation had an imperial destiny."[33] There were advocates of isolationism who tried to calm the imperialist thinking that had suddenly won the day, but they were a minority, and their voices were muffled by the vehement appeals of such imperialists as Albert J. Beveridge, a lawyer from Indiana, who defined "the actual tradition of the nation" as "expansionist" and, referring to the cases of Florida, Texas, and the Mexican War, claimed, "We do but what our fathers did—we but pitch the tents of liberty farther westward, farther southward—we only continue the march of the flag."[34] Interestingly, despite the imperialist subtext of U.S. actions in the Spanish-American War, the war was also the first to be defined as a humanitarian one. Not only scholars claimed this—for example, David F. Trask, who called the war "a humanitarian crusade"—but President William McKinley did so as well, characterizing the war as "a triumph of our humanity," started "for freedom and to relieve our neighbors of oppression."[35]

Viotti underscores the fact that after the formation of the U.S. as an independent state, "the American experience . . . is replete with examples of armed intervention or using force against adversaries." He contends that "a constant in this historical record is readiness to use force, going to war as necessary to defend the interests or objectives set by policy elites." U.S. involvements in the conflicts with Mexico (1846) and Spain (1898) are therefore the results of American "exten[sion] to the Western hemisphere." Moreover Viotti draws one's attention to the emergence of the Monroe Doctrine (1823), which prevented those territories seen to compose "an increasingly American sphere of influence" from falling under European colonization.[36] Thus, according to Ernest R. May, the Monroe Doctrine allotted the U.S. "a duty to act in the Western Hemisphere as a policeman."[37] This military activity of the U.S., maintained throughout the nineteenth century, can also be interpreted as a manifestation of American exceptionalism that allowed the U.S., or to be more specific its political and military leaders, to decide upon and conduct the country's participation in a number of conflicts. This assumption is strongly supported by ideas expressed during those times. For example, in 1898, Beveridge declared:

Wonderfully has God guided us. Yonder at Bunker Hill and Yorktown His providence was above us. At New Orleans and on ensanguined seas His hand sustained us. Abraham Lincoln was His minister and His was the altar of freedom the Nation's soldiers set up on a hundred battlefields. His power directed Dewey in the East and delivered the Spanish fleet into our hands, as He delivered the elder Armada into the hands of our English sires three centuries ago. . . . We can not fly from our world duties; it is ours to execute the purpose of a fate that has driven us to be greater than our small intentions. We can not retreat from any soil where Providence has unfurled our banner; it is ours to save that soil for liberty and civilization.[38]

At the same time, Carl Schurz, a republican reformist, advocating that America focus on its domestic problems, argued that "the problem of democratic government" should be resolved "not only for the benefit of the inhabitants of this country alone, but for the benefit of mankind."[39] Thus he overtly underscored not only the exceptional status of the U.S in its having the privilege to demonstrate the correct example for living and development to the whole world, but also the humanitarianism that the U.S. as a country should embody.

After the Philippine-American War (1899–1902) that resulted from the 1898 Spanish-American War and before getting involved in World War I, the United States carried out several important military operations: the occupation of Veracruz (1914), the Punitive Expedition in Mexico (1916–17), and the invasion of the Dominican Republic (1916–24). In 1917 the U.S. entered World War I, fighting until the war's end in November 1918. Yet by the 1930s, primarily influenced by the tragic loss of American lives in that war but also by the Great Depression, a sizable portion of the country turned again to isolationism in a debate that persisted through the outbreak of the war in Europe and was settled on the side of interventionism only after the Japanese attack on Pearl Harbor on December 7, 1941.[40]

Against the background of the pendulous nature of U.S. militarism —which kept oscillating between isolationism and active interventionism—American exceptionalism continued to play a significant role in the political sphere of the country over the course of the twentieth century, greatly influencing U.S. interventionist policies in that period. Still, it would be rather myopic to think of U.S. interventionism as driven only by the ideology of American exceptionalism. The basis of U.S. foreign policy entangled the desire to maintain peace worldwide— which is, in itself, a humanitarian goal—with the country's rush for global leadership.

Throughout the twentieth and twenty-first centuries, the U.S. interventionist policy was steeped in the ideas of both exceptionalism and humanitarianism. From the country's successful involvement in World War I to its drastic failure in Vietnam, the American nation was considered to be invested with a divine purpose and with the mission of protecting other nations from an evil Other. Speculating from the viewpoint of those who have shared the ideas of American exceptionalism, men and women joined the U.S. military and fought because, first and foremost, they truly believed in the holiness and sanctity of their actions. They were confident that only *they* could solve the critical issues of war. The involvement of the U.S. Army in World War II, for example, was considered "the violent military campaign in which [American soldiers] had participated with the idealized representations of the nation to which they desired to return."[41] Although it might be somewhat unfair to accentuate the violence of the campaign, for war is based on violence, the humanitarian motifs for U.S. involvement in occupied Europe and in the Pacific—to free the world from oppression, tyranny, and concentration camps—are unquestionable. While the involvements in the Korean War and the Vietnam War could possibly be viewed as humanitarian too, for those were fights against another oppression embodied by communism, the Vietnam War, to speak in Donald Pease's terms, symbolized the "fall" of the Myth of the Virgin Land. By way of evidence, Pease draws on the slaughter in My Lai, when hundreds of South Vietnamese civilians were murdered by U.S. soldiers, which de-sanctified the myth.[42] This bloody event fully undermined the purported humanitarianism of U.S. motivations and made many question such means of bringing peace and liberty to foreign lands.

U.S. intervention in 1990 in the First Gulf War signified the beginning of a new military era for the U.S., as well as the revival of U.S. militarism and, importantly, humanitarianism after the drastic failure in Vietnam. While the principles and doctrines of American exceptionalism have remained constant since 1990, the initial grounds for intervening have consistently been humanitarian.

This brief overview reveals the eagerness and unquestionable readiness of the U.S. to intervene in conflicts worldwide throughout history. But exactly *what* is intervention? Examining the notion, Gary Hart suggests thinking about the act of intervening as an "engagement" and, invoking U.S. interventions, argues that no matter what kind of engagements Americans have had in the past, they should feel proud of them because "helping a country," whether politically or economically, "quite often . . . promotes American interests."[43] In contrast, Herbert Tillema asserts that although the term "intervention" has gained certain "moralistic and legalistic baggage," it refers to a "deliberate, forceful intrusion by a state within foreign territory." Calling intervention an engagement that necessarily and in all cases dignifies the nation, as Hart does, is simply one side of the coin. Tillema identifies three constituents of interventionism: first, "specific instruments of foreign policy . . . that necessarily violate standard diplomatic practice"; second, "interventionary behavior" as a "deliberate act of state"; third, "specific actions presumably related to warfare, at least a tangible risk of direct participation within violent international or domestic conflict."[44] Intervention is a complex notion that at its core deals with the "interrelation of force and diplomacy."[45]

In contrast, "humanitarian intervention" can be classified as a positive notion. Focusing on the post–Vietnam War period as a significant phase in U.S. military history, scholars specifically underline the fact that, after the collapse of the Soviet Union, many (particularly on the left) realized that "the vast military capabilities" of the United States "could now be used to save lives rather than destroy them."[46] (This was so also because the U.S. remained the only world superpower and therefore did not need to worry about the reaction of the USSR to U.S. military interventions.) Others talk about that turn to humanitarianism in even more overt terms: "Once the Cold War ended, the United States had to take on a large role as a world leader to guard against human rights abuses, defend democratic regimes, and lead humanitarian efforts."[47] All U.S. interventions that took place after the Vietnam War can be defined as humanitarian interventions (although this issue is not as simple as it might sound and therefore will be examined in more detail throughout this book). What is humanitarian intervention, and what elements constitute it? Distinguishing humanitarian intervention from other kinds of intervention, I seek to identify whether U.S. interventions conducted after 1990 are indeed purely humanitarian or whether they in fact deflect from the course of humanitarianism, shaping a so-called military humanitarianism that can be used as a means to achieve specific (and not necessarily humanitarian) goals.

Is humanitarian intervention defensible politically? Answering this question, James Pattison puts forth the well-founded response that, theoretically, humanitarian intervention is "largely unjustifiable" since it undermines the meaning of sovereignty, that is, "a state's freedom from external interference, so that it can pursue whatever policies it likes within its own boundaries." However, he continues, sovereignty must guarantee that the human rights of those who belong to the state are protected. If they are not, external interference is needed.[48] I draw the conclusion that humanitarian intervention is a form of forced or emergency interference prompted by political and/or social instability within the territory of a foreign state, and its supreme aim is to quell such turmoil so that citizens who have been stripped of their human rights have them restored.

Brendan Simms and D. J. B. Trim construe the term "humanitarian intervention" as follows: "[Humanitarian intervention is] action by governments (or, more rarely, by organisations) to prevent or to stop governments, organisations, or factions in a foreign state from violently oppressing, persecuting, or otherwise abusing the human rights of people within that state. . . . The aims of humanitarian interventions can also relate to wider humanitarian concerns: ending tyranny, stopping slavery, or ensuring efficient and equitable delivery of disaster relief or general humanitarian aid." They further state that a humanitarian intervention is a "response to mortality and brutality" by *humans* toward others rather than to natural catastrophes.[49] J. L. Holzgrefe argues that what constitutes humanitarian intervention is "the threat or use of force across state borders by a state (or group of states) aimed at preventing or ending widespread and grave violations of the fundamental human rights of individuals other than its own citizens, without the permission of the state within whose territory force is applied."[50] Taylor B. Seybolt defines it as action aimed at "help[ing] the innocent."[51]

Aidan Hehir contends that the use of such a "positive" word as "humanitarian" beside the term "intervention" allows such an intervention to be gauged within a specific frame. However, intervention is not limited to acts of direct intrusion but encompasses the measures taken during any given intervention. Therefore I strongly support Hehir's claim that we should distinguish "humanitarian intervention" from "humanitarian action," as humanitarian actions determine the nature of an intervention. Along these lines, Hehir argues that the proclamation of actions as humanitarian measures should be interpreted as an attempt "to legitimize these actions as non-partisan and moral, and hence inherently justified, rather than selfish and strategic, and hence necessarily contentious"; thus the concept "'humanitarian intervention' carries intrinsic normative assumptions."[52] Therefore, when dealing with the term "humanitarian intervention," it is important to think not merely about the food, medicine, and clothing that are the evident signs of humanitarian aid. One must also address the issue of force. To be more precise, one should consider the *interrelation* between the intervening power's use of force and its stated humanitarian goals.

The literary and cinematic examples that I draw on focus on so-called armed humanitarian intervention, when military force is applied. The use of militarism in tandem with humanitarianism has concerned many scholars. For example, David Chandler notes "the blurring of the distinction between military action and humanitarian intervention," whereas Seybolt shrewdly pinpoints the problem of "*military* intervention for *humanitarian* purposes."[53] Seybolt calls it an "oxymoron" and claims that these sorts of interventions are, first, always politically loaded and, second, can only worsen the situation in a war-torn territory because they increase the bloodshed.[54] I want to accentuate the emergence of another issue when dealing with humanitarian intervention, namely the equivocation between the humanitarian aid provided and the military actions conducted during an armed humanitarian intervention. Additionally the motives of the intervening side should be considered: helping the oppressed, preventing or stopping genocide, or eradicating nationalistic or terrorist groups that have become ruling oppressors differs considerably from imposing the governmental policies and views of the intervening country.

Theodore J. Lowi and colleagues underline the direct interrelation and connection between "humanitarian goals" and "military force" in specific cases, asserting that the latter can be used to "achieve" the former.[55] When one considers the twofold nature of humanitarian military interventionism in the examples of specific U.S. military interventions, it is impossible to determine unambiguously whether in all cases the positive result is ultimately greater than the negative consequences. The issue is too complex. Drastic ramifications ensue from every military intervention because "the use of military force is inherently fraught with risk": no matter how well an intervention is considered and planned, its "results can seldom be fully anticipated."[56] And the most apparent "results" in this case, I argue, are casualties—both among civilians and military women and men—as well as the destruction of infrastructure, roads, hospitals, schools, kindergartens, houses, and so on. Even if one assumes that an intervention carried out to liberate a nation from oppression successfully achieved this main aim, the "side consequences" are always terrible. And it would not be overly dramatic to say that much of such humanitarianism has entailed leaving countries in disarray after the primary conflict ends. That said, humanitarian military intervention should not be treated as a separate action sealed off from other actions. Humanitarian military intervention should only be part of a larger humanitarian project whose next stage would facilitate better living conditions for those affected by and involved in war, frequently against their will and without their consent. I do not mean to suggest that the United States has always financially neglected the countries where it has been militarily involved. Regarding Iraq and Afghanistan, for example, the U.S. "invest[s] billions to rebuild [these] countries."[57] Yet whether the countries ravaged by war become fully completed humanitarian projects remains unanswered. Humanitarian military intervention is called humanitarian only because the aim of intrusion is justified in terms of its goal, which is to restore human rights. The actions and consequences that characterize a humanitarian military intervention, however, make it hardly different from any other sort of military intervention. Hence the term "humanitarian" only helps one immediately see the *reason* for the involvement, but it by no means always denotes the *means* by which this or that aim is achieved.

U.S. Interventionism in Film and Literature

U.S. interventionism is a complex issue. It can be analyzed not only as a political but also as a cultural problem, considering the substantial number of texts, including fiction, that center their plots on stories of U.S. military intervention. Both film and literature externalize U.S. interventionism as a pivotal cultural phenomenon, which finds itself reflected in cultural artifacts and also shapes American culture today, at a time when real war has made killing, violence, and torture the objects of a perverse, almost pornographic pleasure, even as the psychological and physical mutilation caused by war has become one of the most common, persistent life problems around the world. War, however, has not only changed the aesthetics of culture; it has also made politics the most intriguing, widely discussed, and omnipresent *cultural* phenomenon. Interventionism has not remained on the sidelines but, I argue, occupies the central place in cultural discourse. The crucial question that arises, however, is this: How do U.S. film and literature represent interventionism? Specifically, do they prefer dealing with the advantages of U.S. interventionism, or do they demonstrate both sides of the coin?

My core argument is that fiction film (and literature) on war should be considered docu-fiction. It seems reasonable to return to ground covered at the beginning of this introduction, but with a particular stress on the cinematic representation of *intervention* and a more in-depth analysis of the extent to which the fiction film can be a reliable medium to understand a political, military, and ethical issue as complex as interventionism. In fictional films, the characters, actions, plot, even location are frequently invented. In the best cases, the audience is told that the film is based on true events, but it is still impossible to estimate how much of what the film depicts has happened in reality. The main character can be a portrait of a real person, and the general story can be close to something that actually happened—or not. The events portrayed in the film—encompassing love, loss, betrayal, revenge, death, salvation, and more—help construct the viewer's opinion about, first, the main event that fuels the plot; second, the main character; and third, the supporting characters. These aspects are equally crucial in the examination of such important issues as the representation of a specific event or person(s) (or both) and the audience's perception and interpretation of a film. Discussing the artistic nature of film, David LaRocca writes, "Film is a forum for negotiation, not a fixed document; it is art, not history. By watching this particular representation of soldiers and strife, moral conflicts and somatic peril, a viewer experiences an internal, nonreferential struggle with war's nature and manifestation. On this reading, war films tell us or teach us nothing about the reality of war—that is something for the firsthand witnesses and soldiers to contend with—but summon us to the complicated business of the (mere, but still significant) representation of war."[58] Although LaRocca discusses particularly the portrayal of war, I find that his assumption can be aptly applied to the representation of interventionism as a political and military phenomenon that, while being a more specific issue, is still tightly connected to the broader and more complex phenomenon of war. Taking into consideration LaRocca's speculations, one might conclude that spectators of films learn no historical truths about war or, consequently, interventionism. Fostering the notion that fictional war narratives in film and literature are best regarded not as pure fiction but as docu-fiction, I of course refute this contention. How can film of a fictionalized nature be regarded as being related to reality? A shrewd observation has been made by LaRocca himself, who, talking specifically about war films (i.e., the key cinematic genre that provides rich material with regard to U.S. interventionism), claims that they "exist at the intersection of geopolitical reality and imaginative fiction, where government and corporate investment meet creative endeavor."[59]

The significant problem that LaRocca eventually raises is the treatment of film not as a purely fictional medium but as one that portrays both reality *and* fiction. As I argued above, fictional films about war draw on stories from real life; therefore each war film, to various degrees, relies on, borrows from, and reflects reality. The war genre is a very specific cinematic genre, not only because of the importance and complexity of the subject that every war film deals with but also due to the ethical and aesthetic representations of military events that result from the endless struggle between reality and fiction taken up by a film director. It is, then, the hard task of the audience, film critics, and scholars to interpret and distinguish where reality is, and where fiction. LaRocca provides a good explanation of the problem: "In contrast with the you-had-to-be-there-to-believe-it sentiment, one hears from returning soldiers that being there [in a real battlefield] is seldom sufficient for having a grasp of the reality of the situation. In short, real bullets—like staged ones—may leave a survivor (or viewer) with an impression of the surreal, the hyperreal, or the unreal; unexpectedly, *the soldier and the cineaste may share this position of indeterminacy.*"[60] The problem of the real consists in the historical facts presented but also in the ability of grasping war as a phenomenon, of understanding its nature and brutality—something that can be equally hard for real soldiers and for the audience. If the nature of war is so ambiguous and, hence, if war film is so equivocal, how does film connect its audience to reality? I argue that just as a screenwriter and director can never fully escape political, geographical, or historical reality (as it is framed by the news, TV, print media, etc.) when shooting what is defined as a fictional war film, so too does the audience not treat the film in an abstract way; instead it inevitably projects the fictionalized representation of war onto real life, thus understanding, judging, explaining, and interpreting real-life events with the help of the fictional film. A similar idea is put forward by LaRocca: "We do not see the world as it is (or as it corresponds to lived reality), but as the film presents it to us—an interface for investigation, interpretation, and insight."[61] I, however, partially refute LaRocca's statement, specifically disagreeing that what film shows us does not "correspond to lived reality." The scholar aptly notices that in film, "we do not see the world as it is," a form of partial blindness that, I suggest, results from the dominant fictional side of film. However, the picture on screen can always be matched with the lived reality, although, as LaRocca himself remarks, film may display this reality in such a way that, at first sight, it would look like fiction.

Fictional literature too has much to add to one's understanding of U.S. interventionism. Like their counterparts in film, works of literary historical fiction should not be treated as narrations of pure facts that took place in the past. On the contrary, they employ a subtle combination of history and imagination so as to enrich the final product both factually and emotionally. The aim of fictional literature—and the fictional literature on war in particular—is not to provide its readers with concrete historical data but rather to plunge them into the time of a specific war and, in doing so, draw them into the atmosphere of the conflict, where military operations and hostilities become everyday reality while psychological tension and paralysis, along with strong and conflicting emotions, are the natural state of those enduring the situation.

There are two aspects that I find important here: one must, first, distinguish among the types of war literature and, second, analyze how and in what ways they succeed in either revealing or concealing the reasons for U.S. involvement in various conflicts. Does literature tend to focus on the political premises of U.S. intervention at all? Is it important for authors to place their novels accurately in terms of the time and location of the war? Or is history obscured in the fictional world while other aspects move to the foreground? What factors become composite elements, the pieces of the mosaic of the author's imagination that make narratives so distinct? What stance do authors take in their works? Do they give precise answers, judge, criticize, or censure war, and, especially, external interference in conflict zones? Do they approve of and assent to military actions, or do they take a neutral position, leaving further analysis and judgment to the reader?

Before proceeding to the types of literature that deal with war as a subject, one must elucidate the general problem of literature that narrates war events. To what extent can one use such terms as "fiction" and "nonfiction" when discussing such literature? This subgenre of literature is undoubtedly serious, even if specific works contain elements of irony or comedy. The pivotal aspect here is that the plot relies on a specific war, and regardless of whether a war story, novel, or poem has a happy, dramatic, or tragic ending, the central problem remains war—a brutal, hostile, merciless, and traumatizing event that entails casualties, degradation, psychological problems, and material and moral loss. Therefore, no matter the plot, the tone, who the characters are, and what the ending is, every literary work that deals with a real war contains an element of nonfiction. Yet the characters, along with the described events, can be fictional. The tone of the work can frequently guide the reader and help her or him understand whether or not it attempts to narrate real events. However, authenticity is part and parcel of such fictional works, because reality inevitably finds its reflection in literary works that touch upon the very real problem of war and the particular events of specific wars.

I divide the literature that presents war into two core categories: literature that is created during a war by a participant, and literature that is written about war from the outside. I classify war films in the same way. I argue that *some* texts that belong to the first type of literature can be characterized by their authenticity and historically correct narration of events. Such literature, however, can be both objective and subjective, depending on the type of publication. For instance, soldiers' diaries usually focus on their authors' experiences and, generally, involvement in war, and thus often present a rather subjective viewpoint of events. Yet this must not be regarded as a shortcoming or as being detrimental to the significance of such literature. Because the events are filtered through the perception of a particular soldier, and because a personal diary does not need embellishment (which frequently takes place when information is conveyed to a mass audience), as it usually addresses a limited audience, this type of war literature can also be quite objective. It can aptly be compared to combat films. Additionally its genuineness may remind readers of a documentary.

However, the other type of war literature—which, like films on war, is central to my analysis—makes up the other platform that has accumulated significant writings about specific wars. My suspicion is that such literature unites all the novels, short stories, and other narratives that have been created to enhance the reader's perception of war. Just as in case of film on war, the task that literature on war undertakes is to mix history with fiction, so that the literary world of war gains specific trajectories toward the disclosure of new elements that are obviously lacking in war literature. Madhumalati Adhikari calls literature on war "fictionalized history," a thoroughgoing means to see into past events with a "new and deeper awareness."[62] Such an observation is intended to underscore the fact that by using imagination while creating a story, authors aim to stimulate their reader to do the same while reading: the reader should use imagination both to abstract from and to better understand history, to try to re-create events as they might have been, to identify with soldiers, to analyze the situation at that very moment, in that particular place, as part of a specific squad as it is being recounted in the text. It is precisely this sort of reading that extends one's perception of war. While Adhikari calls fiction a "concoction of imagination," I contend that certain truths are rooted in every fictional story. And such truths are arrived at through interpretation. Adhikari states, "History can never articulate the final word, as it has to be rewritten, reconsidered with the addition of new experiences and new perspectives."[63] Thus the narration of history is an ever-changing sequence of attempts to combine pieces and solve a puzzle. Literature on war, explicitly or implicitly, attempts to interpret history, specifically war history, too.

Film and literature together constitute a full and intricate platform that can provide a cultural representation and interpretation of such a pivotal yet involute issue as U.S. interventionism. But although they deal with specific U.S. interventions, neither fictional films nor literature can provide a full explanation for these involvements and wholly demonstrate their multisided nature. As a rule, one specific text insists on a particular standpoint, thus unveiling only a small bit of the complex picture. Nevertheless, when combined and juxtaposed, these bits can together form a solid cultural portrayal of U.S. interventions, uncovering the reasons for American involvement in conflicts, as well as their follies, successes, losses, traumas, triumphs, and truths. Dealing with wars that have taken place, fictional film and literature challenge history and politics. Such texts in themselves are the proof of the role that politics and culture play in the process of reimagining when it comes to certain historical events. The political and cultural anxieties of specific eras certainly influence the restaging of history in fiction, either directing the audience into the darkest corners of politics or, on the contrary, deceiving it. The intrusion of the U.S. State Department and the military in the film production doubtless contributes to the creation of "preferred" history and generates interpretations that might not be objective.[64] The film and literature I examine are frequently antiwar, provoking criticism toward certain military policies. While these texts provide their audience with a sociocultural commentary on specific historical and political events, they should be analyzed in context, with reference to the political views existing at the time portrayed.

Examining a substantial number of films and literary works, this book aims at showing that fictional works that deal with U.S. interventions in the Middle East and Eastern Europe since 1990 are docu-fictions because they succeed in conveying the history of recent U.S. wars as well as revealing, although not always explicitly, the change in U.S. interventionist policy over the past several decades, in which human-itarianism plays a key justificatory role.

1

Conceptualizing (War) Docu-Fictions

Theories of Truth

The cultural depiction of various historical events in film or literature, whether in a documentary or a purely fictionalized form, raises
several significant issues, including the reliability of the narrative or
visual portrayal. One might think that the films and literary works that
claim to belong to the documentary or biographical genres are direct
reflections of history, but this is not always the case. At the same time,
in treating fictionalized narratives that deal with real-life events as
pure invention, as this work argues, one can fall prey to a fallacy. The
problem's complexity reveals one major issue that I analyze in greater
detail: How does a consumer (i.e., a viewer or a reader) distinguish
between fiction and nonfiction? To answer this question, one should
consider the relationship between these two modes and understand
the difference between reality and fiction. The mediating concept that
might help illustrate this difference most vividly is truth.

What is truth? I raise this question not to find a single, universal
answer that would cover a term as fraught as "truth" but rather to see
how truth has generally been interpreted and, eventually, to demonstrate
the connection between truth and reality. Truth is a relative notion, and

its having been the major concern of philosophers through the ages only proves how ambiguous it is. It is rather hard to provide an accurate definition of truth because it is not a specific object that can be touched, seen, or otherwise perceived in a physical way; it is a phenomenon that is conditioned. Yet despite the difficulty of defining or characterizing truth, philosophers have succeeded in singling out certain boundaries within which truth exists. Their opinions and ways of interpretation, however, vary, giving rise to a whole panoply of theories.

The attempts to define truth go as far back as Aristotle, who claimed, "To say of what is that it is, or of what is not that it is not, is true."[1] Aristotle understood truth to be the ultimate ground that divides phenomena into false and not false. While this understanding seems plausible, it provides no characterization of truth; that is, it does not set truth in a relationship with falsity or inaccuracy, and instead provides rather plain, general, even superficial parameters for the definition and understanding of truth as such. Plato claimed that "truth was universal and existed independently of individuals"; that is, "everything was already known."[2] Augustine believed, "To be true is the same as to be."[3] Aristotle's, Plato's and Augustine's definitions suggest truth's inconceivable nature and seem to simplify "truth," on the one hand, even as, on the other hand, they underscore the term's complexity, of a sort that cannot be fully grasped by the human mind.

Nevertheless scholarly endeavors to perceive truth have never ceased; later, in the seventeenth century, Descartes interpreted truth as "a pursuit of the individual."[4] Benedict Spinoza made a contribution to its study, developing a coherence theory of truth. Reading Spinoza in the twentieth century, Ralph C. S. Walker comments:

> A coherence theory of truth is a theory about the nature of truth; a theory about what truth consists in. It is not simply a theory about how we find out what is true; that we often make use of coherence as a test of truth, and reject as false a belief that fails to cohere with the rest of the things that we believe, is not very controversial. The

coherence theory is not the theory that coherence is a likely guide to truth, but rather the view that coherence is all there is to truth, all that truth amounts to.[5]

Coherence theory therefore proposes exactly what Aristotle's understanding of truth lacks: Spinoza does not treat truth as an identifier of what is true or false; he examines truth to understand its monolithic structure and thus define its essence. According to his coherence theory, "truth consists in nothing more than a relationship of coherence between beliefs," whereas "the coherence theorist can accept that there are facts, and that true beliefs correspond with them, provided he can give his own account of what the fact and the correspondence ultimately consist in: they ultimately consist in coherence."[6] The connectedness of facts constitutes truth universally. The philosopher comes to argue that "truth is its own standard" and is, moreover, "the standard both of itself and falsity."[7] Hence, for Spinoza, truth is independent in the way that it does not need an external agent to determine its reliability or, as Walker puts it, "A true idea needs nothing outside itself to guarantee its truth or to constitute its correspondence with reality."[8] Walker's formulation aptly introduces the connection between truth and reality, facilitating the discussion of truth as a phenomenon that exists in the real world rather than in its illusion. I shall come back to this issue later in the chapter.

Deconstructing the essence of truth, Spinoza writes:

As regards that which constitutes the reality of truth, it is certain that a true idea is distinguished from a false one, not so much by its extrinsic object as by its intrinsic nature. . . .

Thus, that which constitutes the reality of a true thought must be sought in the thought itself, and deduced from the nature of the understanding. . . .

Thus falsity consists only in this, that something is affirmed of a thing, which is not contained in the conception we have formed of that thing.[9]

Spinoza succinctly and accurately distinguishes between true and false, underscoring the firm codependence between the two concepts, yet foregrounding truth as the key agent in this relationship, which makes falsity fully subordinate to truth.

In the eighteenth century George Berkeley attempted to correlate truth and reality; according to Walker, the philosopher "does deny that the truth of a belief can ever consist in its corresponding to some reality which is metaphysically independent in the sense that its nature is not determined by the coherent system of beliefs, for if it did then the coherence of the belief system could at best be a guide to truth and not what truth consisted in."[10] At first sight, Berkeley's interpretation seems to challenge the connection between truth and reality, yet it only reinforces this linkage, illustrating the tight correlation of reality itself to beliefs and, as a result, to truth.

An interesting interpretation was provided by Immanuel Kant—"The nominal definition of truth, [is] that it is the agreement of cognition with its object"—who relied on Spinoza's understanding of truth and particularly his postulate that "a true idea must agree with its object."[11] Kant attempted to understand the "'material' correspondence of a cognition with its object," claiming that "although our knowledge may be in complete accordance with logical demands, that is, not contradict itself, it is still possible that it may be in contradiction with its subject."[12]

A century later Friedrich Nietzsche introduced a theory of truth and belief, working with such notions as truth, falsity, error, and illusion. Nietzsche complicates the understanding of truth, contending that "truth is the kind of error without which a certain species of life could not live." He adds, "Those beliefs we normally take to be true are really false but without these beliefs we could not live." More than that, the philosopher questions the quality of the truth that is to be validated: "How is truth proved? By the feeling of enhanced power—by utility—by indispensability—in short, by advantages. . . . But that is a prejudice: a sign that truth is not involved at all." Although Nietzsche questions the nature of truth and criticizes the viewpoint that truth can be, by some means, measured or classified, he does not deny its existence—though he seems to suggest that truth is artificially created; that is, it is not a universal, self-proclaimed phenomenon, but rather it was determined in a certain form and eventually imposed. The following claim vividly illustrates this conclusion: "The most strongly believed *a priori* 'truths' are for me *provisional assumptions*; e.g., the law of causality, a very well acquired habit of belief, so much a part of us that not to believe in it would destroy the race. But are they for that reason truths? What a conclusion! As if the preservation of man were a proof of truth!"[13]

Nietzsche differentiates truth from its essence, claiming that the latter can accurately be described by what he calls a "valuation": "I believe that this and that is so." In turn, he defines truth as "a kind of belief that has become a condition of life," and adds, "'Truth' is . . . not something there, that might be found or discovered—but something that must be created and that gives a name to a process, or rather to a will to overcome that has in itself no end—introducing truth, as a *processus in infinitum*, an active determining—not a becoming-conscious of something that is in itself firm and determined. It is a word for the 'will to power.'" This interpretation of truth only reinforces the earlier claim that truth is, indeed, artificial because it did not emerge of its own accord but was created by humankind. As Nietzsche posits, "We can comprehend only a world that we ourselves have made."[14]

A more recent endeavor to study truth is that of Jacques Lacan, who claims that although "established truths" exist, "they are so easily confused with the reality that surrounds them that no other artifice was for a long time found to distinguish them from it than to mark them with the sign of the spirit and, in order to pay them homage, to regard them as having come from another world." Therefore, "a truth . . . is not easy to recognize once it has become received." Lacan rejects the existence of absolute truth and falsity, claiming that "the discourse of error—its articulation in action—could bear witness to the truth against the apparent facts themselves."[15] Lacan's reference to "*a* truth" demonstrates that he does not treat the notion as a universal concept, a unique phenomenon that synthesizes all beliefs; rather, for Lacan, truth is a narrow concept that can be applied only to a particular phenomenon. There is no such global phenomenon as "truth." One should instead speak of a collage of truths—comprising facts that are independent and disconnected from one another.

Lacan's other main concerns are the relations between truth and language and between truth and science. With regard to the former, he sees a tight connection between language and truth, asserting that, virtually, truth does not exist prior to language and becomes possible only with the help of language (in what he calls "the birth of truth in speech"): "The dimension of truth emerges with the appearance of language." The relationship between truth and science, in turn, is chiefly grounded on such a phenomenon as "truth as cause." As an example, Lacan refers to an unnamed philosopher who insists, "The truth of pain is pain itself."[16]

Another significant connection investigated by Lacan, primary to this analysis, is that between truth and fiction. He argues that truth "makes the very existence of fiction possible," inviting the approximation of fiction to truth rather than to falsity. At first he does not deal with truth and falsity as the major domains. He does not talk about falsity in relation to fiction. Instead he correlates truth with fiction, thus positioning fiction closer to truth than to falsity. Returning to the earlier examination of truth and reality, that "truths . . . are so easily confused with the reality that surrounds them," which unveils a tight connection between truth and reality, one can speculate that if fiction is close to truth, then it is also close to reality. This showcases a complex bond between fiction and truth as well as between fiction and reality.[17] This question will be analyzed in greater detail later in this chapter.

More recent interpretations of truth provided by Marxists, poststructuralists, and postmodernists reveal the inextricable bond of the concept to power and conceive truth to be "generally constructed out of particular social interests."[18] For example, Michel Foucault relates the concept of truth to politics, overtly singling out the tight connection between truth and power.[19] Philosophers' relatively recent interest in truth as a manifestation of power is not surprising since the cultural studies discourse of the twentieth and twenty-first centuries is shaped by power—whether it be social power or governmental authority—as a mechanism that facilitates the spreading of certain views or ideologies. That is why one can speculate that in its most recent understanding (broadly speaking), truth is a relatively flexible phenomenon; it is the powerful, dominant group that determines the meaning and degree of truth. Wendy Helsby's assumption that "in a postmodern media world we may ask: whose truth is dominant?" supports this theory most vividly.[20]

This brief overview of theories of truth demonstrates humankind's persistent concern to find answers to the question of our world's organization, which is based on the existence of and interrelation between truth and falsehood. As Hartry Field states, "we want a notion of truth" because it "aid[s] us in utilizing the utterances of others in drawing conclusions about the world."[21] Yet this overview also reveals the development of the general understanding of truth as a concept. Paul Foulkes may claim that there is "no answer" to the question "What is truth?," though "many think that they can find one," but the theories just presented illustrate an opposing view.[22] Although Foulkes's criticism of various theories of truth seems to be logical and deserves consideration, it cannot be taken as fully correct for one simple reason: it contests the very existence of the study of truth.

The interpretations provided by Aristotle, Spinoza, Berkley, Kant, Nietzsche, Lacan, and other philosophers, however, demonstrate a wide array of approaches that have been applied to analyze the term "truth." Whereas these philosophers' interpretations might sound imperfect or incomplete and at times inconclusive, their shared endeavor to provide an understanding of such a complex phenomenon as truth shows, at the very least, how strong the need has always been for an understanding of the concept. The existing theories of truth uncover and eventually help us understand the complex relations among such phenomena as truth, reality, and falsity and their connection to fiction, nonfiction, and cultural representation. Foulkes's assertion that we need theories of truth "to secure guaranteed objects of knowledge" is convincing.[23] Yet there is more at stake than just the question of ensuring the existence of such "objects"; there is also the need to understand the connections and relations among them. Truth not only defines knowledge in general but also develops it. And while truth is indeed difficult to define, mainly due to its intricate nature, theories of truth help us perceive the philosophy of truth and reality, as well as the issues that are connected or related to it.

Representing Truth and Reality: From Jean Baudrillard's Simulacrum to Roland Barthes's Myth

Having discussed some of the key theories of truth and provided various definitions of truth, I now move to the analysis of questions that concern how truth becomes a cultural issue and whether it can be represented. In this regard I also raise other significant questions: What is the connection between truth and reality? Is truth the same as reality? Is truth only part of reality, or is reality part of truth? Discussing the issue of authentic representation, it seems that one must inevitably make a distinction between truth and reality.

Truth is by no means reality; likewise reality is not truth. These two phenomena can coexist, but, importantly, they do not necessarily depend on each other. "A proposition is true in this sense when things in the world are as that proposition says they are. Some aspect of reality must simply be a certain way—if it is, then the proposition is true; if not, the proposition is false." In other words, "truth has a nature and . . . its nature is objective: whether a proposition is true (in most cases) does not depend on what anyone believes."[24] Truth can become part of reality in particular situations. Reality, however, is not based fully or only on truth. In this relationship, falsehood takes a place equal to truth and therefore can be part of reality too. But, most important, "truth is agreement with reality."[25] William James makes the strong point that to "agree" in the widest sense with a reality, can only mean to be guided either straight up to it or into its surroundings, or to be put into such working touch with it as to handle either it or something connected with it better than if we disagreed. Better either intellectually or practically! And often agreement will only mean the negative fact that nothing contradictory from the quarter of that reality comes to interfere with the way in which our ideas guide us elsewhere. To copy a reality is, indeed, one very important way of agreeing with it, but it is far from being essential. The essential thing is the process of being guided. Any idea that helps us to deal, whether practically or intellectually, with either the reality or its belongings, that doesn't entangle our progress in frustrations, that fits, in fact, and adapts our life to the reality's whole setting, will agree sufficiently to meet the requirement. It will hold true of that reality.[26]

Truth therefore assists one in understanding reality; truth becomes a tool that helps reality be constructed and perceived.

However, when it comes to the relation of truth and falsehood to reality, it is important to understand that, just like truth and falsehood, reality has a complex and abstract nature. What is reality? Is it our everyday life? But what about the historical past? Is not that reality too? What about various performances and plays? Do they not create specific realities? One can speculate that there is no universal reality; instead one should think of reality as a phenomenon that consists of multiple parts—perhaps "subrealities" would be the right term for them. But while reality in itself is so multifaceted, it is not quite so with truth. Hardly anyone can claim that there are subtruths; truth is a more universal notion than reality. Nevertheless, what allows one to subdivide truth is based not on the nature of truth itself but rather on the variety of beliefs that can be true. Bertrand Russell, for example, claims that "'What is true?' and 'What is falsehood?'" and "'What beliefs are true?' and 'What beliefs are false?'" are two absolutely different problems, and the solution to one can by no means be the solution to the other.[27]

Frank Plumpton Ramsey makes a similar distinction, raising "What is *truth*?" and "What is *true*?" as two separate questions.[28] It seems that true and false beliefs are in a tighter connection with reality than truth and falsehood.

Since I aim in this work to analyze particular war representations and assess their validity, it is pivotal to examine how one can represent reality and whether, or to what extent, representation (specifically verbal and visual representation) can be authentic. Ludwig Wittgenstein argued, "What any picture . . . must have in common with reality in order to be able to depict it—correctly or incorrectly—in any way at all is logical form, which is the form of reality."[29] The representation of reality is possible, yet the issue is not simplistic in nature. Another important question that emerges in this discussion is that of authenticity and its relation to truth and reality. My analysis adopts the idea that authenticity and truthfulness are equal phenomena or perhaps even criteria, according to which one can define representation. In this regard I agree with Dimitrios Theodossopoulos, who interprets authenticity as a phenomenon that "encompasses diverse sets of meaning that range from genuineness and originality to accuracy and truthfulness." He concludes that "authenticity encodes the expectation of truthful representation," thus underlining a similarity between the two terms.[30]

Before focusing on the representation of reality, it is important to deal with the issue of representation in general. Thoroughly examined by Stuart Hall, the term "representation" in its most basic sense can be interpreted as "the production of the meaning of the concepts in our mind through language. It is the link between concepts and language which enables us to *refer to* either the 'real' world of objects, people or events, or indeed to imaginary worlds of fictional objects, people and events." Interestingly, the concept already makes reference to the problem of truth by means of including the real and the imaginary. "Language" here is to be understood not merely as a verbal means of communication but also as a whole system of "signs" that includes both verbal and visual references, that is, "the 'language' of facial expressions or of gesture . . . or the 'language' of fashion, of clothes, or of traffic lights." In other words, anything that is "capable of carrying and expressing meaning is . . . 'a language.'"[31]

Hall singles out three "approaches" to how representation functions. First, it "reflect[s] or imitate[s] the truth that is already there and fixed in the world" ("reflective" or "mimetic" theory). Second, a particular meaning can be "impose[d]" by somebody ("intentional" theory). Third, "things don't *mean*: we *construct* meaning, using representational systems—concepts and signs"; that is, nobody and nothing "can fix meaning in language" ("constructionist" theory).[32] These approaches to representation raise the question of authenticity, namely, how true representation is. This issue, however, can also be considered from a different perspective: whether reality or, speaking more generally, truth can be represented. It is obvious that the "reflective" or "mimetic" approach to representation most accurately reveals the tight connection between reality and its representation, literally proclaiming that what is represented is a mirrored reality. That proves that representation can be authentic and thus that reality and truth can be represented. The second approach—an "intentional" one—demonstrates that representation can be an obtrusion of one's ideas or opinions. For example, in film and literature such a mode of representation can work in the following way: the director or author imposes his or her own opinions on the viewer or reader. In this case, it is impossible to talk about an authentic representation of reality; rather representation becomes distorted, and so truth may be mutilated and contorted. Finally, according to the "constructionist" approach, reality and truth cannot always be reflected in an authentic way either, because, constructing our own meaning, we risk interpreting things differently, which means that in some cases representation too can be skewed. It is evident that the relationship between representation and reality and truth is very complex. Indeed it is hard to assert that representation *mirrors* reality as it is: every representation is unreliable, to a greater or lesser degree.

When dealing with representation, the problem of meaning becomes essential. Both representation and meaning "belong . . . to the interpretative side of the human and cultural sciences"; that is, each makes sense only when interpreted or deconstructed, because one's understanding of particular objects or phenomena is built only through interpretations. Therefore it is reasonable to speculate that while the representation of truth and reality can be authentic, its interpretation can prove the opposite and vice versa; while one might interpret a particular representation to be authentic, the representation itself might not reflect truth or reality correctly. Yet in relation to this problem, one must consider an important peculiarity of interpretations: they "never produce a final moment of absolute truth." The argument overtly suggests that no interpretation can ever reach truth; that is, while truth and reality can be represented, a particular meaning of representation that one comes to by means of construing is never fully correct. Thus, while truth and reality can be represented, one's interpretation can never be considered the only one, or, as Hall pinpoints the crux of the matter, "Interpretations are always followed by other interpretations, in an endless chain."[33]

Since in my analysis of representation I will primarily adopt the constructionist approach, it is worth examining this theory in greater detail. The constructionist theory of representation employs two approaches to the examination of representation, namely "semiotics" and a "discursive" approach.[34] Both deal with the problem of meaning, specifically examining how representation conveys meaning(s). While the first orientation is primarily based on the concept of myth proposed by Roland Barthes, a "discursive" approach centers on the questions of "power" and "knowledge" as they have widely been discussed by Michel Foucault. Foucault's treatment of meaning as a product of the cofunctioning of and codependence between "power" and "knowledge" accentuates "the production of knowledge through a whole network of relationships (discourse) rather than just the meaning of a text." The key purpose of this theory is to investigate "who produces the knowledge" and, consequently, "who controls the message." Importantly, the theory also employs the idea of truth, seeking to understand how truth is represented and even how it is created: "If you possess a particular knowledge and you have the power to express this knowledge, it can become the truth by which others will lead their lives. The knowledge might change over time, and hence the beliefs will change and we will behave differently according to the new ideologies. The person/institution who has the 'knowledge' will also have the power to represent the new truth or discourse. . . . Obviously the larger the body circulating the truth, the more influential it is."[35] The theory reveals the tight connection between truth and representation, overtly claiming that representation itself can create new truth(s). Truth, in this case, is a very flexible phenomenon; instead of being absolute, truth is artificially created and imposed on minds through the invention and representation of new forms of knowledge that are advantageous to those in power. One can therefore conclude that truth is not just changeable and unstable; there is no such notion as independent, universal truth. Truth is a social phenomenon that exists only to serve those who need to create it to guarantee their own power:

> Truth isn't outside power, or lacking in power. . . . Truth is a thing of this world: it is produced only by virtue of multiple forms of constraint. And it induces regular effects of power. Each society has its regime of truth, its "general politics" of truth; that is, the types of discourse which it accepts and makes function as true; the mechanisms and instances which enable one to distinguish true and false statements, the means by which each is sanctioned; the techniques and procedures accorded value in the acquisition of truth; the status of those who are charged with saying what counts as true.[36]

Hall suggests that, for Foucault, "things meant something and were 'true' . . . *only within a specific historical context*," which again largely challenges the idea of truth as a constant.[37] That is, truth changes not only due to who is in power; it also transforms over time.

Foucault's theory is a significant contribution to the understanding of representation, primarily regarding the social side of representation.

In examining representation, specifically the representation of truth, it is important to deal with the issue of authenticity, which Foucault emphasizes in his theory and his idea that knowledge is created and imposed by the agent in power. Yet, while not refuting Foucault's approach, I seek to understand, first and foremost, the connection between meaning and representation in a way that shows how meaning can be constructed through interpretation. In particular, it is important to examine which meanings representation can generate and to what extent these interpretations reflect the truth of representation—if there is any. To examine these issues, I will now discuss the idea of myth as suggested by Roland Barthes, as well as Jean Baudrillard's concepts of simulacra, simulation, and hyperreality.

Introduced to explain how representation and particularly its meaning can be interpreted, Barthes's concept of myth is crucial for the examination of the representation of truth. Analyzing a famous example—"the Negro-giving-the-salute"—to discuss French colonialism, Barthes concludes, "What is invested in the concept is less reality than a certain knowledge of reality; in passing from the meaning to the form, the image loses some knowledge." Barthes suggests that we consider various meanings that a particular representation can stimulate. He claims that this diversity of meanings is constructed out of various myths that society has to create in order to explain certain phenomena as well as connect them to history, so that meaning itself is not an isolated phenomenon but rather is put into a context. However, when considering the issue of the representation of truth in connection with Barthes's concept of myth, it is problematic to accept that an authentic representation exists; or rather it is hard to say exactly which meaning is true. One traditional definition of "myth" is the one provided by the *Merriam-Webster Dictionary*: "an idea or story that is believed by many people but that is not true." Barthes argues, "Myth hides nothing: its function is to distort, not to make disappear." He elaborates: "Myth hides nothing and flaunts nothing: it distorts; myth is neither a lie nor a confession: it is an inflection." Barthes underlines the view that myth should not be confused with a deception, for myth is not an untruth. Is myth then truth in itself? Consider the following: "Myth does not deny things, on the contrary, its function is to talk about them; simply, it purifies them, it makes them innocent, it gives them a natural and eternal justification, *it gives them a clarity which is not that of an explanation but that of a statement of fact*." Thus, while myth "distorts," that is, deviates from truth, it is also not a lie, because myth deviates from falsity as well. One can conclude that, according to Barthes, myth in itself constitutes a specific meaning that is neither true nor untrue. Yet the idea that myth "gives [things] a clarity" suggests that myth, still, is a certain truth; hence myth is an interpretation of an authentic representation, which leads to the conclusion that truth or a particular reality can be represented. According to Barthes, "what the world supplies to myth is an historical reality, defined, even if this goes back quite a while, by the way in which men have produced or used it; and what myth gives in return is a natural image of this reality."[38] Thus myth is reality; myth is truth.

The notion of simulation proposed by Baudrillard—"the generation by models of a real without origin or reality: a hyperreal"—is another important concept to consider when examining the relations between representation and reality. Baudrillard's main concern is reality itself; he argues that it is impossible to find meaning in today's reality because it is filled with various texts that construct this very reality: "The real is produced from miniaturized cells, matrices, and memory banks, models of control—and it can be reproduced an indefinite number of times from these." Thus reality itself no longer exists; instead, one lives in the world of the "hyperreal": "It is no longer really the real. . . . It is a hyperreal."[39]

Claiming that everything around us is simulation, Baudrillard seems to reject the existence of truth. If there is no reality, if every meaning is simulated, that means that truth a priori cannot find a place in the world of our new reality (or hyperreality). Indeed the scholar calls the current reality a "space" that is "no longer that of the real, nor that of truth." "Simulating is not pretending," he argues and hence comes ever closer to the problem of truth, claiming that "simulation threatens the difference between the 'true' and the 'false,' and the 'real' and the 'imaginary.'"[40] Whereas the aim of pretending is to make someone believe in something, simulation is an imitation. And if such an imitation is close to reality, is not simulation reality in this case? Yet it is difficult to claim that simulation is reality here, because Baudrillard rejects the existence of any reality and thus any meaning. For him, hyperreality is a new reality, with simulation as its main mechanism. But is not simulation, if not reality, its very close imitation?

Examining the relationship between simulation and representation, Baudrillard writes, "Whereas representation attempts to absorb simulation by interpreting it as a false representation, simulation envelops the whole edifice of representation itself as a simulacrum." Does representation then become simulation? Yes, it does; more than that, representation in this case is not untrue: "It is no longer a question of a false representation of reality (ideology) but of concealing the fact that the real is no longer real, and thus of saving the reality principle." Refuting the existence of reality, Baudrillard logically comes to the conclusion that "illusion is no longer possible" either. Therefore, in a world where everything becomes relative, for neither what is true nor what is untrue can be discovered anymore, "it is *now impossible to isolate the process of the real*, or to prove the real."[41] Thus Baudrillard does not reject truth, and neither does he state that truth is minimized or avoided; instead he suggests that truth is simply difficult to discover, for within the abundant simulations it becomes barely distinguishable from what surrounds it. Truth exists, but it is hard to identify.

Considering representation, both Barthes and Baudrillard accentuate the problem of finding its meaning. In their discussions they inevitably deal with the issue of reality and true representation. Foregrounding the problem of identifying truth, each thinker, as a result, questions the representation of truth and reality—not because it is not possible but rather because it is hard to find out which particular representation reflects truth. And here it seems appropriate to bring in Foucault's notion of power and its connection to knowledge. In line with Foucault, Trinh T. Minh-ha claims that "truth is produced, induced, and extended according to the regime in power." She continues, "Truth and meaning: the two are likely to be equated with one another. Yet, what is put forth as truth is often nothing more than *a* meaning."[42] The connection linking representation, truth, and meaning is thus apparent. What Trinh seems to propose, however, is that we consider every meaning to be true. While Barthes and Baudrillard question the idea that truth can be easily found, introducing, respectively, the theories of myth and of simulation, Trinh somewhat simplifies the issue of truth, claiming that every meaning can be considered true. At the same time, an interesting argument she attempts to advance here is that truth in itself is just one of those meanings. It is therefore apparent that a representation is interpreted by an audience, and truth as a manifestation of meaning is also found out by an audience. "There is never a single discourse, however, as all media texts can be read in a variety of ways and with many meanings that can only be constructed with our active consent as readers."[43] Yet determining which meaning is true is the task that is to be completed by the audience.

Another significant question that arises in relation to the representation of truth is that of the mode of representation itself. Are there various types of representation, some of which tend to be more reliable than others? Is there a specific scale of representing, and do certain representations tend to reveal truth more than others? Which cultural representations are to be considered the most truthful?

Documentary and the Authentic Representation of Truth and Reality

Representations differ in form and content. That is why one can talk about a so-called scale that would serve to value how authentic a particular representation is. The most important, albeit rather general concepts to be discussed in respect to authentic representation are fiction and nonfiction. There are different ways that reality—whether fictional or nonfictional—can be represented. The most apparent means is photography, as each photograph is an image of a certain truth and a particular reality. Whether these are pictures of torture in Abu Ghraib, of dead civilians after a drone strike, or simply those depicting the soldiers' routine on a military base—all reflect a certain truth about war. Yet one can question the reliability of the truth that a particular photograph intends to render. Once taken out of context and presented under a specific title or with a particular description, the photograph can distort truth and reality. (Or rather the description distorts the meaning of the photograph.) Consider examples of propaganda, when photographs are used to change facts in favor of those who, for various reasons, try to impose their own truth. The problem that Trinh formulates discussing documentary is the need to distinguish between "what is 'honest' and what is 'manipulative.'"[44] Thus although photography is meant to be the most reliable means of representation, it is obvious that its claims in this regard can be questioned. In this respect, Susan Sontag, although considering a photograph a "narrowly selective transparency," thus underscoring the connection between an image and a real event, contends, "Even when photographers are most concerned with mirroring reality, they are still haunted by tacit imperatives of taste and conscience. . . . In deciding how a picture should look, in preferring one exposure to another, photographers are always imposing standards on their subjects."[45] Every photograph can be staged, yet it can also be used in a wrong context, which ultimately thwarts an attempt to connect an image to real events.

Other means to represent reality include film and literature. What kind of representations do film and literature adopt and eventually project? Both offer examples of fictional and nonfictional representation. In the broadest terms, and also perhaps in the most primitive way, one easily distinguishes a fictional from a nonfictional representation, according to the visualized or verbalized story, the chosen characters, and the events that take place. As Jacques Derrida puts it, "Common sense will always have made the distinction between reality and fiction."[46]

For example, when one watches or reads the story of Harry Potter's adventures, one readily understands that it is fiction. On the other hand, when one watches a documentary film about John F. Kennedy or reads a biography of him, one clearly understands that—at least for the most part—this is nonfiction. The viewer or reader largely relies on the story that is being shown or narrated and its correlation with reality; it is understood that the characters are actual people and the events described took place; if this is the case, he or she classifies the story as an authentic representation of current reality or events of the historical past. Gregory Currie, however, laments, "As consumers of fiction, we have become skilled at recognizing unreliable narratives; as theoreticians, we are less well able to say what constitutes unreliability and how it is detected."[47] Although this argument is somewhat problematic, as it neglects the fact that the reader or viewer can simply be tricked and eventually believe that a fictional narrative is, for example, a documentary, it does stress one important fact: that it is frequently possible for the audience to understand whether the presented narrative is fiction or nonfiction because each text is marked. By the term "marked" I do not, however, mean only genre-marking, when a cinematic or literary text is classified as fiction by the writer or director prior to one's reading or viewing, but I also include various means that this or that text employs, such as special effects in films and storytelling in literature. One might speculate that a realistic effect is often achieved by the inclusion of photographs (whether in a film or a book) of real people and events or by the reproduction of newspapers and documents. Indeed documentary proof is perhaps the best and easiest way to persuade the audience and make them believe what is being shown or narrated. Does this mean, then, that when one talks about nonfictional representation, one should consider documentaries and (auto)biographies to be the main media? Not necessarily. Even documentaries and autobiographies are not always true. It is worth remembering Hall's intentional and constructionist theories of representation, both of which question the concept of true representation, arguing that a certain meaning is either imposed on a reader or viewer or it is subject to multiple interpretations, which is the case with the narratives that some falsely tend to classify as always nonfictional.

To understand to what extent a work in the documentary genre (whether a cinematic or literary account) can be a reliable representation of truth, it is important to analyze the term "documentary" and track the development of the genre. Yet it is also significant to specify that in utilizing the terms "fiction" and "nonfiction," I am not referring to a particular form (although my chief focus is of course film and literature); I am discussing the discourses of fiction and nonfiction. When one deals specifically with the discourse of nonfiction, one considers, as Carl Platinga suggests, "a broad grouping comprising films, essays, biographies, news reports, recounting the day's events to one's spouse, and so on."[48]

What is documentary? For Paul Ward, it is "a form that makes assertions or truth claims about the real world or real people in that world (including the real world of history)."[49] Bill Nichols, talking specifically about a documentary film, calls it a "discourse of sobriety."[50] That is, it is a "discourse that claim[s] to describe the 'real,' to tell the truth." In line with Nichols, Godmilow refers to documentary films as "edifiers," thus underlining the films' ability to instruct more broadly rather than to teach only about facts.[51] Trinh provides a similar definition: documentary "takes real people and real problems from the real world and *deals with* them."[52] Julie Jones, examining documentary films, claims that they "turn on questions of evidence and testimony—documentation—to support the contention that they provide insight into actual phenomena."[53] A somewhat similar understanding of documentary can be noted in Hillary L. Chute's analysis of comics as documentaries: "Documentary operates as a set of practices that is about and instantiates the presentation of evidence."[54] Frances Bonner defines documentary as follows: "Documentaries, whether film or television, are non-fiction texts. . . . At some level a documentary makes a claim on the truth, asserting that what it talks about and shows is 'real,' not a made up story like the typical Hollywood thriller or romantic comedy."[55] This last definition I find very problematic or, rather, superficial: its view of the documentary genre is primitive. How precisely are documentaries "non-fiction texts": are they such because of their form, content, or everything altogether? What about the fact that most documentary films are staged: the director films particular events or scenes, interviews a number of people, but then starts to cut various pieces and shift the others around so that the documentary's final product differs greatly from what it had intended to be in the beginning? In this regard, is a documentary really all that different from a so-called fictional Hollywood film? It still *does* differ from a fictional film, of course—most vividly, as has been noted, in terms of plot. A documentary focuses on a real event or person or an actual problem, whereas in a typical Hollywood film—although it can also have this emphasis—this is not its paramount goal. In relation to a documentary's way of staging reality, it is important to refer to the famous phrase of John Grierson, quoted often by documentary studies scholars: a documentary is a "creative treatment of actuality."[56] Grierson insisted that "documentary needed to make a strong claim on the real," yet he "did not want it to be a mechanical, automatic claim arising from nothing more than the very nature of the apparatus."[57] Bonner shrewdly observes, "We usually think of 'creative' as being associated with fictional work, not with that claiming to represent actuality." Thus, when a documentary is staged and when a film itself is eventually reworked, this is done for one purpose: to follow the aesthetics of a regular film so as to draw the attention of the audience, or, to borrow from Bonner, "filmed actuality has to be treated creatively for it to become documentary film or television."[58] This is perhaps what Godmilow calls a "satisfying form," the form that every documentary must take in order to "survive, to take public space and attention," to be able to compete with fiction, which tends to be more entertaining and thus more popular.[59]

Yet a documentary maker should realize that his or her main goal is still to reflect real problems. The work "has to bother . . . about being right" rather than "beautiful."[60] And in this respect, it is important to remember a crucial moment in the development of the documentary film that took place in the 1960s thanks to "a series of technical innovations in sound and camera equipment." At that time, the documentary genre was represented by direct cinema, cinéma vérité, and observational documentary. American and Canadian direct cinema and French cinéma vérité "valued immediacy, intimacy and 'the real'; they both rejected the glossy 'professional' aesthetic of traditional cinema, unconcerned if their images were grainy and wobbly and occasionally went out of focus—in fact, these 'flaws' in themselves seemed to guarantee authenticity and thus became desirable, eventually developing into an aesthetic in their own right." Yet the representatives of cinéma vérité, among them Edgar Morin, Jean Rouch, and Dziga Vertov, believed that "the camera was able to reveal a deeper level of truth about the world than the 'imperfect human eye.' They interviewed their subjects and intervened constantly in the filming." In contrast, Robert Drew, who represented direct cinema, argued that it is "a 'theatre without actor,'" and thus one "could record 'reality' without influencing it."[61] In this respect, observational documentary followed the tradition of direct cinema. Documentary filmmakers thus were always concerned with questions of reality and truth and searched for their own ways to deal with these issues in their works. It was important to create a documentary film that would not be confused with a fictional film.

Another important technique that a documentary can employ and that makes it closer to a fiction film involves the presence of actors and the use of scripts—the phenomenon that Bonner calls "re-enactment."[62] When this is done, does not a documentary turn into something akin to a fiction film, where the events are staged, the roles are assigned, and the lines are distributed? Too many factors are involved to claim an unequivocal yes or no to this question. If the people shown are not the actual individuals but instead are portrayed as "real" characters by actors, and the text is written specifically for the film, does the film still fall into the documentary genre? Ward appeals to a "commonsense suggestion," stating that "the aesthetics somehow *distort* or *change* the reality being represented." He adds that the shooting of a documentary the way one would a fiction film, that is, the staging of it, "invalidates the documentary status of what we are looking at." Is it not so that "truth could only be represented via the literal unfolding of events, captured as if the camera and crew were not present"?[63] One witnesses very complex relations between documentary and fiction for the reason that both seem to borrow particular elements from each other. Michael Renov writes, "Nonfiction contains any number of 'fictive' elements, moments at which a presumably objective representation of the world encounters the necessity of creative intervention." More than that, both fiction and nonfiction aim at touching the imagination of their audiences: "It would be unwise to assume that only fiction films appeal to the viewer's Imaginary, that psychic domain of idealized forms, fantasy, identification, reversible time, and alternative logics." Thus, in terms of perception, the audience has to switch on its imagination to interpret and understand a particular representation, whether it be fictional or nonfictional. In other words, with regard to the representation of reality and the search for truth, it is the task of the audience to find out where the truth is. Renov's argument seems very appropriate here: "The two domains [fiction and documentary] *inhabit* one another."[64] That, in turn, reveals that "blurred boundary" suggested by Nichols and unveils the difficulty of distinguishing fiction from nonfiction in particular cases.[65]

Bonner contends that in such films, "there are still truth claims being made."[66] In line with Bonner's argument, I suggest that the documentary genre is relatively flexible. In its most traditional form, a documentary records events in real time, without actors, invented lines, or specially designed decorations, and presents a particular reality. But many examples show that the documentary genre has not stopped at one specific type of filmmaking but, rather, has adopted an array of means to represent truth and reality. Stella Bruzzi criticizes the view "that the minute an individual becomes involved in the representation of reality, the integrity of that reality is irretrievably lost." She contends that the documentary is a "perpetual negotiation between the real event and its representation. . . . The two remain distinct but interactive."[67] The techniques employed notwithstanding, documentary is a form that attempts to present reality, and therefore it is perceived "as non-fictional" by the audience.[68]

In discussing the connection between fiction and nonfiction in the documentary genre, it is important to address the issue of narrativity that Hayden White has meticulously examined in relation to the representation of reality. White suggests we must "distinguish between a historical discourse that narrates . . . and a discourse that narrativizes." While the first "reports" the events, the second "feigns" them; hence "narrative should be considered less as a *form* of representation than as a *manner of speaking* about events, whether real or imaginary." Therefore documentary is first of all a narrative; the representation does not function on a visual level only. White touches upon a serious issue when introducing his understanding of narrativity: he foregrounds storytelling as the main element in the composition of representation. Representation is, first of all, a story, whether that story is true or fictional. White argues, "By common consent, it is not enough that a historical account deal in real, rather than merely imaginary, events; and it is not enough that the account in its order of discourse represent events according to the chronological sequence in which they originally occurred. The events must be not only registered within the chronological framework of their original occurrence but narrated as well, that is to say, revealed as possessing a structure, an order of meaning, which they do *not* possess as mere sequence." He concludes, "'The true' is identified with 'the real' only insofar as it can be shown to possess the character of narrativity."[69] Dealing with documentary (and history in general) as a form that can be told and retold, one cannot but notice the overlap between nonfiction and fiction in this process. Specifically, one can speculate that the ability to be narrated and take the shape of a story unites both fiction and nonfiction genres. Yet, at the same time, the types of stories told—fictive, imaginary, fantasy, or real—set the two genres apart.

Nevertheless documentary is a complex form that to various degrees employs both fictional and nonfictional elements, and this eventually leads to difficulty in distinguishing one from the other. Speaking once again in Nichols's terms, one can talk about a "blurred boundary" between fiction and nonfiction in the documentary genre.[70] Discussing the problem of meaning in a documentary film, Trinh even insists, "There is no such thing as documentary—whether the term designates a category of material, a genre, an approach, or a set of techniques."[71] Ulrich Kurowski believes that "there is no such thing as 'documentary film'" because "the image cannot be reality."[72] Both scholars challenge the existence of a realistic depiction, even as they imply, in unison with some other academics, that because there are so many nuances in representing reality and interpreting truth, the term "documentary" has become archaic.

Is it possible to distinguish between documentaries that depict the truth fairly closely and those that do not? Trinh argues, "Good documentaries are those whose subject matter is 'correct' and with whose point of view the viewer agrees."[73] This is, however, a very controversial claim, as it makes one question the notions "good" and "correct." Let us start with understanding what would make a documentary "correct." One can say that it is correct when it deals with an actual person, event, or issue; this aspect is quite clear. But for a documentary to be correct, to what extent does the narration have to coincide with the opinion of the audience? What about documentaries that raise controversial political issues, inevitably provoking debate and dividing the audience into supporters, opponents, and those who remain neutral? To some members of the audience, a particular documentary can be correct, but does this necessarily mean that if others disagree with the views expressed, then this documentary is automatically incorrect? How can we grasp the meaning of the "good" documentary? "Good" in this context can be related to the notion of a "correct" work, as a correct documentary is a good one. It is logical that the documentary that depicts false views or promotes wrong opinions is an "incorrect" one and is therefore "bad," again in terms of its subject matter. However, dividing documentaries into good and bad is wrong when considering that a correct documentary can only be one "with whose point of view the viewer agrees." In this case, the problem of authentic representation is put into question. Does it mean that the representation is true if it coincides with the opinion of the audience? Trinh makes an interesting remark: "The real? Or the repeated artificial resurrection of the real, an operation whose overpowering success in substituting the visual and verbal signs of the real for the real itself ultimately helps to challenge the real, thereby intensifying the uncertainties engendered by any clear-cut division between the two. In the scale of what is more and what is less real, subject matter is of primary importance."[74] The authentic representation of particular events, and one's evaluation of this representation in terms of truthfulness, strongly depend on the subject matter. Still, it is important to draw a line between a documentary's subject matter and the audience's response to it, since in relation to the authenticity of representation these aspects are polar.

Scholars insist on the complex entwinement of fiction and nonfiction in any documentary work. This becomes apparent when we realize that any documentary represents a reality that is artificially shaped by a film director or a book author. Each documentary, just like each work of fiction, has a story to tell. This story does not exist in this particular form in reality, to be simply taken up and appropriated; rather there must be a creator (or creators) who tackles the issue from a certain perspective in order to collect, shape, and present the truth in what is deemed to be the best way. Consider the following: "You must re-create reality because reality runs away; reality denies reality. You must first interpret it, or re-create it. . . . When I make a documentary, I try to give the realism an artificial aspect. . . . I find that the aesthetic of a document comes from the artificial aspect of the document. . . . It has to be more beautiful than realism, and therefore it has to be composed . . . to give it another sense."[75] Thus documentary *is* fiction in the sense that it is created or rather "re-create[d]," yet since its task is to present truth, it should not be considered *fictional* in the common understanding of the term. Documentary is a hybrid. It employs both truth and fiction, but by employing fiction it does not undermine truth because, to borrow from Trinh, "to give the filmed document another sense, another meaning, is not necessarily to distort it."[76] Yet if fiction is relatively harmless, so to speak, to documentary, can documentary be successfully involved in fiction too? When dealing with this question, one must return to the problem of truth and true representation in general. As it has already been argued earlier, truth helps one understand reality. In turn, true representation helps one accurately imagine the real event that is at the center of representation. Yet, in line with Foucault, I contend that, once being part of a specific representation, truth can turn into an instrument of power. Moreover it can lead to creation of other truths. Therefore, when considering that a representation (whether documentary or fictional) may consist of both truth and fiction and so may be hybrid, one is to examine the role of fiction in a documentary representation and the role of truth in a fictional one. My contention is that when implicating these traditionally unusual elements in the two genres, the author or director strives for achieving narratological power; that is, the creator turns to fiction or truth in order to transform a traditional genre and ultimately intensify the message that the text seeks to transmit. This certainly works for both genres, yet I am particularly interested in how this transformation influences a fictional narrative.

From Documentary to Fiction: Introducing the Concept of (War) Docu-Fiction

There is a considerable debate about how much fiction there is in documentaries. Yet here I would like to reverse the perspective and examine an issue from the opposite side, namely: Can fictional works (particularly those of film and literature) adopt elements of documentary, and, if so, can they thus reflect reality and truth and eventually bring fiction closer to the documentary genre? If, as Bruzzi states in relation to documentary, "there has been a relaxation of some of the boundaries between documentary and fiction," cannot such a "relaxation" be noticed in the sorts of fiction that manages to incorporate documentary?[77] Was not Henry James right after all when he claimed that "the only reason for the existence of a novel is that it does attempt to represent life"?[78] Finally, can fiction, with its realistic representations, be a serious mode, just as documentary is?

Going back in history, film documentaries that appeared before 1909 were considered entertainment, and only with the emergence of fiction films did documentaries start to lose this status.[79] It is, however, impossible to claim that they were completely transformed into a serious product as such, especially considering Bruzzi's term "factual entertainment," which emphasizes the possibility of combining fact and entertainment.[80] After all, documentaries are films, and film's main purpose is, now as always, to entertain. Some might find certain documentaries to be much more entertaining than particular fiction films. David L. Wolper's attempts "to make documentaries that were entertaining as well as informative" and to reach the emotive side of his audience, by creating films that are "emotional and entertaining," vividly illustrate this argument.[81] If documentaries were (or still are) considered entertaining, it is interesting to examine whether fiction film (at least its particular examples), whose chief aim is to entertain, can be considered serious cinema.

Works neither of fictional film nor of literature are treated as reliable sources when it comes to questions of truth and reality. Marc Ferro laments, "The fiction film is despised, because it dispenses only a dream, as if the dream formed no part of reality, as though the imaginary were not one of the driving forces of human activity."[82] As complex as documentary is, fiction is not an easy issue to deal with either. How does one determine whether a particular representation is documentary or fiction? Some scholars underline the difficulty of doing so, claiming that "there is no textual property that will identify a stretch of discourse as a work of fiction."[83] Thus it is impossible to say definitely whether a given representation is only a work of fiction and does not show reality or the truth about reality. Ward distinguishes between nonfiction and fiction, claiming that while nonfiction is "a realm where there is a basis in the world of actuality," in fiction "places and characters may be completely fabricated."[84] In contrast, Platinga argues, "All films are fictions, equally reliable—that is, not reliable at all, becoming fabrications expressive of our wishes and desires and reflecting not reality but our self-interest."[85] This is a pivotal observation that I will take as the central argument to support the idea that any representation (and not only the cinematic examples that Platinga discusses) is fictitious in its nature; these fictions skillfully combine imaginative and documentary parts.

Using the example of the soap opera, which presents its audience with "the 'reality' . . . [that is] typical of 'everyday life,'" Nick Lacey claims that "realist texts can, of course, be fiction."[86] That is, while soap opera imitates our everyday reality, it is not a form of documentary because it invents a whole new world of its own, with characters, events, and sometimes even places that do not exist. This is perhaps what Barthes meant when he wrote, "It is well known how often our 'realistic' literature is mythical (if only as a crude myth of realism) and how our 'literature of the unreal' has at least the merit of being only slightly so."[87] And although Barthes analyzes literature, his understanding can aptly be applied to every type of fiction and nonfiction. Thus while particular modes of representation are disguised as realism but in fact are absolute fictions (like soap operas), others that are taken to be pure fiction at first sight can in fact represent reality. In this respect, "mainstream cinema . . . is realism."[88] Yet the division is, of course, not so simple.

Unlike documentaries, explains Lacey, "realist fictional texts do not claim to be representing actual events, but rather things which could happen, or might have happened." While documentary "represent[s] *the* world," fiction depicts "*a* created world."[89] It is certainly difficult if not impossible to confuse a fictional with a documentary text; the audience hardly ever has such a problem. Yet can one claim that some fictions more than others remind their audience of documentaries? I assert that one can. Lacey accentuates the importance of time and space in the creation of realistic fiction. He argues that, first, "convincing characters must exist in a particular time and place" and, second, "the setting, whether historical or contemporary, [must] signif[y] itself to be accurate."[90]

Derrida does not refute the possibility that fiction can represent truth in his analysis of the following questions: "What happens . . . when a text, for example a so-called literary fiction . . . stages truth? When it defines analytical reading, assigns the analyst his position, shows him in search of truth, and even finding it, holding a discourse about the truth of the text and then pronouncing in general terms the discourse of truth, the truth of truth? What happens then to a text allowing for such a scene and, excelling in its program, in situating the analytical bustle at grips with truth?" He eventually concludes, "'Literature' can thus produce, stage, and advance something like truth. Its power thus extends itself beyond the truth of which it is capable." Yet, while analyzing Lacan's understanding of the relationship between truth and fiction, Derrida makes a crucial observation: "'Truth inhabits fiction' should not be understood in the somewhat perverse sense of a fiction which is more powerful than the truth which inhabits it and is inscribed in it. In truth, truth inhabits fiction as the master of the house, as the law of the house and as the economy of fiction. Truth brings about the economy of fiction. It directs, organizes and renders fiction possible."[91] Derrida then refers to the Lacanian argument that truth "makes the very existence of fiction possible" and writes:

> The question is thus to ground fiction in truth to guarantee it within truth and to do so without stressing, as is the case of *Das Unheimlich* [sic], this resistance, always renewed, of literary fiction to the general law of psycho-analytic knowledge. Lacan never poses the different question of what distinguishes different literary fictions. Even if all fiction were founded on a truth or made possible by a truth, the question may remain pertinent to the type of fiction from which something like literature . . . arises, and to the effects literature might have on the very thing which seems to render it possible.[92]

Later, Derrida observes, "Truth commands the fictional substance of its manifestation which allows it to be or become what it is, to be confirmed. It commands this substance from its origin or from its telos, which ultimately subordinates this concept of literary fiction to a rather classical interpretation of mimesis: [as a] detour towards the truth, more truth in fictive representation than in reality, increased faithfulness, 'superior realism.'"[93] Thus Derrida accurately underlines the absolutely symbiotic relationship between truth and fiction, arguing, in line with Lacan, that fiction would never have existed if there had been no truth, and stresses the fact that there is truth in fiction and it is exactly truth that ultimately determines fiction.

What sort of text is generally called fiction? Paisley Livingston declares, "A work is fictional just in case it is the product of the right sort of fictive intent: that is, its author(s) must have a communicative intention that some target audience adopt the attitude of imagining toward the work's propositions."[94] This is quite obvious, though, since every work is a unique creation of an author and it is the author who decides how to shape and narrate the idea(s) that he or she intends to present to the audience: the choice of topic, the characters and events, and the choice of words, elements, and techniques are always individual and are determined by the creator alone. What is important in what Livingston says, however, is the idea of the author's intention: the degree to which a fictional work is fiction has been determined by the author. That said, the author decides how much realism his or her work will contain. But how objective is the realism that the author depicts in the work? Is it not then what Lacan calls "[a] truth," that is, not absolute truth but rather a particular piece of knowledge, or even only one's understanding and interpretation of a matter that one attempts to present as truth or as an authentic account of reality?[95] More than that, it is not necessarily the case even that the author is presenting his or her personal viewpoint; instead the author may create a "fictional author" whose opinion and outlook do not necessarily reflect those of the real author.[96] This is what Currie earlier called an "implied author," arguing that "her mental economy does not necessarily correspond to that of the actual author."[97] Livingston underscores that it is more important to find out what the real author thinks about the subject than to rely on what an invented one puts forth.[98] One can speculate that this is because in fiction, truth is frequently disguised and is not narrated explicitly; instead the audience is presented with facts that are to be deconstructed, questioned, and analyzed.[99]

When dealing with the problem of truth in fiction, along with reality, one has to consider illusion. Is it the case that when one thinks that fiction is endeavoring to display truth, this is only an illusion, and in fact there is no truth in fiction at all—that this is only a false appearance or impression of reality? Does fiction in such cases employ what Christopher Brooke calls "a special skill in illusion," namely "the capacity to deceive the viewers or the readers into thinking that something especially real has been put before them"?[100] How can such an illusion be constructed? Ward offers a basic distinction between nonfiction and fiction: if "the events and persons depicted exist (or did exist) in the real world of actuality," then it is nonfiction; if, however, "the events and persons are . . . fictional or made up," then it is fiction.[101] Discussing the relationship between reality and illusion in film, Currie refutes the argument that they can be combined and instead proposes that film is exclusively a "realistic medium." While the scholar "accept[s]" that "the experience of film watching approximates the normal experience of perceiving the real world," he is "neutral" about the fact that "film is transparent in that we see 'through' it to the real world, as we see through a window or a lens," and he "reject[s]" the idea that "film is realistic in its capacity to engender in the viewer an illusion of the reality and presentness of fictional characters and events portrayed." Currie therefore disagrees with the view that "film induces the illusion that fictional events are real and that the viewer is directly witnessing them."[102] While the second concern is more psychological in nature, involving the relationship between the viewer and what is being viewed, his first concern seems to be related more to the problem of realistic fiction. How does a consumer of a realistic fictional text understand what is factual information and what is fiction? Does not realistic fiction prompt confusion in this regard, making one question facts and believe in fiction at some point? Indeed such a reaction happens, and this is the biggest flaw of realistic fiction.

Analyzing docudrama and mock-documentary (or mockumentary), Steven N. Lipkin, Derek Paget, and Jane Roscoe foreground the problem of fictive or, rather, "mislead[ing]" films that pretend to be documentaries. Unlike a drama-documentary that "uses the sequence of events from a real historical occurrence or situation, and the identities of its principal protagonists, to underpin a film script intended to provoke debate about the significance of the events/occurrence," a docudrama "uses a wholly invented sequence of events, and fictional protagonists, in order to illustrate the silent features of actual occurrences or situations." Is not docudrama, then, the best example of fiction that attempts to represent truth? Especially considering that, as these scholars suggest, it "obeys the rules of the fictional film"? That is, docudrama is a hybrid of fiction and documentary that combines the features of both genres in equal proportion. The examples the scholars provide in regard to docudramas include Marvin J. Chomsky's miniseries *Holocaust: The Story of the Family Weiss* (1978), Steven Spielberg's *Schindler's List* (1993), Spike Lee's *Malcolm X* (1992), Roman Polanski's *The Pianist* (2002), and Ridley Scott's *Black Hawk Down* (2001), because these films and miniseries re-create specific events that took place in history, they unfold in places that really exist, and they present characters who (at least some of them) are or were actual people.[103] While I agree that these films stand out from most other Hollywood films because they are not pure fictions, I find it problematic to classify them as docudramas. Still, there is quite a solid criticism directed toward fiction films that attempt to deal with historical facts: they "unabashedly use the assertion of a real historical subject to satisfy box office demands, and those box-office demands often generate films that are either ahistorical, unexamined, and ideological, or heroic/tragic dramas, like *Schindler's List*." Such films, in this view, do not become reliable historical documents but instead become "pornography of the real."[104] Yet it is crucial to understand that none of these films pretends to be documentaries. A harsh criticism that is frequently spewed at them is, however, understandable: dealing with some of the most horrific events, including slavery, genocide, and war, they frequently neglect the ethical side of the matter, turning humanity's traumatic past into its entertaining present. These films are documentaries to a certain extent, yet one should never ignore that they are also fictions. Therefore, for such films, I propose the term "docu-fictions," seeking not only to reveal their hybrid nature but also to underline the fact that these representations (and this applies to films and to literature) are documentaries *and* fictions. While the events that they present "occurred *much like* what we see," as Lipkin, Paget, and Roscoe claim, it is important to keep in mind that the events were not *exactly* as portrayed;[105] therefore the term "docu-fiction" is more apt in this context than "docudrama." Importantly, these texts are not "fictive documentaries" but "documentary fictions" because they were originally intended to look like fictions and their main purpose is still to entertain and only secondarily to educate. However, the very fact that they include elements of realism makes them hybrid works wherein documentary and fictional forms are combined. I do not use two discrete words to define this genre but rather merge them together as "docu-fiction" so as to demonstrate the unified nature of the final product; I use a hyphen to indicate that for the most part this is *fiction*, which contains history and reality.

I am, of course, not the first to notice that fictional texts "'based on' or 'inspired by' 'true stories'" stand out from the genre of fiction, for they take "their roots in actuality."[106] What, then, is so special about the genre of docu-fiction? It is obviously more credible than fiction per se because it attempts to represent history. It is, of course, not a mode of pure documentary, and so the audience should not fully rely on what it is told or what it sees or reads. Thus one might wonder what the purpose of docu-fictions is. If documentary, speaking in rough terms, presents history, and fiction seeks to entertain, why would one need to create docu-fictions, since, one might speculate, such works would neither be able to fully educate nor, perhaps in some cases, to satisfactorily entertain, and would thus only confuse the audience? Here it seems important to raise again the questions asked by Ward with respect to the historical documentary: "Who is telling this story? To whom? And why?"[107] As has been noted, the *fictional* part of docu-fictions is still important. As Ward, borrowing the example from Platinga, shrewdly points out, "If someone uses a toaster as a weapon to hit an intruder, it would still be described as a 'toaster,' despite its unconventional usage on that particular occasion. A similar conventional usage prevents someone from simply understanding a fictional film as nonfictional (or vice versa): if we were to watch *The Matrix* (Andy and Larry Wachowski, 1999, US) as nonfiction we would be misunderstanding the film's status."[108] It is clear, though, that in such cases the audience decides what is—or rather can easily distinguish between—fact and fiction. As Platinga himself states, "If George Lucas had indexed *Star Wars* as nonfiction, I doubt whether the viewing public would have received it as a nonfiction film simply because Lucas introduced it as such."[109] This is what Noël Carroll calls "label[ing]" or "index[ing]": "Standardly, when one attends a film, one does not have to guess—on the basis of how it looks and sounds—whether it is fiction or nonfiction. Nor does one typically guess whether a written narrative is a novel or a memoir. The film and the writing come labeled, or, as I say, *indexed*, one way or another, ahead of time."[110]

In investigating the representation of reality, it is important to correlate realism and verisimilitude and to distinguish between them. In this, the analysis provided by Taylor Stoehr seems most useful: "Fiction does not imitate life in the way that mirrors do . . . nor does it pretend to be real in the way wax bananas do." This argument once again emphasizes that it is important to understand that not only is fiction not reality, but it does not attempt to be such. "Truth-to-life is not valued in the same way as truth," and why should it? When fiction creates its own reality, it is, of course legitimate, but that does not mean that one should consider that reality to be real, that is, to be actual reality. Certain facts can be created, and they would not disturb the process of perception. For example, Stoehr claims, "What do we care if the sperm whale is not really the largest of mammals? For the purposes of reading *Moby-Dick*, at most we wish it were." Indeed, one does not read *Moby-Dick* to get factual information about whales, and although such information is included, it is hardly the reason why one reads this novel. If one wants to get detailed scientific information about whales, one most probably turns to an encyclopedia. Stoehr foregrounds two main terms that are crucial in the analysis of realistic fiction: "realism" and "verisimilitude."[111] In fact the distinction is pivotal in the analysis of truth and reality as reflected in fiction. One might falsely think that verisimilitude is only an *imitation* of reality, and thus equivalent to an illusion; that is, it is an *illusion* of reality. That, however, is not exactly so. The French *vraisemblance*, which stands for "verisimilitude," is reminiscent of the English word "resemblance." One might claim that verisimilitude is the *resemblance* of reality. Yet *vraisemblance* also means "probability." And here it is worth referring to Stoehr, who describes verisimilitude as a "tool of realism," but not an imitation, "a trick of the practiced ear or eye by which an author enhances his illusion of life." To achieve realism in his or her work, the author uses various "devices" but not verisimilitude per se. Yet while Stoehr claims that "the techniques of realism are the best means of achieving verisimilitude," I would consider the problem from the reverse perspective (without, however, refuting Stoehr's position): namely, that verisimilitude is a means that the author can use in the service of achieving reality in his or her work.[112] Creating narratives that resemble truth and reality, the author or director does not exactly invent truth; rather he or she projects it into the work, which eventually makes it closely resemble what is real. Thus the connection between verisimilitude and realism is apparent.

Of course, truth in fiction is not as significant as it is in scientific literature and film; however, if the author or director wants to make the work reflect a real situation or be perceived by the readers or viewers that way, he or she has to follow specific rules. These are the rules of mimesis, among which Stoehr singles out "familiarity," "particularity," "plausibility and probability," and "simulation and illusion." The first two rules deal with "the relation between language and reality"; in other words, "the availability of words to 'stand for' objects" is crucial. However, "particularity" also implies "using a high proportion of names of physical objects and spending time characterizing [them]." Quite obviously, "plausibility and probability" presuppose the inclusion of specific events and actions that can take place in real life. Finally, "illusion" is compared to "identification"' that is, readers are always "caught up in the story" to such a degree that they believe that what they read exactly mirrors their own thoughts: "The expressed thoughts of a character are our own thoughts; reading them is thinking them, though not thinking them up." "Simulation," in turn, is achieved by such "devices" as "the autobiographical mode, the epistolary narrative, the quotation of invented (or genuine) documents, newspaper articles, manuscripts, letters, poems, and so forth." Thus reality is simulated while the reader is persuaded that this is the case.[113]

In this regard, I would like to briefly return to Baudrillard's analysis of "simulacra" and "simulation." Using the examples of Disneyland and Watergate, Baudrillard writes about the "effect of the imaginary concealing that reality no more exists outside than inside the limits of the artificial perimeter."[114] Can one argue that in simulating reality, fiction (whether film or literature) creates a reality that attempts to be more "real" than actual reality? In other words, in simulating reality, or in reflecting reality and thus inevitably creating a new reality, the author or director has to intensify the realism of the work only to make sure that the fiction will be taken as something that reflects truth and reality. Therefore, applying Baudrillard's terminology of being "inside the limits of the artificial perimeter," one can contend that film and literature make up this "artificial perimeter," within which reality is created and eventually given a prescribed form. This, compared to our everyday reality, represents another dimension. One can speculate that the endless creation of such realities in fiction changes their authenticity. To borrow from Baudrillard, "From the most fantastic or mythical to the realistic and the hyperrealistic."[115]

Scholars have noted that some fiction films "pay tribute to documentary techniques"; they do so "us[ing] a certain shooting style and dialogue which evokes 'documentaries' in order to bolster their claims to authenticity."[116] The same takes place in literature when authors combine "the more creative forms of mythic discourse" with history.[117] In this way, docu-fictions somewhat break with White's reflection that "narrative becomes a *problem* only when we wish to give the *real* events the *form* of story. It is because real events do not offer themselves as stories that their narrativization is so difficult."[118] Docu-fictions, in this sense, manage to "narrativize" history by combining it with fictional events and creating a streaming story. Carroll discusses the problem of fusing "history" and "narrativization," pointing out that while "historical reality" can be present in fiction, the story itself ("the plot") "has no reference to reality."[119] But that, I argue, is exactly what makes a docu-fiction what it is: the presence of both "historical reality" (docu-) and "the invented plot" (fiction).

Certainly no one would dispute that documentary and fiction are different, yet it is important to notice the extent to which the two genres overlap and how the elements common to both help produce distinct subgenres and even new genres, such as docu-fiction.

Fiction can reflect everyday and historical reality. Ferro, for example, claims that fiction film can be used to analyze society and vice versa, that fiction film can be analyzed *through* society, thus underlining their tight relationship; their connection is even stronger than that between documentary and society. Pinpointing the serious nature of film, he also insists that "every film has a value as a document."[120] Fiction is not just the product or expression of someone's fantasy; it is a serious genre. This idea can be reinforced only if one is to discuss historical fiction, the genre that successfully combines documentary with fiction. Both of Ferro's arguments can also be applied to literary fiction because, just like film, literature can be analyzed through society and can help examine society; literary texts can be considered documents. Ferro's argument can thus be somewhat generalized and utilized for the analysis of fiction in general.

Yet fiction can and should be classified. When saying that docu-fiction exists, I do not propose that we think that every fictional text reflects (historical) reality (although such texts do create their own realities). I suggest instead a careful analysis, because even if fiction can present reality, the proportion of fact to fiction varies among works; thus the "quantity" of authentic material defines the documentary level of a given representation. In this respect, I contend that subject matter assumes the most pivotal role here, and I consider war fiction and specifically the fiction of interventionism to be one of the most authentic subgenres in this regard. When literature or film deals with a particular war or military operation, regarding it purely as fiction is inappropriate, or rather inaccurate; instead such a fictional work should be referred to as docu-fiction. Although this book focuses only on wars (and particularly U.S. interventions) that took place after 1990, I do not claim specifically that only the literature and films that deal with these wars are docu-fiction. The works that consider U.S. interventions prior to 1990 are docu-fictions too. Such works create an archive, a concept that I borrow from Derrida, who interprets it as follows: "It keeps, it puts in reserve, it saves"; or simply, it is "a record of the past."[121] But in this particular case, *the archive of war docu-fiction*—the storage that accumulates multiple works of film and literature—is what contains and eventually produces the cultural knowledge of U.S. interventionism.

What makes literary and cinematic works on war docu-fictions? First, of course, the topic itself. Implementing in its narration real wars, real campaigns, real operations, real people, and real geographic locations, war docu-fiction inevitably creates a strong basis for the story it has to tell. This very basis is what turns ostensible works of fiction into works of docu-fiction. Whether one reads Kurt Vonnegut's *Slaughterhouse-Five* (1969) or watches Stanley Kubrick's *Full Metal Jacket* (1987), one clearly orients oneself in time (World War II and the Vietnam War, respectively) and space or place (Germany and Vietnam, respectively). That is, one reads or watches a war docu-fiction as a projection of a particular military event rather than of an invented conflict. Second, the techniques used in film and literature to represent specific wars authentically are very often reminiscent of the ones used in documentaries about combat. To be specific about film: such films are often either partially shot in the style of a combat documentary (to create an impression that nothing has been staged, which is frequently achieved by the shaking images recorded by a camera as if it were in the midst of actual combat; this mode has very successfully transmitted a sense of the brutality of war in contemporary cinema) or include the use of cameras (usually when soldiers film their experience) to suggest that what is shown in the film is indeed real, and it is this reality that soldiers have recorded. It is worth mentioning that many of the current conventions of realistic combat portrayal were established by a single film: Steven Spielberg's *Saving Private Ryan* (1998). In literature such examples include the use of letters (or their excerpts) from soldiers to their friends and relatives and of images that suggest authenticity of the narrated story. A docu-fiction might invent a story, but particular aspects of such a story prevent one from labeling the text as mere fiction. One can clearly spot what Ferro dubs "areas of overlap" between fiction and documentary. I claim that this overlapping is most apparent in docu-fiction; "one has only to learn to read it."[122]

To corroborate my argument that war docu-fiction should not be classified as mere fiction because it combines fiction and documentary, I would like to address the issue of entertainment. Although my analysis of documentary and fiction rejects the idea that there is a strict division between the two on the basis of entertainment, it is still possible to claim that in general terms a documentary's task is to provide factual information, to educate, whereas the task of fiction is, to a large degree, to entertain. What is the purpose of docu-fiction: to entertain or to educate? Lacey's example of films on the Iraq War seems very appropriate in this context: "the audiences weren't interested in seeing representations of such an important event," chiefly because, according to Lacey, "cinema is seen primarily as an entertainment medium, [and] audiences didn't want to be reminded of the death and destruction occurring in Iraq."[123] This example vividly demonstrates that when directors and authors base their stories on such a complex and, most importantly, tragic and traumatic event as war, their products (i.e., films, miniseries, novels, short stories, etc.) can no longer be exclusively regarded as entertainment. This does not, of course, guarantee that they are automatically to be regarded as educative media, yet, as I have argued, since these films and literary works play with facts, they *do* become educative, for they reflect or bring to the fore particular truths about wars. Therefore docu-fictions with war as their subject, as those on the Iraq War prove, can be perceived as not being (exclusively) entertaining because they are not pure fiction; they project or resurrect the memories of real-life events in the minds of their audiences.

In addition, Lacey provides a brief analysis of Brian DePalma's *Redacted* (2007), a film that, as I will analyze later in greater detail, is "a fiction inspired by true events."[124] The film, as Lacey correctly observes, is a collage of various events that "(might have) happened."[125] The uncertainty is crucial because, as this film, along with many other narratives that will be examined in the following chapters, demonstrates, docu-fictions of war are conspicuous for their ability to mix fact with fiction in a way that makes it hard to know what is what. In the case of *Redacted*, the viewer understands that he or she is witnessing events that took place in Iraq, most certainly that American soldiers raped an Iraqi girl, but at the same time one can question everything else that accompanies the main plotline. Since the story is based on true events, one assumes that some American soldiers did indeed rape an Iraqi girl and accepts this story to be true. Yet how much of the rest is true is impossible to measure. Lacey also addresses the way the film is shot and concludes, "While it might seem that it is a realist text, the multimedia mixing instead draws attention to the artifice of what is shown.

This may suggest that such horrendous events *cannot* be convincingly rendered by realism."[126] Nevertheless the final (real) photograph of a dead Iraqi girl seems to sum up the story as true. Additionally, the image of the dead girl can be viewed as a symbol of the destructive side of the intervention in general; that is, it gives a potent visual form to represent all the other innocent victims of the war.

Rendering the brutality of war, docu-fictions emphasize their dual nature. On the one hand, they are documentaries because they attempt to depict real wars and real actions. On the other hand, they intensify the fact that the brutality of war demands fictional means for its representation when events are verbalized or visualized because the savageness of war is simply beyond sane human perception. Moreover one can speculate that the inclusion of fictional elements in war narratives helps one interpret the events from an unofficial perspective. It does not mean that there is no truth in such narratives, however; quite the contrary, they demonstrate *truths*—the term suggested by Lacan—of war, either subjective or objective. The inclusion of fictional elements does not allow one to call docu-fictions of war purely authentic representations, yet authenticity is present in them, mostly due to their serious subject matter, which is obviously related to (historical) reality. Further analysis of works of film and literature on U.S. interventions after 1990, namely the First Gulf War, the wars in the Balkans, the Afghanistan War, and the Iraq War (the Second Gulf War), will demonstrate that these texts display a (cultural) history of the interventions and thus deserve the status of docu-fictions. Overtly dealing with the problem of American interventionism, they reflect the change in U.S. policy regarding its interventions, showcasing the involvements after 1990 as mainly humanitarian missions yet also paying attention to the reasons behind such purportedly disinterested help, largely focusing on the issues of oil, national security, world leadership, and Western supremacy. While the representation of U.S. interventions in the selected cinematic and literary examples will primarily be examined through the prism of Lacan's theory of truth, according to which there is no unified truth but instead various truths—which only reinforces the complex and intricate nature of cultural representations of war—it seems plausible that the truths reflected in all these examples can be described as subjective and are dependent on the genre.

2

The First Gulf War

The History of the War

In 1990 the United States became involved in the Persian Gulf War (or, as it is often referred to, the First Gulf War). The premise for the First Gulf War was the increase of Iraqi troops at the border with Kuwait in the middle of July 1990, prompted by the Iraqi desire to influence Kuwaiti oil production and its price. Although the George H. W. Bush administration disregarded the probability of outright conflict, it agreed to provide military help when asked by the United Arab Emirates. The aim was to demonstrate to Iraq that the United States was able to withstand and suppress any Iraqi military actions. Although Saudi Arabia organized a sequence of meetings with Iraqi and Kuwaiti representatives, and it seemed that the continuation of the conflict had been prevented, Kuwait was occupied by the Iraqi military on August 2, 1990, and the incursion provoked U.S. concern that the Iraqi threat might spread to the other Gulf states. That would lead to Iraqi domination of the world's energy markets. In response, the United States initiated Operation Desert Shield on August 8, 1990, with the intention of freeing Kuwait, restoring its government, providing safety for the Gulf states, and protecting U.S. citizens who lived in the affected territory. The buildup of U.S. military forces lasted until the middle of January 1991, when Operation Desert Storm began: a six-week campaign involving aerial bombardment and one hundred hours of ground fighting. As a result, by the end of February, Iraqi forces had been driven out of Kuwait and the combat stopped. According to the U.S. government's assessment, the aims of American intervention had been fulfilled.[1]

In terms of conducting war, the U.S. strategy during the First Gulf War had clearly changed: it differed from the attacks on civilian populations during World War II, as well as the indiscriminate bombings during the Vietnam War.[2] Presumably because of this change, Americans were generally not against their military engaging in combat during the 1990s. In addition, television and the nascent internet made information on the wars accessible and available, which contributed to general national approval of the military involvements.[3] Seeing other people suffering or living under terrifying and dangerous war conditions made Americans support the use of U.S. military force in other countries, including Iraq, as the only efficient means of salvation. At the same time, free access to information on the war was fraught with other consequences, some of them undesirable for the U.S. government. To wit, "a revolution in information and communication . . . forever changed the roles of governments, militaries, the public, and the media," and the frequent translation of the events "ma[de] the world much smaller and more accessible."[4] Therefore governmental decisions had to be weighed and balanced, as every action was exposed to global public opinion. This meant that every right step would guarantee the United States support, from domestic and world audiences alike; every mistake or failure, however, could cost the United States in general and the government in particular their political reputation.

According to Edward Said, in the case of the First Gulf War, the media's main accomplishment was its convincing representation to U.S. domestic audiences that Iraqi culture was alien and dangerous, and this portrayal biased Americans generally against Iraq. More than that, Said accentuates the narrowness of the cultural picture that the media presented to the Western public: "All roads lead to the bazaar; Arabs only understand force; brutality and violence are part of Arab civilization; Islam is an intolerant, segregationist, 'medieval,' fanatic, cruel, anti-woman religion."[5] Nevertheless what the media undoubtedly achieved was "making the average American feel that it is up to 'us' to right the wrongs of the world." Hence Said insists on the cultivation of U.S. exceptionalism during the First Gulf War. The main motive that stands behind the ideology is, he argues, "a desire for mastery and domination" of "a stern White Man [an American, a Westerner], a kind of Puritan superego whose errand into the wilderness knows few boundaries and who will go to great lengths indeed to make his points."[6]

But exactly what "points" were made? Was the intervention as "colonial" as Said describes it, or can one spot other reasons behind the action? Bush's grandiose project of "a new world order, where diverse nations are drawn together in common cause to achieve the universal aspirations of mankind—peace and security, freedom, and the rule of law," crashed into pieces when Iraq invaded Kuwait.[7] One of the reasons for U.S. intervention—which openly characterized the involvement as a humanitarian effort—was to restore the model of a world that would live together peacefully and in a civilized fashion. Freeing oppressed Kuwaitis from the Iraqi military occupation was another humanitarian reason. Yet one other reason for U.S. involvement that should not be neglected—and that clearly is not a humanitarian rationale—was oil. Bush himself acknowledged, "Our own economy is suffering, suffering the effects of higher oil prices and lower growth stemming from Saddam's aggression."[8] Stephen G. Walker and Akan Malici remarked at the time that a successful Iraqi invasion of Kuwait would endow Saddam Hussein with considerable power over the United States, "which was heavily dependent on imported oil."[9] In this respect, Toby Craig Jones has made a very shrewd observation:

> The United States did not wage war out of old-fashioned imperial calculation or ambition. American oil wars have not been about

establishing direct control over oil fields nor about liberation or freedom, at least not political freedom for the peoples of the region. Instead, they have primarily been about protecting friendly oil producers. The objective has not necessarily been to guarantee that Middle Eastern oil made its way to the United States, although meeting basic domestic energy needs remained a vital part of the broader calculation. Keeping prices stable (not low) and keeping pro-American regimes in power were central to U.S. strategic policy.[10]

Therefore U.S. intervention in the Gulf region, although sometimes interpreted in a "blood-for-oil" sense, as Andrew J. Bacevich argues, had the purpose of guaranteeing "the ever-increasing affluence that underwrites the modern American conception of liberty." Hence strengthening militarization was nothing more than a demonstration of "the American will to be free."[11] Despite Jones's argument that the U.S. interest in oil was much stronger than the country's desire to bring democracy to the Middle East (and prevent the genocide of the Kurds and of the Shiites in the northern and southern parts of Iraq, respectively), one should understand that in fulfilling its economic aims, the U.S. also liberated Kuwait.[12] And although some scholars claim that "the presence of so much oil in the region no doubt was a prime factor in western willingness to take on this battle," the war nonetheless had a humanitarian aspect as well.[13]

The United States could not assent to Iraq's national assertion. Yet some scholars claim that the protracted U.S. involvement in the Middle East, including its participation in the First Gulf War, should not be reduced solely to its interest in oil and control over its extraction and production.[14] After all, the military intervention resulted in the liberation of Kuwaitis. Yet scholars' concerns about oil are too evident to be neglected. For example, Richard C. Thornton, examining rival Russian and American pushes for oil, argues that after the end of the Cold War, a new war started, a "struggle for power and influence, especially in the energy sector."[15] Therefore, one of the tasks this project undertakes is to scrutinize how oil as a decisive phenomenon in the conflict is represented in film and literary fiction and to determine what cultural niche it has found via certain visual and narrative forms. Additionally I seek to unveil the role that oil played in the war as it is portrayed in film and literary fiction and whether it is culturally represented as the central reason for U.S. involvement in the Gulf region.

While J. Bryan Hehir argues that the First Gulf War is characterized by the U.S. exercising a "hegemonic style of leadership," Michael D. Gambone makes the point that after the disintegration of the Soviet Union, the United States had to adapt to its new role in the world—the role of "the sole remaining superpower" whose duty was to maintain the world balance in a time of geopolitical flux.[16] By making frequent references to World War II and the Vietnam War and underlining the role of American soldiers in those conflicts, the American government drew the attention of national and international communities alike to the significance of the U.S. role in the First Gulf War.[17] Bush overtly compared the president of Iraq, Saddam Hussein, to Hitler, which charged Americans with the moral responsibility to help those burdened by Hussein's oppression to free themselves from the evil he embodied.[18] However, relatively fresh memories of the Vietnam War exerted a large influence on the public, so it was important not to repeat the failure of Vietnam in the Gulf region. The First Gulf War had to be represented as "the perfect war," especially when compared to the Vietnam conflict.[19] It was crucial to discredit the myths surrounding the war in Vietnam. President Bush's speech on March 17, 1991, foregrounded this connection between past and present wars: "You [U.S. soldiers] know, you all not only helped liberate Kuwait, you helped this country [the U.S.] liberate itself from old ghosts and doubts. And when you left, it was still fashionable to question America's decency, America's courage, America's resolve. No one, no one in the whole world doubts us anymore."[20]

Was this U.S. intervention in the Middle East a humanitarian intervention? Stephen G. Brooks and William C. Wohlforth claim that U.S. interference in Iraq and precisely "the use of force [were] widely seen as clearly lawful before the fact."[21] Friedrich Kratochwil goes further and asserts that it is wrong to call the U.S. participation in the First Gulf War a humanitarian intervention: "After all, the classical meaning of humanitarian intervention was to thwart specific crimes against humanity and to rescue actual and potential victims of an ongoing massacre. It was not designed to overthrow 'tyranny' or to spread democracy in the hope that such regimes might be more peaceful and cooperative in the future."[22] At the same time, Bill Clinton, who succeeded Bush as president and sought, in the words of Guy Westwell, to "rebrand Bush's foreign policy as his own," has claimed that the intervention in Iraq was undertaken because "the moral responsibility of America" entailed that it had "to ensure stability and promote democracy on *humanitarian grounds.*"[23] Analyzing the cultural representations of U.S. involvement in the First Gulf War, I aim to find out whether the works of film and literature addressing the war have portrayed the intervention as a humanitarian mission. Was the intervention a failed attempt on the part of the U.S., or can the war be justified due to its humanitarian nature? What other factors do docu-fictions of the First Gulf War present to the audience while narrating events from the history of the war?

Film and U.S. Intervention in the First Gulf War

Iraq's Invasion of Kuwait: Humanitarian Devastation and the Struggle for Oil in Werner Herzog's Lessons of Darkness (1992)

This chapter mainly focuses on the U.S. participation in the First Gulf War. But it is also important to see how film has presented the conflict on the local level, for it makes it evident that international (U.S.-led) involvement was in fact really necessary. Werner Herzog's *Lessons of Darkness* (1992) is one of the most famous documentary accounts of the war, which has contributed to our understanding of the Iraqi invasion of Kuwait and its destructive and ruinous consequences. Released a year after the war ended, the documentary could not, of course, influence people's minds during the conflict or help stop it. Nevertheless,

Lessons of Darkness serves as a justification of American involvement in the First Gulf War. It implicitly demonstrates that help was needed and that U.S. military operations were prompted not by the United States fighting for world leadership but because Kuwait needed an army of saviors.

Werner Herzog is a German-born filmmaker who is particularly famous for his documentaries. His understanding of documentary is somewhat unique, as he defines the genre "with particular emphasis on its contested relationship to knowledge." He is largely interested in the "vast areas of human experience that are not in themselves visual, and therefore tend to be either overlooked or neglected by scholars of documentary." And "has often rejected the distinction between fiction and documentary as an illicit one."[24] This is crucial to understanding Herzog's documentaries as cinematic products that overtly employ fiction, for the filmmaker finds the process of mixing fact with fiction essential in film production.

Lessons of Darkness has been classified as both a documentary and a science-fiction film that in visual, symbolic, and metaphorical ways shows Kuwait City before and after the attacks of the First Gulf War.[25] The director creates the film's apocalyptic world not only visually but also verbally, by including a voice-over and by conspicuously dividing his film into chapters. Structured in such a way, *Lessons of Darkness* pretends to be another version of the Bible, an analogue that focuses on peaceful life and its destruction provoked by human beings. Classical music, along with the lofty and elevated tone of the voice-over, adds much to the sense that the film is akin to Holy Writ.

The film starts with a quotation of Herzog's own, which he spuriously ascribes to Blaise Pascal: "The collapse of the stellar universe will occur—like creation—in grandiose splendor." By using these words to open the film, Herzog intends to bring his spectators to a "high level," which, he explains, is important to occupy from the very beginning of the viewing. A phrase that could plausibly be attributed to the renowned philosopher would grasp viewers' attention and make them understand the seriousness of Herzog's project. However, what the director ambitiously says about these pompous opening words is that "Pascal himself could not have said it better."[26]

In the beginning Herzog focuses on the filming of the capital as an idyllic setting. He pictures a sort of Gulf-region Eden: beautiful buildings, green trees, and, most important, everyday life zipping along. The director does not devote too much time to this part; as soon as the camera points at the deep waters surrounding the city, as if sinking in them, the screen turns black and a new part begins, titled "The War." The spectator is immersed in horrifying and at the same time fascinating, surreal pictures of the war-world—a world of human and ecological disaster. The new city that emerges on screen represents a scorched earth: it is a desert filled with smoke, oil, bones, and death. Eden is replaced by Hell, terrifying and shockingly mesmerizing. This new world becomes the major focus of Herzog's film, which implicitly judges humankind for committing crimes of this kind—crimes whose perpetrators have inflicted destruction not just on others but on themselves. For a long time the viewer can observe oil fires burning in Kuwait City and the hard work of firefighters who are trying to extinguish them. The end of the film, which contains images of oil fires on the horizon, does not allow one to underestimate the film's main message: that human violence and self-destruction are like a vicious circle, never ending. The First Gulf War may be over, but the director, as if prophesying, makes the case that this was not the final war and is definitely not the last act of human violence that will be committed against other human beings and against nature. As Herzog himself puts it, *Lessons of Darkness* demonstrates "a crime against creation itself." It is, however, interesting that the film was classified not just as a documentary but also as a science-*fiction* film, which the director interprets as follows: "There is not a single frame in *Lessons of Darkness* in which you can recognize our planet; . . . [it is] as if it could only have been shot in a distant galaxy, hostile to life."[27] Calling this film a work of science fiction (or perhaps even a docu-fiction) accentuates the fictional element in it. One can speculate that this classification demonstrates how unready people are to accept the destructive reality of war, its violence and brutality in general, and the First Gulf War in particular.

Apart from dealing with the ecological disaster caused by the conflict, Herzog pays attention to the ramifications of the Iraqi invasion on the Kuwaiti people. The audience hears the story of a woman whose sons were tortured and killed right in front of her, which caused her to be struck dumb. Another example of Iraqi violence is the story of a young woman whose little son is now unable to speak because an Iraqi soldier stomped on the boy's head; the parents had to watch this act of savagery, completely helpless to do anything because rifles were being pointed at them; in the end, after shooting the woman's husband, the Iraqi soldiers let the boy go. Those stories occurred more than a year before their telling in *Lessons of Darkness*, but the pain the people feel due to their losses and the fear resulting from what happened to them obviously still live with them.

Thematically Herzog's film stands out for one rather obvious reason: it combines issues of war, ecology, and humanity, unveiling the intricate relations among these fundamental problems. The film's thematic uniqueness makes it clear why I have chosen it to start my analysis of the cultural representations of recent U.S. interventionism. Focusing on an ecological disaster along with the murdering of civilians, *Lessons of Darkness* distinctly tackles the issue of a *necessary* humanitarian intervention. As a result, the film allows the discussion of U.S. involvement in the Middle Eastern conflict as a humanitarian instance. As I have already argued, by displaying Kuwait in an apocalyptic way both aesthetically, as one observes ruins and sites of demolition, and content-wise, since both nature and human beings die in this war, Herzog's film justifies U.S. intervention, making it seem an explicitly humanitarian endeavor.

Yet there is another, more profound implication in the film that hints at the need for external help. Showcasing the death of people and nature, Herzog obviously shifts the focus to the latter, revealing the threat to nature to be an even more important problem caused by the Persian Gulf War than the havoc affecting human beings. This choice can, of course, be interpreted in various ways, for example, that in conflicts between nations, people forget that nature involuntarily becomes part of such conflagrations. Nobody seems to care; dead animals, scorched earth, and polluted basins become just side-effects that humanity thinks can be restored on their own. Herzog explicitly demonstrates this to be a delusion. Moreover, by stressing the ecological disaster that can be dangerous not only for Kuwait, and not even just for the whole Middle East, but for the whole of planet Earth, Herzog makes the soldiers who come to stop this destruction assume the role of saviors; they save not only the Kuwaiti people but all humankind. Thus Bush's claim that "the hopes of humanity turn to us [Americans]" in terms of bringing liberty becomes somewhat prophetically illustrated in this film.[28] Here, however, humanity does not explicitly plead to be set free; rather it mutely asks to continue its existence. U.S. intervention, as illustrated in *Lessons of Darkness*, takes on a rather allegorical meaning, as U.S. soldiers stand for saviors. They rescue more than one nation from the ecological disaster caused by the war: they save the whole of humanity. Thus American soldiers, who are shown to be carrying out a humanitarian mission, symbolically turn into the ministers of God who have prevented the real apocalypse, stopping the descent into hell on planet Earth and providing human beings with a chance to rethink their existence, to cease engaging in warfare, and to live in peace, in a free, democratic society.

"Every War Is Different. Every War Is the Same": The Reflection of the First Gulf War in *Three Kings* (1999) and *Jarhead* (2005)

Apart from documentary accounts of the First Gulf War, a number of fictional—or rather docu-fictional—films were released that, through their invented plots, dealt with U.S. involvement in the conflict: the role of soldiers, the means applied to achieve the liberation of Kuwait, and the goals set by the U.S. military. The examples include David O.

Russell's action film *Three Kings* (1999) and Sam Mendes's war drama *Jarhead* (2005). The two films raise different issues concerning U.S. intervention and use different means to address the audience and draw its attention to the most salient aspects of the U.S. participation in the war. *Three Kings* presents an adventurous journey of Americans in the Middle East, narrated in a rather comic way, while *Jarhead* evokes feelings of incomprehension, sympathy, revolt, repulsion, compassion, and empathy. These two films may be quite different in genre and in the cinematic techniques they employ, but there is one aspect that unites them: they both question U.S. interventionist policy during the First Gulf War, taking a skeptical attitude toward the reasons for and consequences of sending soldiers to the Middle East, as well as the role of American soldiers in that war. Yet neither film gives up on presenting the intervention as a humanitarian mission.

DAVID O. RUSSELL'S *THREE KINGS*

Russell's *Three Kings* is set in Iraq in March 1991, right after the First Gulf War has ended. The film starts with Troy Barlow (Mark Wahlberg) seeing an Iraqi soldier and asking one of his comrades, "Are we shooting? Are we shooting people or what?" Another soldier does not know whether they are still supposed to shoot, since the war is officially over. No one from the group is interested in what is going on, so the soldier suggests that Barlow think for himself. Barlow responds, "I don't know the answer! That's what I am trying to find out!" Eventually he decides to shoot the Iraqi because he notices a rifle in his hands. "Congratulations! You shot yourself a raghead!" comments one of the soldiers while they all run to the dead man, suddenly deeply interested in what has just happened. Barlow, on the contrary, feels ashamed of what he has done, having realized that the man only wanted to surrender. The scene undermines the purported humanitarian intention of the intervention. However, Elizabeth E. Martinez finds the scene problematic, arguing that Barlow's aim was just to learn if they were ordered to shoot, not to find out whether shooting was "the right thing to do."[29] The scene explicitly demonstrates that the soldiers were instructed to kill in war. It is fruitless to think that every soldier analyzes whether the killing of an enemy in war is "the right thing to do." On the battlefield, if a soldier does not kill, he or she may not survive. Yet Barlow "do[es]n't know the answer" when the war ends because nobody has taught him what to do in that situation. American soldiers had been fighting against Iraqi soldiers for some time; how could they be expected to suddenly become indifferent to or even now be friends with their former enemies? Hence, while the scene attempts to portray the soldiers as murderers and thus not at all as humanitarian saviors, it essentially fails to do so, presenting a very dubious situation.

Later, U.S. soldiers celebrate the end of the war: they are dancing and the music is playing loudly when a journalist asks a group of soldiers, "They say you exorcised the ghosts of Vietnam with a clear moral imperative?" and gets a pretentious answer from one of them: "We liberated Kuwait!" Considering how the soldier says this slogan, the phrase can be interpreted in two ways: first, the soldiers not only freed the U.S. from its "Vietnam syndrome" but also brought *freedom* to another country; second, they did not care much about what they did to negate the failures of Vietnam because their mission was to "liberate Kuwait" *instead of* expiating guilt for the country's past. Either way, the soldiers believe that their main achievement is to have brought freedom to an oppressed people.

The film's main plotline starts, however, when, while stripping down Iraqi prisoners of war for examination, Conrad Vig (Spike Jonze) finds a map in the "ass" of an Iraqi soldier that shows where a cache of Kuwaiti gold is hidden. With the help of this map, the soldier, along with Major Archie Gates (George Clooney), Sergeant Barlow, and Chief Elgin (Ice Cube), set off to procure the treasure for themselves.

As *Three Kings* continues, the soldiers are driving through the desert, throwing baseballs in the air and shooting them, and then Vig puts some explosive into one of the balls. The ensuing explosion scares the other three soldiers. Vig justifies himself: "We didn't get to see any action, sir." Major Gates, desiring to show him and the others evidence of "some action," gets out of the car and leads the group farther off the main road. They observe lots of dead bodies, and Gates makes the comment, "We dropped a lot of bombs out here"—an obvious reference to the six-week aerial bombardment during Operation Desert Storm. However, the charred corpses do not scare the soldiers, especially not Vig, who is boyishly craving to participate in some sort of military action. The soldiers decide to shoot a cow that is standing nearby when a fragmentation shell explodes. The scene is suddenly filled with splashes of blood, pieces of the cow falling down from above; bloody stains appear on the car as well as on the soldiers. Such an unexpected combination of different and what may seem incompatible styles and aesthetic characteristics obviously serves to set the viewing off balance, thus, to borrow a description from Ben Dickenson, "never letting the audience settle into a comfort zone of familiarity." Another crucial moment in the scene is a bullet being shot, accompanied by a detailed visual explanation of what happens to the body's tissue when penetrated by a bullet. Dickenson notices that the colors used when the inner organs are revealed contrast "the heat of desert warfare" to "a paleness and coldness."[30] Such polarity is a metaphor, standing for the director's vision of war as a merciless and destructive phenomenon. Vig, for whom the scene is "like a cartoon," gets very excited after having witnessed such "action." The scene therefore reveals the duality of a soldier, who is compassionate toward the loss and pain of the locals but also craves to see combat action (or something akin to it) and to take part in war.

Having made sure that nobody has been hurt, the four men get back into their car and continue their journey. It is significant that aesthetic means make their implicitly criminal, clandestine "mission" to steal the gold an explicit crime: these U.S. soldiers are covered with blood (as is the car they are in), which visually makes them appear to be aggressive military men. The blood is not human, but the audience and especially people whom the soldiers meet later perceive them nonetheless as a danger and a threat because of it. Crucially, the locals, unlike the audience, do not know the source of the blood that covers the soldiers. Additionally the use of sudden close-ups, loud (though not inappropriate to the action) music, and fountains of blood (not just from the cow but also from the Iraqi soldier Barlow killed in the beginning, his head blown off and a fountain of blood coming up out of his neck, as Vig remembers it), as well as the plotline itself: all turn the film into a criminal comedy. Thus the First Gulf War, and specifically the U.S. participation in it, is portrayed not as a saving mission but as a quest for easy profit—a metaphor for U.S. interest in Arab oil.

When the soldiers arrive in the village that is their destination, they force the people sitting next to the bunker, where they assume the gold is going to be, to leave, pointing guns at them. At that moment one of the local men says, "They're butchers covered in blood," referring to the cow blood on the soldiers' faces and clothes. This observation and the way the locals perceive the soldiers dramatically resonate with Vig's shouting into a megaphone, "We are the Army of the United States of America! We are here to protect you! . . . We are here for your protection and safety!" When Gates, Barlow, and Elgin get into the bunker, they find there two Iraqi men, one of whom, scared to death, repeats, "I love the United States of Freedom." These words overtly mock the policy aimed at bringing freedom at the point of a gun. The man asks the soldiers whether they are "look[ing] for [a] chemical weapon," when Barlow replies, "No! We look for the gold!" The whole scene aptly illustrates the material interests of the United States in the war. When local women rush to the soldiers, asking for food and medical help for their children, the soldiers openly ignore them. Yet the happiness of the locals and their trust in the United States, and specifically in the soldiers, are genuine. They truly believe that the soldiers are there to help them fight Saddam Hussein in order to restore a normal life in the country. The U.S. soldiers are, however, concerned only with their mission to rob the people: they aggressively rush inside the bunker, pointing guns at the civilians, showing they are obviously ready to murder anyone who would try to stop them. Martinez claims that in *Three Kings*, the

U.S. soldiers' main anxiety is that there will be Iraqis who will prevent them from finding the gold; this corresponds to a "critical view" of the strategy of U.S. policy, that is, "protecting and amassing wealth in the region, not freeing the Iraqi people from an evil leader."[31]

The film illustrates the soldiers' material interests in another scene, when they are led to a garage that has been filled with the most elite cars of those transported from Kuwait. They end up avidly discussing the cars instead of protecting the people who were "left to fight against Hussein's regime without the military support of the Bush administration."[32] The problem of venality is raised once again, when Barlow is tortured by an Iraqi soldier and is made to drink oil. The moment overtly invokes the American interest in the oil of the Gulf region as one of the reasons the U.S. took military action against Iraq. Yet the scene also touches upon another complex issue, namely the death of local noncombatants at the hands of the U.S. and its allies—the intervention's collateral damage. Mark J. Lacy suggests that the scene displays an act of revenge for the death of the Iraqi soldier's son.[33] Indeed the Iraqi blames Americans who come to his country to bomb it and kill Iraqi children just to get access to oil. "Can you think how it feel inside your heart if I bomb your daughter?" the Iraqi soldier asks Barlow. The audience then observes Barlow, imagining his house in the U.S. exploding while his wife and daughter are inside. The scene questions the "historical role" of the United States in the First Gulf War, not justifying the involvement or presenting U.S. soldiers purely as liberators but questioning the intervention and the actions of soldiers and revealing the U.S.'s veiled (and sometimes not so veiled) interest in Gulf oil.[34] The problem of the soldiers' material interests, which clearly prevail over the humanitarian imperatives of their mission, is corroborated later when their attempt to leave with the gold is impeded by Iraqi soldiers. These men warn the Americans that if they do not leave the gold, they will shoot a civilian woman. Despite the woman's entreaties and the screams of her husband and daughter, the fatal shot resounds, as Gates has started the car to leave. The moment is crucial in the movie because, as Martinez has argued, the shooting symbolizes a change in the U.S. soldiers' attitude toward the war and their role in it.[35] They are no longer interested in the gold but pursue the initial goal of their presence in Iraq: to liberate people, not to steal their wealth.

And it is exactly the film's ending that, through its raising of moral issues, rehabilitates the U.S. soldiers, who now have changed their attitudes toward the war, the locals, and, most important, their own role in the conflict. It is precisely what the audience of *Three Kings* sees after the shot that deals with the U.S. soldiers' newly found good intentions, thus displaying the intervention to be, at its core, a humanitarian mission. The soldiers organize a rescue operation for Shia refugees and try to help them get over the border to Iran. As a television crew arrives to witness this effort, the journalist Nora Dunn (Adriana Cruz) asks Major Gates, "Did you get the gold?" She gets a very righteous response: "No, but we helped a lot of people. Right now we have to get them over the border." The answer—which one might interpret as being quite far-fetched, given the soldiers' initial greed and cupidity—demonstrates the shift in the soldiers' consciousness. This shift, on the one hand, serves as a critique of the U.S. interest in Arab oil; on the other hand, it tries to justify the intervention, showing that despite all the flaws of its interventionist policy, the U.S. needed to be involved because of the slaughter and oppression that took place in Kuwait and Iraq during the First Gulf War. No longer ordinary criminals, the soldiers become saviors who care for the lives of the locals. And it is exactly the brutal murder of the civilian woman that the soldiers had to witness that made them grasp the danger the locals experience every day. It also triggered the soldiers' sense of moral responsibility for what happened and what still can happen—and made them act to help the people.

Despite the morality with which the director burdens his film, presenting the intervention as a humanitarian effort, he still underlines the imperfection of the U.S. Army, bringing the problem of corruption to the surface. The help the soldiers provide to the refugees costs them demotions, and they are arrested. Gates explains to Colonel Horn (Mykelti

Williamson) that they have the gold, and if Horn allows the refugees to cross the border, Gates will tell Horn where the gold is so that he can return it to Kuwait later and "get another star." Additionally he explains that the refugees helped them find and transport the gold, and for that the soldiers had promised to get them over the border. As Gates puts it, "It's a soldier's honor. We can't fuck them now." The scene is problematic not only because it returns to the issue of American material interests in the First Gulf War but also because it suggests that there were soldiers who were ready to perform their mission only because they believed it would bring a financial reward. Yet despite the bribery and corruption that the scene overtly touches upon, it still does not refute the idea of the humanitarianism of the intervention, because the focus is on Gates, who is now determined to save the people.

Some critics, especially Colin Harrison, argue that the film offers a disclaimer of the First Gulf War's actuality. Influenced by the writings of Jean Baudrillard who, in turn, elaborated on the First Gulf War via an unconventional interpretation of the events—he contended that the "war could not take place" because it was "so highly choreographed and scripted for the screen"—Harrison states that the military men of *Three Kings* "live out Hollywood fantasies."[36] Scholars obviously come to such a conclusion because of a number of contentious and, at times, inappropriate scenes for a war film. Harrison also refers to the bullet scene that I briefly analyzed earlier and argues that no matter how pretentious certain sequences in the film are, or how close to real combat they bring the audience, the bullet piercing the soldier's body is just a "simulation . . . a clever piece of cinematic illusion."[37] In defense of *Three Kings*, one can argue that we should not see the film as trying to record and reveal the events in a *documentary* mode (indeed, this is a docu-*fiction*); instead it aims at achieving its goals aesthetically, visualizing the war as a phenomenon that can be perceived not as a pure set of facts but as a graphic episode whose colorfulness, exaggeration, and unattainability speak for themselves. This is clearly not a drawback of *Three Kings* as a narrative on U.S. involvement in the First Gulf War.

On the contrary, the choice to display the intervention in such an exaggerated manner does not make the war itself unreal; it underscores one of the most common truths about war, its incomprehensibility. While being a primarily fictional story, *Three Kings* raises multiple issues that regard war in general and U.S. intervention in the First Gulf War in particular, including the influence of the failure in Vietnam on U.S. actions, U.S. economic interest in the region, the problem of refugees and migration, technologization of war, and some others. *Three Kings* is therefore a perfect example of a docu-fictional text that through a fictional story tells the truth about the war.

Jake Horsley calls *Three Kings* a "politically subversive" film; Lacy argues that it "contribut[es] to the active forgetting of history" and that "justice and order have been restored in Iraq by our [U.S.] heroes."[38] For my part, I conclude that *Three Kings* very successfully accounts for the flaws of American intervention even as it does justice to its positive aspects and achievements. The characters' radical transformation is not entirely credible, but nonetheless *Three Kings* does not give up the hope of justifying U.S. involvement in the First Gulf War as a humanitarian intervention.

SAM MENDES'S *JARHEAD* (2005)

Whereas *Three Kings* portrays quite an "idealistic picture of soldiers" who succeed in changing their mission from an illegal escapade to a purely humanitarian mission in the days following the end of the Gulf War, Sam Mendes's *Jarhead* is concerned with the depiction of an "alienated soldier" who joins the army and "tr[ies] to do his job" in active duty. Thus the two films discuss the "politics of war" in two separate dimensions.[39] Mette Mortensen compares *Jarhead* to Steven Spielberg's *Saving Private Ryan* (1998), a film set during World War II, arguing that both cinematic examples offer a view of the "myth of soldiers united in their fight for each other and for their nation." Mortensen claims that both films do so by avoiding a "clear and unequivocal image of the enemy," thus abstracting themselves from the respective wars during which the films are set.[40] However, Mendes's choice to narrate the events of the First Gulf War through the confined perspective of a random soldier is purely advantageous. *Jarhead* does not aim to showcase the war from all possible angles, providing a(n) (un)conventional image of U.S. intervention, and hence answering all the *whys, whos, whens,* and *what fors*. It never purports to tell the full history of the war or to impose an already known viewpoint, or a new one. The history of the First Gulf War in *Jarhead*, to borrow from Westwell, can be realized "through the limited personal narratives of spiritual growth and therapeutic transcendence."[41] The development of the war's history parallels the moral and psychological development of the soldier. He fights to realize and accomplish his mission; in doing so, he constructs, as it were, the history of the First Gulf War. More than that, this is not the tale of a politician or a journalist whose stories are well publicized and whose points of view have been long understood; it is this particular soldier who appears on the screen, not merely to narrate what he sees and participates in but to *understand* all those *whys, whos, whens,* and *what fors*. Going through his personal moments of fear, incomprehension, rejection, hatred, and fury, the soldier's story structures the events, constructing, brick by brick, the veiled internal history of the U.S. participation in the war.

Jarhead opens with this preface: "A story. A man fires a rifle for many years. And he goes to war. And afterward he turns the rifle in at the armory. And he believes he is finished with the rifle. But no matter what else he might do with these hands—love a woman, build a house, change his son's diaper—his hands remember the rifle." The film thus reveals at the outset its main concern: what war does to its participants on an individual, psychological level. Despite Martinez's argument that "the job of every soldier is roughly the same: follow orders and kill people who are defined as the enemy" and that war is, generally, perceived by soldiers as a "job," one can speculate that *Jarhead* attempts to submit this problem to even closer scrutiny through one soldier's personal story.[42]

The central character of *Jarhead* is Anthony Swofford, who at the very beginning of the film confesses regret in joining the U.S. Marines and, addressing his commander's question in training camp—"What the fuck are you even doing here?"—answers honestly (and with clear irritation), "Sir, I got lost on the way to college, Sir!" The audience later gets quite a lame explanation from Swofford of his decision to become a marine: "But for me there was nowhere else. That was the truth. After all, I was made in a war!" The last statement is a reference to his being conceived during the Vietnam War. It is clarified in the film that Swofford takes part in the initial stages of the First Gulf War, in Operation Desert Shield. The soldiers' camp where he is stationed is in Saudi Arabia. They are commanded to protect the oil fields that belong to Kuwait.

Jarhead plausibly reflects the atmosphere and the conditions of U.S. soldiers in the Middle East. The audience observes mostly only the desert, stretching far and wide; the images on screen are distorted, which indicates unbearable heat; the picture is usually blinding because of the dazzling sunlight. Driving through the desert on an open military truck, the marines discuss the purpose of their mission. One of them questions the aim of the war: "I've been around these old, white motherfuckers all my life. They got their fat hands in Arab oil. Motherfuckers drink it like it's beer. That's why we are here. To protect their property." The soldier obviously judges the U.S. government's interest in oil as the only weighty reason for U.S. involvement in the First Gulf War. His comrade responds, "Fuck politics, all right? We're here. All the rest is bullshit." Martinez says the soldier's words prove that the state, not "the individual soldier," is responsible for making decisions.[43] While the powerful elite are considering the goals of intervention, the job of a soldier is to follow the orders of the state, more precisely of its powerful elite, and fight—in this context, even if it is merely for a material purpose. Martinez makes a very accurate observation about a soldier's role in war: "On a micro level, the soldier engages in concrete action, enacting violence, but does not theorize the justifications for war."[44] The slang for marines, "jarheads," which, as Swofford says, stands for the soldier's head being "an empty vessel," is very symbolic in this context, as it reveals how the government simply uses soldiers to fulfill particular tasks and reach specific goals.

The film clearly demonstrates that the First Gulf War marked a new era in U.S. military experience. It reveals the difference between films on the Vietnam War and films on the First Gulf War—a difference based on technological progress.[45] Not being involved in real combat, the soldiers in *Jarhead* have to pass their time in any way possible, and although "President Bush sends in more troops," Swofford lets us know, the audience does not see soldiers fighting. What one can realize from the film and from Swofford's comments, however, is how the soldiers' experience in the Middle East resembles their routine in a U.S. training camp: "Six times a day we gather for formation. And we hydrate. We patrol the empty desert. And we dehydrate. We throw hand grenades . . . into nowhere. We navigate imaginary minefields. We fire at . . . nothing. And we hydrate some more. And we look north towards the border. And we wait for them. This is our labor—we wait." Next the audience observes soldiers betting on a scorpion fight in a self-crafted ring. The film continues to offer Swofford's meditations on how to spend one's free time in wartime:

> Suggested techniques for the marine to use in the avoidance of boredom and loneliness. Masturbation. Rereading of letters from unfaithful wives and girlfriends. Cleaning your rifle. Further masturbation. Rewiring Walkman. Arguing about religion and meaning of life. Discussing in detail every woman the marine has ever fucked. Debating differences, such as Cuban versus Mexican, Harleys versus Hondas, left- versus right-handed masturbation. Further cleaning of rifle. Studying of Filipino mail order bride catalogue. Further masturbation. Planning a marine's first meal on return home. Imagining what the marine's girlfriend and her man Joey are doing in the alley or in a hotel bed.

Later, to demonstrate to a reporter how the soldiers' "NBC suits work," Staff Sergeant Sykes (Jamie Foxx) orders them to continue playing football (again—no fighting—the soldiers spend their time playing football) in "full chemical gear." The soldiers obey at first, but then, unable to stand the heat, they start to strip, imitating sexual acts with each other, drawing the reporter's and the cameraman's attention. Sgt. Sykes has to yield and leaves with the survey squad. He later punishes the soldiers by ordering them to make a pile of sacks and then dismantle it in a torrential rain. The soldiers' routine in the Middle East that the film so abundantly focuses on overtly questions the purpose of the intervention; at the same time, it neither judges nor justifies it because, as yet, no outright military action has been taken.

In the next scene the soldiers get drunk celebrating Christmas and set one of the tents on fire—the one where projectile airburst is kept. As punishment, Swofford has to clean the camp lavatories and burn feces. From that moment on, the tension that saturates the camp becomes explicit: there is a skirmish between Swofford and Private Fergus O'Donnell (Brian Geraghty) when the former, angry with his comrade (who started the fire on Christmas night), loads his rifle and threatens to shoot Fergus. Swofford behaves the way he does not because he has to clean the latrines but because he thinks the war will never start for him. "I'll end this fucking waiting," he hopes, "and I'll know what it's like to kill a man." Martinez argues that these scenes symbolize the insecurity of a soldier who performs the role of a "worker" and "wants to do his job but is not entirely sure whether his job is to shoot people or to waste time."[46] Until that moment the intervention has been portrayed as an ambiguous event without an aim, which influences the atmosphere in the units, destroying the soldier—who came to fight but instead has to wait—psychologically.

Finally Operation Desert Storm begins. After their unit is bombed, the soldiers examine the area and stumble across the dead bodies of civilians and their burned cars. One of the marines finds a small girl, burned, sitting on a burned bus. The scene is replaced with oil fires that, according to Martinez, stand for the "focal point of the war": "the struggle over oil."[47] The soldiers are shown moving into gray-black smoke and becoming immersed in it. Oil drops cover their faces; when Swofford opens his mouth to catch some drops, another soldier tells him not to, "it's just poison"; Swofford replies, "The earth is bleeding." This metaphor places *Jarhead* in parallel with *Lessons of Darkness*, in that both films focus on the First Gulf War not only as causing great harm to humans but also as ravaging and destroying nature. This theme is echoed when Swofford encounters an oil-covered horse walking through the desert. He tries to comfort the suffering animal, although he understands that it is going to die. *Jarhead* accentuates the truly unbearable conditions under which the soldiers had to fight and survive. A pelting rain of oil covers them, soaks their clothes, gets into their eyes. The soldiers walk through a mess of sand and oil. When the oil rain stops, they can discern oil fires. The nightmare continues till the next day starts.

As it is presented in *Jarhead*, the role of U.S. soldiers in the First Gulf War is challenged again in the course of a sniper mission assigned to Swofford and Troy (Peter Sarsgaard). When Swofford takes aim at an Iraqi soldier, following Troy's instructions, he is stopped from shooting by Major Lincoln (Dennis Haysbert), who explains that if Swofford fires, he will kill only one soldier, and the other Iraqis will escape. He sits down next to Swofford and Troy, as if in a cinema, prepared to see the action performed by the air support, which can do a better job than only two soldiers. This enrages Troy; he starts screaming that they have to shoot because that is what they are there for. Nevertheless the marines do no shooting; instead they watch the bombing by the aircraft overhead. Scholars argue that this scene serves as proof that the First Gulf War was a new type of war where technology played a more important role than soldiers did: the bombing stands for a "technological advance in warfare" that is preferred over one sniper shot.[48] One can also speculate that the scene emphasizes the problem of soldiers' inactivity in a time of new, technologically advanced wars. Although American troops were brought into the Gulf region as part of the military buildup of

Operation Desert Shield, the soldiers, as *Jarhead* demonstrates, did not understand the aim of the intervention. They joined the military to fight against Iraqi tyranny, but instead, according to Swofford, they just changed locations and were left there in the desert to play football and think about their girlfriends. Even when the soldiers are given a chance to shoot the enemy, the opportunity is immediately taken away. The paradoxical tragedy for Swofford and Troy is that when they return to their camp, their comrades, including Sykes (who even offers them a cigar), are partying because their contract is over and they can finally go back home. Swofford and Troy do not share the soldiers' happiness because they cannot understand the purpose of their coming to this war in the first place. They are given their last chance to shoot, and shoot they do—into the air.

Zeroing in on the life of the soldiers on a military base and only occasionally displaying them participating in a military action, this docu-fictional film aims at portraying the war not as a collective experience but rather as a fragmented one, consisting of thousands of individual stories. In doing so, *Jarhead* contributes to the war film genre, since the inner fight of a soldier is one of the most frequently raised issues in war narratives. Yet it also provides glimpses into the world of the First Gulf War, for example, by choosing to represent the fountains of oil and U.S. soldiers covered in that oil, which metaphorically stands for U.S. economic interest in the region, or when displaying the dead bodies of the locals, among whom are children, to accentuate the devastating impact of the military actions on the local population prior to and during U.S. intervention. In Lacanian fashion, *Jarhead* seems to argue that there are several truths that can be told about that war, and the film ultimately focuses on some of them, thus turning from a traditionally fictional narrative into a docu-fictional one.

Jarhead ends on a very melancholy note. The marines are on a bus, returning home. Outside, a crowd has gathered, cheering, welcoming them home. Joining the marines on the bus is a Vietnam War veteran, who greets the soldiers in appreciation and welcomes them back. It is obvious the man wants to experience at least a bit of the nation's appreciation and support that he did not get upon his return from Vietnam. The scene is pivotal: in bringing a Vietnam War veteran together with the soldiers coming home from the First Gulf War, *Jarhead* implicitly reveals the shift in U.S. interventionism—from the drastic failure in Vietnam to a successful operation in the Middle East in the 1990s. The national approval of the war signifies that the war was regarded as necessary and just.

Literature and U.S. Intervention in the First Gulf War

Frederick Forsyth's *The Fist of God* (1994): Realism, Adventure, and the Cold War Fear of Nuclear Weapons

To trace the way U.S. involvement in the First Gulf War was reflected in literary fiction, this section will thoroughly consider Gabe Hudson's collection of short stories *Dear Mr. President* (2002) and Tom Paine's novel *The Pearl of Kuwait* (2003). However, before scrutinizing these two examples, I would like to examine Frederick Forsyth's thriller *The Fist of God* (1994) because it aptly reveals the war in the Gulf region from multiple perspectives. First, skillfully mixing fact with fiction, Forsyth narrates events from the tense and brutal history of the Middle East that preceded the First Gulf War—namely the war between Iraq and Iran and the Iraqi use of chemical weapons on Kurds and Iranians—and therefore presents the underlying premises for international involvement when Iraq invaded Kuwait. Second, although mainly focusing on the role of Great Britain and British soldiers in the war,[49] the author also covers the roles of Israel and the United States. Third, *The Fist of God* comprises war scenes and military attacks, accounts of political planning and manipulations, and dramatizations of secret operations, which demonstrates that the author is not only interested in depicting combat but has also attempted to explain the reasons behind the war and the conflict's buildup and has investigated how it was resolved. The use of a third-person omniscient narrator underlines the epic nature of the war, which involved a large number of characters, and, at the same time, makes the novel a more reliable narrative as the author does not impose someone's opinion on the reader but instead allows the reader to observe the situation through his or her own eyes. Fourth, Forsyth's past as a pilot in the Royal Air Force, a war journalist, and a spy for the British government in the Republic of Biafra during the Nigerian Civil War (1967–70) and for many years after the conflict, while clearly not making his war and political novels fully reliable narratives, does make this author unique and allows one to question the genre of his "fictional" writings, considering that he has also written a number of explicitly nonfictional texts.

What draws my attention is how the novel portrays the role of the West in the First Gulf War. However, before proceeding to this discussion, it is important to investigate the grounds for the external attention toward the conflict itself. The novel does not showcase oil as the central factor that is worth fighting for. Oil is not, of course, avoided completely, but the real threat that Iraq represents to the world, as depicted in the novel, is nuclear warfare. The twists and turns of the plot are braided around a secret weapon that Saddam possesses, "hidden away, stashed deep underground," "inert but ready to be called to fly," called "Qubth-ut-Allah" or "The Fist of God."[50] According to the specialists, the Iraqi president had been "trying" since 1982 to collect the ingredients for "a basic uranium-based bomb" (181). Hence the fear of the menace that Saddam poses to the whole world compels Western countries to interfere in the conflict with Kuwait, which, as is obvious now, was not restricted to Iraq's illegal annexation of Kuwait's territory but had global dimensions. This perspective is raised quite explicitly in a memorandum from the Political Intelligence and Analysis Group to the U.S. Department of State: "The destruction of the Iraqi war machine and particularly the weapons of mass destruction must now become the overriding aim of Western policy. The liberation of Kuwait has now become irrelevant, serving only as a justification" (209).

The key Western player in the First Gulf War was the United States.

Describing the country's military potential as well as the measures it intends to take, the author by no means criticizes or judges the intervention. On the contrary, he focuses on describing Americans as belonging to a strong nation with a well-equipped army, and the U.S. as the country that "will not allow" Saddam to win (93). Take, for example, this description of the United States: "In any case, no one can see how [Saddam] can humiliate America. The Yanks have all the power, all the technology. When they're ready, they can go in there and blow his army and air force away" (114). More than that, it is frequently stated that the United States is careful when leading military actions and consciously tries to preserve as many lives of its own soldiers as possible; therefore the attacks are always scrupulously planned. Contrasting the United States, its president, and military commanders with Saddam and his methods of conducting war, one of the novel's characters, Dr. Terry Martin, who specializes in Arab studies, says, "America can take many things, but she cannot take massive casualties" (114). Later the issue is raised again by the American banker Saul Nathanson: "Before it is over many young Americans may well be dead, fine young men who do not deserve to die. We must all do what we can to keep that number as low as humanly possible" (202). If this is impossible and if the situation develops so that "anything were done or not done that might increase those casualties, America's memory would be long and her revenge unpleasant" (203), as we read in the thoughts of one of the novel's characters, Israeli deputy foreign minister Benjamin Netanyahu. Another interesting remark in the novel concerns the U.S. obligation to win the war, invoking its disastrous failure in the Vietnam War: "America cannot lose, must not lose. It is simply not acceptable. Look at Vietnam. The veterans came home, and they were pelted with garbage. For America, terrible casualties at the hands of a despised enemy are a form of loss. Unacceptable loss. Saddam can waste fifty thousand men anytime, anyplace. He doesn't care. Uncle Sam does. If America takes that kind of loss, she'll be shaken to the core. Heads have to roll, careers to be smashed, governments to fall. The recrimination and the self-blame would last a generation" (317–18). Along with the films analyzed in the previous section, Forsyth's novel raises the problem of American guilt, shame, and loss in Vietnam. Iraq is considered a second chance for the United States—to wash off the disgrace of Vietnam and provide the current generation and those who come after it with another honorable example of America's might and righteousness.

American soldiers (along with British) are considered saviors who can liberate the oppressed people. The sense of pervasive oppression and tyranny can be grasped from the novel's numerous descriptions of chaos and fear that reign throughout the Middle East. For example, Saddam's wish is to control the world via the intimidation of other nations with the threat of nuclear weapons; he is indifferent to the fate of the people of Iraq and Kuwait, which is strongly contrasted to Western policy and the desire to prevent his actions and save the people. Americans too are cast as saviors in the dialogue between a Kuwaiti man and a British special agent: when the Kuwaiti asks, "How much longer must we suffer?" and receives the response "The Americans and the British will come. One day," he reacts by saying, "Allah make it soon" (194). The author thus underscores the desperate situation of the local people in Kuwait as well as the power of the West to free them; more than that, the intervention is characterized as necessary, pleaded for. However, the intervention that is described as "the greatest invasion . . . since Normandy" (309) inevitably entails negative consequences. For example, Forsyth emphasizes the judgments and criticisms of U.S. actions by the local people who were exposed to American bombing and who suffered losses. The reader is informed that the Americans bombed a shelter, which caused hundreds of deaths; during the burial of his father (who died from torture), the Iraqi colonel Badri is asked by the people at the cemetery if the old man "died from American bombs" (493). And though he did not, it is made apparent that the U.S. bombing killed a considerable number of innocent people too, and thus the help given by the U.S. elicits a split response: it is regarded as necessary, but at the same time it is deplored.

All in all, Forsyth's *The Fist of God* presents the participation of the United States in the First Gulf War as indispensable and, significantly, as a humanitarian intervention—for the aggression that Saddam exercised on the people of Iraq and Kuwait had to be stopped and his mad idea to become a world leader by threatening to activate a nuclear weapon needed to be prevented. The West is portrayed as a force of good, in contrast to Saddam, who is depicted as the incarnation of evil. U.S. intervention, although it was sorely necessary, had its flaws, as it is described in the novel, chiefly because the intrusion caused the deaths of civilians and young American soldiers. However, the book leaves the impression that the intervention was justified since the central menace, the atomic weapon, was not used. Although the allied armies suffer losses, the operations are considered successful because the mission to liberate Kuwait from Saddam's tyranny has been accomplished.

From Criticism to Humanitarianism:
Gabe Hudson's *Dear Mr. President* (2002)

One of the most powerful literary examples that censured U.S. intervention in the First Gulf War is an outstanding collection of short stories by Gabe Hudson entitled *Dear Mr. President*. In his profoundly critical and sarcastic work, Hudson mocks U.S. foreign policy, berates the government, and demonstrates the senselessness of war in general, underscoring the dehumanizing, degrading, and devastating impact on those who participate in it. Although the short-story cycle, for the most part, destroys the illusion that there was a moral goal that the U.S. was pursuing in the First Gulf War, scraping off the ethical and ideological covers that helped justify U.S. participation in the war, it nonetheless reflects the issue of humanitarianism, narrating the war's history so that both the advantages and the disadvantages of the U.S. intervention come into view. It is significant that the stories are revealed from the first-person point of view. This makes them unreliable, as the reader can see each situation only from the perspective of one character. Yet it is exactly the multiple *I*'s that appear in the cycle (the narrator is a different person in each story) that enable the writer to unwrap the many-sided view on U.S. intervention in the First Gulf War, involving those who were for the involvement and those who were against it, thus constructing the truth about the intervention as seen through the eyes of those who fought the war and those who—either literally or metaphorically—lost their family members and friends in it.

The collection is divided into three sections, each of which contains from one to four short stories. The first three stories, constituting the first section, are aimed at uncovering the problem of a postwar syndrome. The explicit parallels can be drawn between the first two stories. In "The Cure as I Found It," Hudson introduces the Gulf War veteran Larry, while in "Cross-Dresser" the reader meets Captain Dugan. Both characters face similar problems when they return home from Iraq: how to go on living despite the deaths that they observed and were themselves responsible for in the Middle East; how to psychologically reintegrate into civil society and into the families that once were so close to them; and how to forget their war experience. The men's stories illustrate the saying "Everybody's Gulf War Syndrome is a little bit different."[51] Larry, only twenty-four, goes gray and then bald, and later finds out that his bones are breaking into fragments inside of him and that he runs the risk of soon turning into a "human blob" (5). Captain Dugan starts wearing women's clothing because the spirit of his dead thirteen-year-old daughter has gotten into him. War destroys the characters from within, changing their inner nature into something extrinsic: the war's ongoing effect manifests itself through gender confusion for Dugan and, for Larry, a complete inner destruction that literally takes place and also stands for more significant, moral problems now suffered by the veteran.

In both stories the veterans have difficulty reintegrating, first and foremost, into their family and most intimate circle. Larry's girlfriend Gloria, although "an angel with a heart of pure gold . . . [who] makes all this other crap worth it" (7), fails to support him in this hard period. Subconsciously she does not allow Larry to forget about his experience.

She constantly reminds him of the war; for example, during their sex play she asks him, "Do you want to come up and make me your prisoner of war? I think I've got some rope" (13); when having sex she moans, "Oh G.I., G.I." (12); when persuading him that he can hold his own in a fight with local bullies she tells him, "You were a rifleman in the army for fuck's sake. You blasted those Iraqis at Al Mutlaa Ridge. Don't pretend like you didn't wax those guys. You want to know what you should do. Go hunt down these punks and cut all their tongues out and make a necklace with their tongues. Then we'll see who gets the last word" (8). It is especially striking how she imagines Larry's experience in the war, casting him as a cruel and merciless soldier; the war has made him such a heartless person that he could make a "necklace" out of human tongues. Larry is not just a loving boyfriend but is now also a cutthroat and a thug for her, which obviously makes her feel proud, as he can pose a menace and protect himself and her. For Gloria, the First Gulf War has turned Larry into a supernatural hero who can easily overcome any obstacle in his way: "Like you're not some kind of badass warrior? . . . You're too much of a man to let this get you down," she says, referring to his illness (13). Larry's complicated affliction, according to Gloria, can be managed with the macho masculinity he gained on the battlefields of Iraq. From Larry's personal perspective, however, the situation does not seem so optimistic. The truth is that "war makes people commit horrible acts" (13). No matter how remorseful of his deeds Larry may be, it is impossible to change the past; the author makes this explicit. No matter what the reason, Larry has contributed to the killing of humans.

An additional problem that arises is soldiers' state of awareness of such murders; that is, to what extent, and how deeply, do soldiers grasp their role in war, and what do they think about themselves as soldiers? Are they saviors or murderers? The polarity of views and the inner fight between good and evil are obviously intrinsic to every human and, specifically, to every soldier. *When* the moment of understanding comes, however, can be interpreted differently. The story provides its version, namely that no soldier considers the philosophy of his or her behavior and deeds while engaging in war but can only do so *afterward,* when back in civilian life. Thus, in Larry's imagination he defends himself in front of the Doorman, arguing for his place in Heaven: "I'm sorry for what happened at Al Mutlaa Ridge, it was my duty, and truly I didn't want to kill those guys. I was scared. *I did what I thought I had to do*" (14; my italics). The response of the Doorman reveals that there is no salvation for Larry; nothing he does now in civilian life can bring redemption for what he did as a soldier: "Larry, you've got to *pay for killing* those Iraqi soldiers. Truth be told, they weren't even going to hurt you; they were *just having fun,* and now their children are fatherless. *You're a murderer, plain and simple.* Don't try to get out of it. . . . You know, you're not the first person to try and pull this stunt. It wasn't that long ago that Hitler was up here saying the exact same thing, and so I'll tell you the same thing I told him" (15; my italics). This extreme comparison of Larry with Hitler is used to intensify the short story's implication that a murderer is a murderer, no matter how many people he or she has killed. Clearly, however, the author underplays the role of the Iraqi soldiers in the war. Saying that the Iraqis "were just having fun," the story implies that it was the Americans who were the aggressors; moreover his phrasing explicitly justifies the actions of the Iraqis. Yet while the passage seems to undermine the humanitarianism of the American mission, it does so not because it seeks to justify the actions of the oppressors; rather, softening the image of the enemy, the author can more easily demonstrate that the war was a destructive force for American soldiers. This technique helps Hudson focus on how war influences individuals—which is clearly the main purpose of the short-story cycle—rather than on how war can bring good or evil collectively.

A similar theme is touched upon in "Cross-Dresser," when Captain Dugan admits that having to kill other people left indelible marks that forever changed his nature: "I . . . fly up into the sky and kill people. Or at least I have, in the Persian Gulf . . . and I'm sure I'll have to kill some more people when I get out of here. This is what I do for a living, and I try to have fun with it, since it's my job" (24). He sees himself as a minister of God, an exceptional human being who is fulfilling the will of God, and thus doing the right thing: "When I'm up there in the sky it's like I'm straight out of God's head, a divine thought inside a divine thought bubble, totally invisible" (24). The idea that the soldiers have exceptional power and might is skillfully mocked by the author in the previous story, when Larry, unable to get into Heaven, has to face a cruel reality: "My wings suddenly disappear and I begin to fall" (15). Making the character of the first story want to fly while the protagonist of the second story is already up in the sky, the short-story cycle demonstrates that both are facing a hopeless, doomed situation: neither will ever be able to come close to God or to pretend that they are fulfilling God's will, no matter how close to God they may feel, because both men are murderers, that is, sinners, and the only destiny awaiting them is to suffer as lost souls in the world of human beings who used to be their family, to struggle with Gulf War Syndrome and never be able to overcome it.

Just as Larry wants to get rid of all his war memories, Dugan tries to erase his soldier past. He imagines "a dark blue dress" and "red high heels" (24); "I let my hair grow out. I put on lipstick that I made from tree sap. I spent most of my time looking down at my reflection. . . . I made a two-piece bikini bathing suit" (35); "I tape my penis down between my legs and put on a pair of flowered panties. I put on one of my mom's dresses [thinking of himself as his thirteen-year-old daughter] and too much lipstick and eyeliner and admire myself in the big mirror in the living room. On special occasions . . . I put on long white gloves that come up to my elbows" (37–38). These confessions demonstrate Dugan's desperate desire to forget his past and his masculine military persona. De-masculinizing himself, he kills that past self in hopes of starting his life over.

Whether there can be normal life for a veteran after the First Gulf War and whether Gulf War Syndrome is ever cured are other questions the reader may ask with regard to both stories. Hudson gives a single, unambiguous answer: no. Larry's own grenade explodes and perhaps kills him when it is accidentally activated by one of the bullies, and Dugan is taken to a psychiatric asylum. Both endings can be interpreted quite pessimistically; either they symbolize the characters' insanity, or they demonstrate that these characters have no chance of leading normal lives upon their return to civilian life. Both characters become examples of the lost generation of war veterans who cannot overcome the nightmare of combat experience and fail to resume their previous lives when back in the United States—the country whose interests and values they were defending and fighting for.

The central story, "Dear Mr. President," most explicitly criticizes and disapproves of Bush's policy toward the Middle East and U.S. intervention in the form of a letter. The sarcasm that Lance Corporal Laverne starts his letter with is entwined in the narrative up to its end, creating moments of comical allusion, sad acceptance, truthful realization, and ruthless mockery at the same time. What initially seems to be sincere patriotism—Laverne begins his letter to the president with the words "The day we met will always shine bright in my mind, like a beacon as I sail through the stormy waters of my life" (41)—we soon realize is a form of deep mockery, unveiled as such when Laverne starts apologizing for the state of his letter: "I'm sorry for how messy this letter is because I just now had to wipe some bird poop from it with a wet napkin, and as you can see it smeared a little when I wiped it" (41). The author of the letter thus demonstrates that he despises the president, the commander in chief presiding over the intervention in the Middle East. He reveals how, by playing with citizens' sense of patriotism and their trust in the state, the government can manipulate people and make them fight for the state's values, without thinking about the consequences that the war experience will exact on themselves, as well as on their relatives and friends.

The author's attitude can be further observed in a sarcastic description of and Laverne's speculation on the events that took place when

President Bush visited the soldiers in Iraq. Hudson's remarkable sense of humor shows itself when, for example, he compares the soldiers to "one of those herds of zebras you see on the nature channel, running away from the lion" (43) as the president's helicopter is landing, or when the president appears in front of the soldiers wearing a gas mask, while no one else has any protective equipment. These images aptly illustrate the gap that exists between soldiers and the government (epitomized here by its figurehead), when the former are to fulfill the orders of the latter, no matter how dangerous the tasks assigned them.

The obsession of the U.S. administration with biological weapons that Saddam might have used seems an ungrounded fear and is mocked again when Laverne explains to the president why the soldiers had no masks:

> The corpsman gave us red experimental anti-biological-warfare pills every day so that we didn't have to wear gas masks. Boy, I took more pills over there than I've taken in my entire life. But don't get me wrong, those red pills could have saved my life if Saddam actually had used biological warfare. If Saddam's biologically laced Devil Air had ever come and tried to crawl down our mouths and noses and into our lungs, the red pills would have been there to say . . . "There's no way you're getting into this American nose and mouth. Nu-uh. Don't you know that America is the greatest country on earth?" (42)

This passage reveals the incompetence of those who designed the U.S. strategy as well as America's negligent treatment of the soldiers it sent to Iraq: the pills are "experimental," so nobody knows about their possible side effects, yet the U.S. continues stuffing marines with them—whether for good or ill. A great number of *ifs* in this piece is a sign of instability and a certain lack of awareness that is characteristic of the way American policy is represented in the short-story cycle. Moreover Hudson skillfully brings up praise of the United States that appears to be misplaced and is not actually very reassuring, given what means "the greatest country on earth" utilizes. Instead of reinforcing his administration's strategies and policies, the only thing the president does, according to Laverne, is give purportedly profound speeches to marines while wearing a gas mask, which turns out to be nothing more than idle talk:

> And when you [President Bush] came out, well, what can I say, that's when you demonstrated your *unbelievable leadership skills*. You could easily have hopped back on your chopper and sailed away and nobody would have thought anything of it, but that's not what *a brilliant leader* does, is it, sir? No, sir. I'll tell you what, sir, *Sun Tzu could learn a thing or two from you*. Because, instead of sailing away, you made your way through the ranks, *boosting morale*, stopping at *each* Marine to talk to him. . . . In case you were wondering, sir, yes, your voice did sound a little fuzzy, but that's because *you had your mask on the whole time*. But not everybody sounds like Darth Vader. No. And that's what you sounded like: *Darth Vader with a drawl, only in a cool way*. (44; my italics)

Casting Bush as a negative character, Hudson points up the wrong turns in U.S. foreign policy as it has been determined by the antihero president; he also showcases, in more general terms, that "the greatest country on earth" is in fact ruled by a villain. More than that, the story draws parallels between Bush and Saddam. Here is Laverne describing his feelings as the U.S. Army frees Kuwait: "I felt for a moment as if this were truly World War III, or, more precisely, Hell, and here we were, endowed by God Almighty—Manifest Destiny come back to the Holy Land to cast out the Prince of Darkness himself" (45). Darth Vader/Bush is compared to the Prince of Darkness/Hussein, and both characters are negatively depicted antiheroes.

The administration's sham morality and its indifference to the soldiers are manifested not only in the scene with the red pills. When Laverne returns home, he is doomed to suffer from a surreal kind of Gulf War Syndrome: He finds a third ear on his body and, later, a second mouth on his wife's head. In the first case, Hudson uses a strong metaphor that is drawn from the writings of the psychoanalyst Theodor Reik: "The unconscious has a built-in system [the third ear] designed to intuit the other's unconscious by decoding interpersonal signals." The so-called third ear "decodes clues through an indirect process of understanding necessitated by the fact that we cannot directly know ourselves or others."[52] In other words, the third ear facilitates one's ability to grasp withheld information. This is exactly what happens to Laverne, who either refused to acknowledge or simply did not see the full picture of what role he played in America's Middle East policy when he enlisted and while serving. But he has come to understand that the government simply manipulated him, used him for its own political purposes, and now, when he is no longer a soldier, back home, it has no use for him. Only upon his return did this realization dawn on him, with the help of the sudden appearance of the third ear. As for the emergence of the second mouth on his wife's head, Hudson invents this trope as a comic analogue to the third ear. While the third ear figuratively helps Laverne *hear*, the second mouth helps his wife *articulate* the truth that she wants to be heard. Mrs. Laverne, certain that the use of biological weapons has caused the third ear to appear, tries to open Laverne's eyes about his exploitation by the government: "The government doesn't give a damn about you. Your so-called good friend George Bush doesn't give a damn about you. You're nothing but a jarhead to him" (51). Yet even though the short-story collection energetically tries to foreground the idea that the only job the government has fulfilled was to send thousands of soldiers to the Middle East, and that it has taken no responsibility for the impact the war has had on them, this view seems somewhat biased: it suggests that the soldiers were literally hypnotized into agreeing to serve, whereas obviously they chose to serve. The book's criticism of the U.S. government and its policies is relevant to one's understanding of interventionism in general and the First Gulf War in particular, yet it patently does not reveal the full picture: it ignores the reasons soldiers joined the military and supported the war in the beginning, as well as the rationale for intervening in the first place. While the book repeatedly censures the intervention, it does not pay closer attention to the reasons for U.S. involvement but tends to take up issues that became known after the fact—for example, the absence of weapons of mass destruction. This emphasis, combined with a portrayal of the intervention as a series of follies—from the soldiers' experience to the overall policy in general—presents a very negative view of the U.S. role in the conflict.

Hudson tries to consistently display all the negative aspects behind U.S. intervention, focusing especially on the psychological trauma that the war's veterans were left to fight on their own. He also seeks to reveal the flaws of American policy. Yet there are traces of the intervention's humanitarianism in the book too. The reader finds out about the liberation of Kuwait in "Dear Mr. President" and the medical help that G.D. provides for "innocent civilians" (134) while checking the roadsides at night in the last story that by itself constitutes the third section of the collection, "Notes from a Bunker along Highway 8." Nevertheless certain other reasons for U.S. soldiers to be in the Middle East are made much more explicit and are stressed more emphatically in the collection. For example, Laverne says, "We are over here to defend the citizens of the United States of America" (44), whereas Larry remembers when he was captured by Iraqi soldiers, one of whom declares a different American interest before starting in on Larry's torture: "Have you come on behalf of America to do some more of your Nation Building? No, you have come to negotiate the price of oil, I suppose? Do you know the price of oil, Mr. America?" (10). Thus national interests, especially the American dependence on cheap oil, are among the major factors that drive American policy. Moreover it is crucial that the Iraqi addresses Larry in this scene as "Mr. America," underlining that oil is not an interest limited to *specific* politicians or soldiers; instead it is a *common*, national interest.

Additionally *Dear Mr. President* touches upon generational conflict. This issue is, however, unusually witnessed through the prism of governmental short-sightedness and failure. It is pivotal in the story "Dear Mr. President," when, finishing his letter, Laverne makes it explicit that relations within his family started to worsen after he returned from the Middle East. Unable to cope with her husband's sufferings from the postwar syndrome, Laverne's wife takes their son and leaves him; thus the family falls apart. Although the letter's style may indicate the family problem is a minor issue, while foregrounding Laverne's patriotism and deep trust in and admiration of President Bush, Hudson chooses to use sarcasm to report about the family difficulties Laverne is experiencing at the moment, something the reader finds out about via Laverne's "humble" request to have the president influence the situation:

> I was wondering if you could do an old friend a favor and write Mrs. Laverne a short note to tell her that she should come home with Jimmy, Jr., so that we can be a family again. Could you tell her that you are proud of me and that I served my country honorably? Could you tell her that I said she should come back so we can start the healing? . . .
>
> I sure would appreciate you writing that letter, sir. . . . *Then maybe I could start to get my life back. I mean if a man doesn't have his family, what does he have?* (56; my italics)

In this passage the tragedy of loss is intensified, as Hudson explicitly reveals the plain but horrifying truth: the U.S. government engages its citizens to fight for the country in order to uphold what is profitable for the U.S. and the purported well-being of the country; it refuses, however, to bear sufficient responsibility for those who return and for their families, eschewing any interest in *their* well-being, psychological, moral, or otherwise. All the veterans get as a reward for their participation in the war and their defense of U.S. interests is their own moral and psychological instability, along with broken families and broken lives. Hudson lets Laverne finish his letter with the stock phrase "It is an extreme honor to serve under you, sir" (57), which is obvious sarcasm. Yet he emphasizes that the U.S. administration's propaganda has skillfully obscured all the negative aspects of its policy, making soldiers believe in the supremacy of their mission and in their own significance, even as such a fundamental phenomenon as family and its cohesion is cast aside in neglect. The author dedicates a whole story, "The American Green Machine," to such a "zombieing" of young men and women into serving their country, and offers as well some highly sarcastic praise of the U.S. Marine Corps. The exaggeration that very closely borders on absurdity in this story is applied, as elsewhere in Hudson's work, to underline the blindness of soldiers and the indifference of the U.S. government toward its own veterans, as it goes about protecting the interests of the state.

It is fascinating that Hudson introduces some of his protagonists as fathers, creating a connection to a new generation instead of positioning the soldiers as abstract objects who do not belong to anything outside their military service. The collection raises the issue of the sons and daughters of those whose fathers fought in the First Gulf War or, to be more precise, it underscores how these children have been deprived of their fathers. It also surveys the problem from the reverse perspective: namely, that the veterans will not be able to raise their children properly because of all the negative consequences and other harmful influences that military service has exerted on them; because of what the war has done to them, they will never be fully able to be fathers. Two instances in the collection dramatize this predicament. The first example is quite explicit: while Captain Dugan was fighting in the Middle East, his daughter was killed in a car accident. The story raises the question of whether she might still have been alive had her father been there with her. The second example is Laverne's son, whom Mrs. Laverne, now doubting her husband's mental stability, takes away from the veteran. The story makes it clear that the father loves his son; Laverne refers to him only in a positive way, and he can only be read as being sincere in his desire for his son to have a happy childhood. Most important, Laverne wants to *participate* in his son's upbringing.

The collection also looks at the filial dynamic from the opposite angle, by sometimes portraying the soldiers in the role of children whose parents have to deal with the fact their sons or daughters took part in the First Gulf War. There are two examples that deserve special attention, as they vividly illustrate this perspective. In "Those Were Your Words Not Mine," Valerie Hackett, the mother of the fallen soldier Chad, tries to figure out what happened to her son. The story's bitter irony is that the woman is blind, so she is unable to read her son's last letter, where, she thinks, she can find an explanation for his death. The reader comes to know that Valerie has asked relatives to read the letter to her; they refused to do so or invented a substitute text in order not to traumatize the woman with an account of the real events. Desperate, she is ready to pay three hundred dollars to the person who reads the letter to her. The story contrasts the attitude of the mother with that of the government. Having viewed the problem through the government's eyes in other stories, the author now adopts the viewpoint of a parent, the soldier's mother, who, ironically, is blind. Does the author judge parents for not convincing their children to stay away from military service? Or does he attempt to say that the parents of soldiers frequently cannot even find out how their children have died while serving in foreign territory? Both interpretations are plausible; what is revealed is the tragedy of military families who lose members and are left to cope with this loss on their own.

The second example of a parent-child relationship can be found in "Notes from a Bunker along Highway 8," when G.D.'s father, a Vietnam War veteran, protests against the First Gulf War, which he calls "another Vietnam quagmire" (111). It is significant that unlike all the other examples I analyze, this story openly makes the First Gulf War equivalent to the Vietnam War, thus—although not really refuting the shift in policy—suggesting that no matter what the reason is for the involvement, war is war. To demonstrate his disapproval of any U.S. intervention in the Middle East, the Vietnam War veteran declares himself to be homosexual. The man, "a highly decorated Vietnam soldier, former Special Forces with a Medal of Honor" (112), demonstrates that he is ready to draw people's and especially his son's attention to the wrongs of American intrusion by any means. Together with G.D., the reader realizes from the veteran's letters that the man considers this war meaningless, since the only reason Americans are being sent to fight there is for oil. He compares the First Gulf War to the Vietnam War, diminishing the brutality of the former by noting that the soldiers spend their days "sitting in the desert, making sand castles" (118); the war, as shown on TV, "looks like a video game" and is "boring" to watch; there is no combat action, and the soldiers "have to pretend to fire . . . [their] weapon[s]" (123). Yet exactly this comparison reveals the differences between the two wars. Indeed the father's words illustrate the advances in technological progress that distinguish the First Gulf War from its precursors. But they also explicitly say that the First Gulf War is *less* bloody and brutal than the Vietnam War. There is hardly any characterization of the Vietnam War as "boring" or of the soldiers who fought that war as doing nothing. In the case of the First Gulf War, the Vietnam veteran allows himself to say that. This, of course, does not literally mean that soldiers did not do anything in Iraq, yet it clearly stresses the shift in interventionist policy, as the outcome of the intervention in Iraq is less brutal than it had been in Vietnam.

However, the father finds it inappropriate to call U.S. involvement *war* not just because of the way the war is being conducted. He judges the war's very premises and questions the right of the United States to intervene in the Middle East. Reminding his son of the extermination of Native Americans and of slavery in American history, the Vietnam War veteran tries to make G.D. see that the country that had shed so much blood in the past while building itself as a nation-state simply cannot have transparently altruistic motives in this current involvement. He asks his son why, if Americans really wanted to liberate people and fight against tyranny, the United States does not intervene in "all the other places in the world where there's oppression" (127). His answer is simple: "Because they don't have oil" (127). The veteran insists that the U.S. government has always presented its actions only from the positive side, enveloping its projected image as a nation in myths: "Our forefathers, those liars, those storytellers, have given America a way to feel morally justified when we do the same thing as every other country: murder, conquer, breed our population, and generate income and luxury" (127). Just as European settlers slaughtered Native Americans, just as Americans used and murdered millions of Africans and their descendants, the American military, according to the veteran, are now doing the same thing with people in Iraq, and because Saddam ordered *every* man to fight, the enemy includes "innocent people" (137). According to the story, every war, including the First Gulf War, is the result of government manipulation, a political ploy that is aimed at profits and enrichment. The explicit sarcastic reference to the government that is persistently made in the book is an important illustration of how *Dear Mr. President* deals with the problem of power. The book openly blames the U.S. government for all the war's negative consequences—from the health problems of the soldiers to the world's critical perception of the political role of the U.S. in the Middle East—demonstrating that the full responsibility lies on the government, and specifically on President Bush, an important character in *Dear Mr. President.*[53]

Yet, ultimately, the father tries only to protect his son. Citing his own example, he explains to G.D. that the government is just trying to involve him in its ploy, using high-flown metaphors and profound speeches to persuade American men and women to go and fight, just as they did when mobilizing men to go and fight in Vietnam, manipulating the future combatants "with all their [governmental] bullshit about the heroics of WWII. They used words like *evil* and *honor*" (138). However, behind the mask of American justice and democracy, peace and freedom, there are ordinary men and women who die in combat or who return home with psychological baggage. According to the short story, the government cares little about whether the veterans can reintegrate into society, whether they can remain mentally stable and overcome the psychosis of war. War is often portrayed by politicians as a heroic event, but behind the lofty speeches, there are thousands of innocent deaths, injustices, murders, and acts of barbarism and savagery that are skillfully veiled by those who start wars. The Vietnam veteran confesses that he himself killed innocent people during the war he fought in, and no politician would ever meditate on what the veteran now knows for sure: "The things you do in war you have to live with for the rest of your life. How am I supposed to live with something like that? You [G.D.] tell me. How am I" (139). He attempts to protect his son from the nightmare he has been experiencing ever since he fought in the Vietnam War, as he realizes that G.D. is destined to live a similar life. No matter what reason is given for a war, its atrocities will surely stay in the soldiers' memories forever.

The veteran's plan to pretend to be gay can be interpreted as a sign of a more general process of de-masculinization. What may seem nonsense to the readers and embarrassment to G.D. is the veteran's protest against the conventional masculinity epitomized by a warrior, his attempt to forget his soldier past by turning himself into a categorically opposite person. And if in the beginning the reader might assume that the veteran's declared homosexuality is a joke, toward the end of the story it is made apparent that the veteran does indeed now live with another man and enjoys his new life. His earlier comment, written beneath a photograph of a naked man that he has sent to his son—"This is still a free country, right?" (112)—is therefore not to be seen as an ironic question about whether he is *allowed* to send what he chooses. Rather it should be understood as a subtext that identifies the hypocrisy that may well emerge in such a situation: that the United States is a country that claims to have lofty values and is eager to spread peace throughout the world by any means, including brutality and the killing of innocent people, but this same "free country" questions whether its soldiers can be gay. In other words, murders are permissible, but sexual orientation presents a problem.

All in all, Hudson's *Dear Mr. President* vividly blames the U.S. administration for sending American troops to the Middle East. The short-story cycle also dramatizes the tragedy on a personal level, illustrating the broken lives endured by veterans of the First Gulf War. Even so, despite all the negative ramifications of the war that are shown and the thoroughgoing critique of the U.S. government, *Dear Mr. President* does not purely reject the idea of the shift in U.S. interventionism and portrays the intervention as being different from previous foreign military conflicts, thus revealing a historical change in U.S. foreign policy. It is perhaps the stories' deep analysis of the philosophy of war, their dealing with war as a phenomenon, that somewhat distracts the reader from the problem of the First Gulf War specifically. Yet the book does fall into the category of war docu-fiction: it does succeed in grasping the cultural history of the American war experience in general and of the First Gulf War in particular. Just like the previous examples analyzed in this chapter, *Dear Mr. President* presents multiple truths about U.S. intervention, from Vietnam War veterans' disapproval of the involvement to the loosely planned military operations in the Middle East and the problem of reintegration of First Gulf War veterans. Undeterred by the large employment of irony and sarcasm, the short-story cycle touches upon some of the most problematic aspects of the First Gulf War, decisively proving that documentary is not the only genre that can tell the truth.

Questioning the Missions, Defining Heroism: Tom Paine's *The Pearl of Kuwait* (2003)

Tom Paine's novel is, in one sense, similar to Hudson's *Dear Mr. President*—American participation in the First Gulf War is mocked and criticized here too. Yet the perspective is different. *The Pearl of Kuwait* is a novel about two marines, Cody Carmichael and Tommy Trang, who go AWOL to save Princess Lulu of Kuwait, whom Trang has fallen in love with. Their task is made more complicated by the outbreak of the First Gulf War and the subsequent instability in the region. When the princess is captured by Iraqi soldiers, the U.S. marines start their adventure to save her from them and from her evil fiancé. The final task of the reunited group is to liberate and bring democracy to Lulu's native country, Kuwait.

Paine's novel is an adventurous story of two young men (revealed from Cody's perspective) who do not understand why they are in the Gulf region. They easily leave their unit to do their own business, which emerges as an infatuation, and courageously (well, it probably would be more accurate to say effortlessly, and with a big portion of luck) overcome all the obstacles standing in their way. Through the example of these two soldiers, the novel's main critique is directed toward the notions of mission and heroism and how they are positioned in the context of U.S. involvement in the First Gulf War. The following analysis elaborates on these two aspects in greater detail.

The concept of mission is explored through the soldiers' consciousness of their presence in the war effort: Why are they here? What do they fight for? Do they support the ideas they are fighting for? To what extent do they realize they can die in war? Are they ready to sacrifice their lives? Are they ready to kill other people? These are crucial questions, and yet they are raised only implicitly and in a philosophical manner so that it is hard to get a single, unambiguous answer. *The Pearl of Kuwait* succeeds in providing answers to these questions, although only with respect to the two soldiers, the main characters. Therefore the following analysis should not be understood as elucidating a theory that per se can be treated as a generalizing one since it does not dictate strict and exclusive parameters governing the way the First Gulf War is represented in literary fiction universally. Rather it should be considered as one among many other possible interpretations and characterizations.

The mission to save the oppressed Kuwaitis and to reverse and stop the actions of Saddam Hussein's regime does not come into view for quite a long time after the novel begins. The first mission assigned to the marines is to collect—to steal, really—pearls from the Gulf's waters. Notably, as this chapter has already made clear, one of the theories that have explained American participation in the war is the country's interest in Arab oil. Paine, although he does not leave out the material aims of the United States, nonetheless avoids making persistent references to oil and, in a sense, makes pearls a substitute for oil, in this way paying attention to the material interest of the intruders. The reference to Lulu as the main "pearl" Trang is willing to obtain is another indication that America's mission is a hunt for specific things—important to Trang, in particular, but also, metaphorically, for the country Trang fights for. However, the novel does make references to oil. It states that "America fights . . . for the oil," and offers descriptions of the air being "full of the smell of oil fires burning," of "the quiet sounds of the oil-slicked waters of the Persian Gulf sloshing up on the beach and down," and of "the oil haze."[54] The descriptions appear over the course of the narration to demonstrate the devastation endured by the region and to remind readers that oil was, if not the key factor, then definitely one of the important motivations for the war.

When they fail to pull off the pearl mission, the marines set out to find and save the princess. After getting into various (either ridiculous or dangerous) situations, the soldiers successfully fulfill this mission. What turns out to be the novel's key mission, though, happens later, when both soldiers, Lulu, Ali (a Bangladeshi boy whom the soldiers have freed from slavery), and representatives of the Kuwaiti resistance movement try to liberate the country from Saddam's occupying army. The mission that was claimed to be the key one in the real war is mocked in the novel in two ways. First, the locals themselves do not quite understand what they are fighting for. Their perplexity is vividly demonstrated when a member of the Kuwaiti resistance movement asks the marines "what *exactly . . . the greatest mission of the war that they were all going on* [is]." Trang has to clarify that they are going to "kill Saddam." Only after this explanation do the Kuwaitis demonstrate their readiness, shouting, "Yea! kill Saddam! Whatever this crazy Chinese [Trang is Vietnamese American] guy says!" (194; italics in original). Second, the operations that are planned can hardly be perceived as serious undertakings since they are dubbed "Operation Flamingo!" (275) and "Operation Broken Glass!" (280); although they are ultimately accomplished relatively successfully, these names indicate that the organizers comprehend their actions as a sort of child's play rather than as serious operations. Hence the mission itself, although—significantly—initially designed with high-minded intentions, turns into a game.

Another problem that emerges in defining the mission is the obvious misunderstanding of the enemy. The reader encounters certain characterizations of Saddam—as "a psycho" (44), "the evil guy" (217), "the badass dude" (308)—as well as his soldiers: "evil bastards" (58), "possessed by something real *evil*" and "true psycho killer[s]" (108; italics in original). However, all these descriptions sound rather abstract and do not provide a clear image of the enemy. Instead they place Saddam and his army out of reach by labeling them as supernatural evil powers that have enslaved the Gulf region, thus demonstrating their superiority and invincibility. This characterization is very important, as it clearly evokes the claim made by many scholars, that the Gulf War can be compared to World War II because of the frequent parallels that were drawn between Hitler and Saddam; both tyrants are portrayed as evil, and their regimes are characterized as powerful evil organizations whose overriding aim was to prove their superiority. One of the most vivid proofs of the evil way the Iraqis conducted their invasion and occupation occurs when the corpses of two men and a girl of five are found on the street and the reader is told that "some real nasty stuff" was done "to the little girl" (289), which one assumes was rape. While the novel intentionally makes fun of the soldiers' presence in the Gulf region and often criticizes their actions, the intervention itself is still portrayed as a humanitarian mission because of the atrocities that have taken place in the affected territories, which clearly need to be stopped. Episodes like the one with the dead girl serve as triggers to act, to get involved, and to prevent tyranny. They make the two marines realize that they "absolutely got to do something" (289). In addition, the novel narrates the devastating consequences of the war on Kuwait: bombed buildings, hundreds of innocent people killed, beatings, the absence of any medical help. And the novel touches upon the forced military service foisted upon Iraqi men. For example, the Iraqis whom U.S. marines meet on their travels are described in the following way: "[Y]ou *never saw a sadder-looking specimen of soldier* than those dudes we passed on the side of the road to Saudi. They were the most *unsat* bunch of dudes! Starving, crapped-up, exhausted—kind of just shuffling their feet. And they all kind of looked like so much the same—most featured the bushy Saddam mustache" (243; italics in original). The U.S. soldiers find two "unarmed" Iraqi soldiers who "sold their rifles for food a few days earlier as they were starving, and they couldn't wait for the war to be over, and had wondered *what the hell had kept America from just busting into Kuwait weeks earlier*" (235; my italics). Here the novel underscores the necessity of U.S. intervention and accuses the country of allowing the atrocities to take place by not getting involved earlier. And when the marines take some Iraqis as POWs, the reader finds out that two of them "had been taken from their house at night to be made into soldiers, and told if they failed their family would be strangled to death" (149). Evil is concentrated in the barbarity of Saddam and the state under his control, and his army includes those who have simply become pawns in the hands of their government.

As for the marines' defining mission, the novel makes it plain: To bring "Liberty and Democracy and Freedom," which the soldiers are "ready to die for" (23), to the Arab world. However, the novel questions whether the Arabs wanted this "American-style freedom" (24); that the Arabs did not want Americans in their territory and "really hated" (47) the Western soldiers is raised as a pivotal issue. The intervention in the Middle East, as depicted in *The Pearl of Kuwait,* parallels the "police action" conducted some decades before, in Vietnam. The inclusion of the Vietnamese American character, Tommy Trang, and the repeated references to Vietnam can be interpreted as the novel's support for the analogy that the First Gulf War was to be another Vietnam for the U.S. Trang's mother was raped during the war and became pregnant with him. One might well wonder: Why would Trang choose to be part of the U.S. Marines? The novel responds to this question in the voice of the character himself: "*America* didn't rape her. And the *Marine Corps* didn't rape her" (55; italics in original). Trang underlines the innocence of the American nation, the U.S. government, and the Marine Corps as an institution with regard to the criminal acts committed during the U.S. involvement in Vietnam, emphasizing that specific individuals, and not institutions, were responsible for the misdeeds and outright atrocities. At this point the novel makes it clear that considering the military to be evil based only on the actions committed by some of its members is wrong; regarding the First Gulf War to be the same as the intervention in Vietnam and thus claiming that every intervention following Vietnam would be another Vietnam for the U.S. is wrong too: the reasons for the intervention change, policies change, the government changes, and soldiers change. Trang worships the government of the United States; he deeply respects its policies; his patriotism, voiced in his sincere belief that "America was totally worth laying down your life for as a marine" (151), and the patriotism of his mother, who asked that her son put an American flag into her coffin when she died, are foregrounded in the novel. Trang often demonstrates his knowledge of the Bill of Rights, which far exceeds the depth of other Americans (e.g., Carmichael confesses, "My Californian family was American as far back as anyone could remember, and I couldn't have told you squat about the Bill of Rights" [151]). Trang's firm patriotism and belief in the U.S. military as a force of saviors make the reader wonder whether the character metaphorically illustrates a historical transformation of the U.S. soldier (whose image in the early 1990s was so different from that of the soldiers fighting in the Vietnam War), or whether the character's trust in U.S. interventionist policy only reveals the naïveté and shortsightedness of those who generally believe in the positive effects of militarism, categorizing all the negative consequences (e.g., rape and murder in Vietnam) as mere collateral damage. In this particular case, it would perhaps be even more correct to ask whether Trang really fully understands the intervention in Vietnam. Does he realize that he himself is the product of that particular fight against evil (which in the case of Vietnam was Soviet communism)?

Another reference to Vietnam is made in the dialogue between Prince

Khalid Ali Abdul Aziz al Saud and the marines, when the prince demonstrates his knowledge of Vietnam as the country "where America lost the war" (101). He is quite sarcastic—"And now you [Americans] come to my country . . . to fight for us. I hope you do not lose this war too" (101)—illustrating Saudi Arabia's uncertainty about whether America will be able to make this war a success. Trang responds in his deeply patriotic manner, declaring that he and his comrades have come "to fight with your people. To be part of a great Allied Coalition to free Kuwait," while the prince mockingly explains that Americans are the "servants" and "slaves" of the Saudis and that the U.S. soldiers are there because the Saudis "have hired America to fight" (101). That last comment is a reference to the political relations between the United States and Saudi Arabia, in which the former is dependent on cheap oil supplies guaranteed by the latter in exchange for, among other things, assurance that its military might will prevent an Iraqi invasion of the whole Gulf region.

Despite the references to Vietnam and oil, which serve to point out the corruption (or at least the nonpurity) of the intervention, the novel does address the war's humanitarian aspect. The tyranny of Saddam's regime must be stopped—this is one of the main messages of the novel. The reader finds out about the oppression of women, the killing of anyone who disagrees with what Saddam says, and the chaos that reigns over Iraq and Kuwait; the existence of biological weapons is mentioned several times. Thus *The Pearl of Kuwait* does provide the reasons that would make external involvement by the West, led by the U.S., seem necessary. U.S. intervention is justified, aimed as it is at spreading America's central values throughout the region. The fight for freedom and democracy that is so vividly described in *The Pearl of Kuwait* brings me to the second element that is criticized in the novel: heroism.

The issue of heroism comes to the surface from the novel's very beginning, when the reader discovers that Trang has a tattoo that says DIE A HERO. Trang believes that he and his comrades have been sent to the Middle East to accomplish a vital mission; afterward they can rest on their laurels as true heroes. Whether the soldiers are fighting for something *they* truly believe in and want to share with others is questioned in the novel several times, for example, when the marines cannot give up the idea that "the Kuwaiti Kingdom . . . will award us [Carmichael and Trang] a medal for heroism" (14–15), when Trang gets "stoked about the Kuwaiti medal for heroism" (15), and when they have to "hurry" before the war comes to its end or else Trang will miss his "chance to win a congressional Medal of Honor" (152). But the final "serious heroic mission" (239), "a mission of historical proportions" (300), makes the reader question their heroism. Carmichael, not ready to give up his life for the freedom of the others, hesitates at the last minute in deciding whether to participate in the liberation. Yet this is not to be interpreted as evidence of the soldier's cowardice; rather here we see the novel censuring the U.S. government, which has sent young American men and women to die for the purported well-being of others. Another incident worth mentioning is an American aerial bombing of Iraqis who have already surrendered but are mistaken for "a still active Iraqi company" (255), demonstrating American incompetence and the intervention's flaws.

Heroism that is to be proved over the course of the war, it turns out, wanes and fades, along with democracy, which is persistently referred to because "America has this powerfully excellent vision to share with the world" (279). Still, *how* does the United States share the values of democracy? Does its way of sharing these values make American soldiers heroes? Can one optimistically call the intruders "the good old boys of the good old USA" (245)? Is it in fact an act of *sharing*, or is it rather one of *imposing* that is carried out by the United States? Who is responsible for the fate of the bombed civilians? Who is responsible for what happened to the U.S. soldiers who were killed, whose families have lost sons, brothers, husbands, and fathers? And does the world even need the "American-style freedom" (310) achieved at the cost of human lives? The novel considers all these questions in order to provide its own estimation of the intervention. Like other literary and cinematic examples, it tackles the intervention from various perspectives, revealing both its advantages and disadvantages. Although *The Pearl of Kuwait* seems, eventually, to take a stance against the U.S. intervention in the First Gulf War—ending with Trang's vigorous exclamation, "We'll write DEMOCRACY with bullets, man!" (310)—there are multiple scenes that portray devastation, sorrow, and atrocities in the region, which show that the intervention had humanitarian grounds. Revealing both pluses and minuses of the intervention, the novel attempts to reflect the broad history of the war and thus becomes a docu-fictional narrative of the U.S. participation in the First Gulf War.

These examples from film and literary fiction assert that the Gulf War resulted in two major outcomes. For the U.S. government, its declared aims were fulfilled; that is, the oppressed nation was liberated, access to oil in the region was preserved, and America was reborn, having shed its lingering "Vietnam syndrome." The soldiers who fought, however, endured physical and psychological mutilation. Hardly any pacifist tendencies can be detected in the analyzed works; there is, to be sure, a strain of protest against war in general, yet the intervention itself is not displayed as only a mistake—in the full sense of the word. It did have its folly, but its humanitarianism, which every director and author inevitably deals with, is apparent and serves to justify the involvement, even if only partially. Through these fictionalized stories, filmmakers and writers document the complex history of U.S. intervention in the First Gulf War.

3

The Balkan War

National Trauma: How It Was

The collapse of the former Yugoslavia is reputed to have started in June 1991, when Slovenia and Croatia decided to secede from the country. That is when Yugoslavia, once a prosperous country in the Balkan region of southeastern Europe, began to decline. While the country still consisted of four other states, namely Bosnia, Serbia, Montenegro, and Macedonia, the government (largely dominated by Serbs) tried to prevent its collapse by sending troops to Slovenia and Croatia. Slovenia managed to keep its independence, while Croatia was stuck in war. The evident explanation for such an unfolding of the events is the proportion of the Serbian population in each place: in Slovenia there were too few Serbs to oppress the Slovenians, but there were enough Serbs to fight against the Croats in Croatian territory. Yet the war in Croatia was only the preamble to a larger war that started as soon as Bosnia attempted to become an independent state. It is worth mentioning that the Bosnians' decision to secede was based on a logical assumption. In that most multiethnic and multireligious state of Yugoslavia, its Muslim population was afraid of Serbian oppression.[1] Eventually it was precisely such oppression that was visited upon them in the ensuing

Balkan War—a war that was mainly fought between Serbs (including Bosnian Serbs) on the one side and Bosnian Muslims on the other.

Samantha Power argues that the interethnic conflict was stirred up by Slobodan Milošević, the Serbian president, who promoted "Serb dominance." While Bosnian Serbs were clearly perceived by Serbs outside Bosnia as friends, and Bosnian Croats could at least rely on military support from Croatia (whose war lasted only seven months), Bosnian Muslims could do nothing but wait for help from outside. The main help eventually provided came from the United Nations. It was aimed at regulating the relations between Serbs and Bosnian Serbs, as well as with Bosnian Muslims, and consisted of imposing an arms embargo in 1991. That left the Muslim population practically without weapons, while the Bosnian Serb Army (consisting of soldiers from the Yugoslav National Army and Bosnian Serbs) took possession of nearly all the arms in Bosnia. There then ensued "ethnic cleansing" in Bosnia, actions aimed at eradicating Muslims from the territory of the former Yugoslavia. Power describes the actions of the Serbs: "They forced fathers to castrate their sons or molest their daughters; they humiliated and raped (often impregnating) young women. Theirs was a deliberate policy of destruction and degradation: destruction so this avowed enemy race would have no homes to which to return; degradation so the former inhabitants would not stand tall—and thus would not dare again stand—in Serb-held territory." Peaceful organizations were involved in the Balkan War practically from the very beginning, and the prospect of military intervention, including U.S. military involvement, was deferred or deemed untenable. Power elucidates that decision by citing the general reluctance of the U.S. to use military force in other countries, especially on "mere humanitarian grounds," since the end of the Vietnam War. The Vietnam experience had turned into a phobia toward foreign military entanglements that was reinforced when policymakers considered that U.S. military involvement in the Balkan region could turn into the country's "second Vietnam."[2] Even the success of the First Gulf War could not fully counteract this anxiety about the repeat of a Vietnam-style "quagmire" in the Balkans. Many policymakers and political figures understood the situation in this way. Richard Holbrooke, an "assistant secretary of state for East Asian and Pacific affairs under President Carter" and a "board member of the International Rescue Committee," who traveled to Bosnia to see the situation with his own eyes, wrote a memorandum to then-candidate Bill Clinton, sharing his anxiety whether "*President* Clinton [would] carry out what *candidate* Clinton proposed."[3] Holbrooke underlined his dissatisfaction with Bush's inactivity with regard to the situation in the Balkans, calling the government's response "weak" and "inadequate." He stressed that the U.S. reaction to the war in the former Yugoslavia should not be limited to the "choice between Vietnam and doing nothing, as the Bush Administration has portrayed it."[4] In the end, Clinton authorized a military intervention in the Balkans—although he did so not at the beginning of his presidency but only in July 1995.[5]

One can argue that the fear of repeating the Vietnam experience is only one part of the explanation for the U.S. adherence to a noninterventionist policy. The American debacle in Southeast Asia, of course, made the country cautious about sending its troops to foreign territories, but what about the huge military effort undertaken in the First Gulf War? Vietnam does not wholly account for American fears about military intervention in the mid-1990s.

Compared to the other wars that are analyzed in this book, I would stress, the Balkan War stands out. Two points make it conspicuous: first, it was a civil war; second, it eventually resulted in crimes against humanity and genocide. Due to the nature of the conflict, UN peacekeepers were its primary boots on the ground at first; neither the U.S. nor any other country that could provide military support was initially supposed to be involved in the war. However, as history demonstrates, numerous conflicts prove that the presence of UN troops is sometimes insufficient to stop war. In such cases, outside military intervention becomes inevitable. The Balkan War was one of those cases when external military involvement was needed. It was eventually carried out by the U.S.

The intervention, as mentioned earlier, came after much waiting and hesitation. According to Dina Iordanova, Yugoslavs thought that "the West would rush to intervene and put an end to the conflict there" and were truly perplexed when it did not.[6] The U.S. government did not rush in because, according to Richard N. Haass, Bosnia was exclusively a "humanitarian tragedy with few or no strategic U.S. interests."[7] In the initial phase, the only help provided by the U.S. and the UN was humanitarian aid.[8] Although the Bosnian War (the longest and the bloodiest of the Yugoslav wars) started in 1992, UN peacekeepers were sent to Bosnia only in 1993. Ultimately it was the slaughter of Bosnian Muslims in Srebrenica (which was supposed to be protected by the UN) in 1995 that provoked a more emphatic reaction from the international community.[9] By that time the genocide had already taken the lives of more than 200,000 Bosnians.[10] Before late 1995 the Clinton administration "continually fed the hopes of the Bosnian government that the United States would actually do something to defend those values that it kept proclaiming."[11] Matthew Parish contends, "After Somalia, the US was reluctant to send ground troops and only resorted to the use of air power to bomb the Bosnian Serbs to the negotiating table. Military intervention occurred in the context of a series of stop-start attempts to negotiate a peace agreement between the warring sides, hampered by the inability of EU and US governments to agree what peace treaty model to push. . . . The lukewarm support of the US government for the EU-led plans caused the war to drag on far longer than it might otherwise have done." And although, with regard to its role in resolving the Balkan conflict, the international community was criticized both in the beginning (for not intervening immediately) and later (for not being able to come to an agreement and stop the war), the efforts of the U.S. and its European allies to end the conflict were colossal.[12] Gale Stokes writes, "The Western powers . . . stop[ped] the massive killing and ethnic cleansing by imposing military force under the auspices of NATO and the United Nations."[13] The war ended in mid-October 1995, and on November 21 a peace agreement was reached in Dayton, Ohio.

Yet in early 1998 war broke out in the province of Kosovo. That conflict was stopped only after NATO military involvement in March 1999.[14]

The reason for U.S. intervention in the Balkans can be interpreted in various ways. Although some scholars argue that the deferral was caused by the U.S. being unwilling "to sacrifice its own soldiers to save Muslim lives," the dangers of entering the conflict should not be minimized, nor should what was at stake be reduced to the religious issue. Yugoslavia was a relatively large country in Europe, and stability in the Balkans was vital for the general stability of Europe. Therefore one can argue that late in the twentieth century the U.S. "returned to Europe to save Europe from itself" for the third time that century.[15] Shortly after peace was negotiated, Holbrooke stated, "it took some time to realize that we are still part of the balance of power in Europe."[16] And although some scholars doubt that the instability in the Balkans can be compared to the kinds of menace posed by Stalin, Hitler, and Wilhelmine Germany,[17] it is reasonable to claim that nobody could have predicted what a destabilized Europe might have caused in the future. The Bosnian genocide should have been a solid enough reason to provoke an intervention. History tells us, however, that the slaughter of thousands of innocent people does not always cause the international community to act.

Discussing the problem of U.S. security and its dependence on the situation in the Balkans, Wayne Bert claims that when the Cold War was over, "the strategic significance of the area [the Balkans] diminished sharply." Therefore the U.S. felt no urge to get involved in the Balkan region, especially when intervention was considered merely on national security grounds. Bert pinpoints two reasons for the delay in intervening. First, the U.S. preferred that Europe deal with the crisis, since the U.S. was "sensitive to charges of impinging on European turf, weary from the recent Desert Storm initiative to eject Iraq from Kuwait, and lacking ready-made solutions." Second, the country's involvement in the Balkan War did not have much support from U.S. citizens or from U.S. foreign policy elites, which the scholar explains via the nation's still fresh memories of Vietnam as well as "the difficulties in Somalia," where eighteen U.S. soldiers had been killed in the widely publicized "Black Hawk Down" incident in Mogadishu in 1993, when the corpses of U.S. servicemen had been dragged through the streets.[18] Thus, although the U.S. was concerned about the escalating war, it did not send military troops for a long time, being unwilling to risk the lives of Americans. Bert aptly elucidates why the U.S. eventually fought in the Balkans: although the U.S. initially accentuated "humanitarian" but not "security interests," "there was a US security interest at stake in Bosnia, since any major threat to the values that underline a US-inspired world order does affect security." In addition, the military inaction of the West (specifically the U.S. and NATO) "would have contributed to the disorientation and weakening of the United States, Russia, the European Community, NATO, and the UN, and would have done considerable harm to the American reputation for maintaining a world order in line with its values."[19]

The Balkan War differed immensely from the other wars the U.S. had fought in its history, chiefly because the enemy was not clearly identified. As Nicholas Morris claims, "all sides in Bosnia saw the humanitarian operation as directly helping their opponents."[20] Nevertheless, Bert states, "what is not in dispute is that each of the main protagonists in the war in Bosnia was involved in ethnic cleansing, each was involved in violence against civilians, each broke its share of agreements and cease-fires, each had paramilitary groups assisting the more standard military units, and each had detention camps." This difficulty notwithstanding, U.S. involvement "was quickly successful and with no loss of American life."[21]

The 1990s is replete with various civil wars around the world, some of which included genocide. The most significant conflicts for the U.S., for various reasons, were those that escalated in Somalia, Rwanda, and Bosnia. The war in Somalia ended for the U.S. relatively soon; after the eighteen American deaths mentioned earlier, the U.S. withdrew its forces. The intervention in Somalia was a purely humanitarian mission, yet it failed to put an immediate stop to the conflict, and American soldiers were killed and wounded. Rwanda was an even more complicated case:

the U.S. did not provide any support to stop the genocide of Tutsi and moderate Hutu in 1994. The unsuccessful U.S. involvement in Somalia likely influenced the country's hesitation in the cases of Rwanda and later Bosnia. The U.S. did not want to intervene in Rwanda because it understood that it might not be easy to restore peace in another African country. When asked about Rwanda and the lack of will to intervene there, President Clinton remarked, "Lesson number one is, don't go into one of those things and say, as the U.S. said when we started in Somalia, 'Maybe we'll be done in a month because it's a humanitarian crisis.' . . . Because there are almost always political problems and sometimes military conflicts, which bring about these crises."[22] The U.S. failure to immediately intervene in the Balkan War was also considerably influenced by the country's involvement in Somalia. Power claims that "one way the administration deflected attention away from Bosnia was to focus on another humanitarian crisis, in Somalia." She concludes that "even though U.S. troops would not deploy to Africa for several months, the Somalia famine had already begun drawing attention away from the Balkans"; the extensive coverage of the humanitarian catastrophe in Somalia, as in a zero-sum game, resulted in fading interest in the Bosnian case.[23]

The Balkan conflict eventually did draw the attention of the West. The war became one of the major military U.S. involvements in the 1990s, aimed at stopping the genocide of Bosnian Muslims and restoring peace in the conflict-ridden area. The focus of this treatment of the Balkan War and the neglect of the two conflicts in Africa is to explain the political and military nature of the war as well as deal with the relatively large involvement of the U.S. in the Balkans. Works of (docu-)fictional film and literature provide a much broader overview of U.S. intervention in the Balkan War as compared to the country's brief involvement in Somalia and its neglect of the Rwandan genocide.

Film and U.S. Intervention in the Balkan War

Barry Levinson's *Wag the Dog* (1997) seems to implicitly tackle the problem of the unrest in the Balkan region, placing at its heart the story of an invented war in Albania that is supposed to draw attention away from a sex scandal involving the U.S. president. Quite obviously referring to the scandal of Bill Clinton's affair with Monica Lewinsky, and making it the movie's central theme, the film manages to reflect a rather complicated political situation in the 1990s. Obviously Albania was never a part of Yugoslavia, but given the large population of Albanians in Kosovo and the confrontation between Serbs and Albanians in 1998, the reference to Albania in the film hints at the 1990s conflicts in the Balkans. Easily selling the American people the sham story about the war in Albania, the film's main characters, who work for the president, point up the fact that the vast majority of Americans know little about the Balkan region and the situation there. Yet the choice of the place where the actual war should be—Albania—is rather symbolic, as it reveals how unstable the Balkan region was in the 1990s.

That *Wag the Dog* figuratively raises the issue of the Balkan War is only a speculation. There are a few films that overtly deal with U.S. intervention in the Balkans. John Moore's *Behind Enemy Lines* (2001), Predrag Antonijević's *Savior* (1998), and Mimi Leder's *The Peacemaker* (1997) will be analyzed in detail. Another interesting example of a cinematic representation of the Balkan War is Boris Malagurski's *The Weight of Chains* (2010), a documentary account that narrates the history of the conflict and attempts to assess the role the West played in the war. The documentary openly argues that the Balkan War was indirectly provoked by the West. In the film, Malagurski explains that the strategy of "privatization through liquidation" imposed on Yugoslavia by its own economists, who were influenced by the West, caused a decline in the country's standard of living that, in turn, provoked tension between representatives of the different ethnic groups. It is interesting that the documentary fully blames the West, completely neglecting the fact that the West could not have imposed ethnic hatred—the grounds for the Balkan War. The ethnic and religious tensions that inflamed the population were the result of social instability in the Balkan region. One cannot therefore blame the West for the massacres organized and carried out by Serbs as well as other ethnic groups. In this context, the words of Iordanova seem very apt: "In the 1990s, it no longer takes aloof foreigners to problematise the Balkans, as the Region is willingly problematised by insiders."[24]

Yet relevant works of film and literature provide a somewhat different interpretation of the role the U.S. played in the Balkan War. While the literature—Douglas Cavanaugh's *Into Hell's Fire* (2007) and Tom Foley's *This Way to Heaven* (2000), which I will take up shortly— tends to criticize the deferral and nonintervention, the films treating the conflict offer a multilateral perspective on U.S. involvement in the Balkans. Moore's *Behind Enemy Lines* primarily censures the American military intervention and demonstrates that the soldiers did not comprehend their role in the war; Antonijević's *Savior* narrates the U.S. war experience from the viewpoint of a vengeful soldier who is morally reborn and becomes a rescue soldier over the course of the war; and Leder's *The Peacemaker* presents the United States as an exceptional country that should intervene in international affairs and solve global problems. Despite the differences in perspective, all the films approach the problem of U.S. intervention in the Balkan War seriously, attempting to narrate the history of U.S. involvement but also to display the nation's humanitarian side.

From Inaction to Action: John Moore's *Behind Enemy Lines* (2001)

Behind Enemy Lines can be divided into two parts. The first concerns the definition of the Balkan War and the role of U.S. soldiers in it, while the second deals with the active U.S. participation in the war. Both are important to analyze in order to define the war as a 1990s (or a post-Vietnam) conflict.

At the beginning of *Behind Enemy Lines*, the director introduces the audience to the protagonist, Lt. Chris Burnett (Owen Wilson), a U.S. Navy pilot who works with a partner, Jeremy Stackhouse (Gabriel Macht). Burnett is an elite pilot, and the chief purpose of his being in the military, as he himself articulates it, is to take part in combat action.

However, his commander, Adm. Leslie McMahon Reigart (Gene Hackman), thinks he is not ready for real war; more than that, no combat is expected in the near future, so Burnett mostly spends time observing training. The audience witnesses him making bets and playing with a baseball or speculating about the Balkan War, ridiculing the role of U.S. soldiers in it. An important scene that vividly illustrates this takes place in the canteen. "Don't you forget what you're doing here," says one of the soldiers to Burnett, and Burnett responds, "What we're doing here? Are you kidding me? Oh, I am eating Jell-O and he [Stackhouse] is wiping his hands." The soldier does not understand Burnett's frustration, for he believes that in the military "everybody has a role to play": his role as a marine is to "take care of the serious business," while the role of a naval pilot is to "eat Jell-O." The difference between the attitudes of the two men is pivotal. While Burnett is annoyed and irritated, seeing his comrades just waiting and doing nothing but pretending to take part in war, the other soldier accepts the rules dictated by the existing chain of military command and thus follows orders, whether they are to fight or to wait. Burnett is portrayed as a potential hero, unwilling to wait but ready to fight and demonstrating a preparedness to destroy the enemy.

In the scene that follows this bit of dialogue, the viewer witnesses two marines in another corner of the canteen, competing to see who can do more push-ups, surrounded by a crowd who is feverishly pulling for them. Burnett makes a comment: "See, that's exactly what I am talking about. Everybody thinks they're gonna get a chance to punch some Nazi in the face at Normandy. And those days are over. They are long gone. I used to think I was gonna get a chance to do it. Now I realize I'm gonna be eating Jell-O." Cynthia Weber argues that Burnett's remark signifies the decisive distinction between a "moral grammar" used for World War II and a different "moral grammar" of the wars in the 1990s; in World War II it was clear who the enemy was, but in the 1990s the uncertainty about the enemy was both "logically and morally" hard for soldiers to grasp.[25] Nevertheless one can speculate that this difference can also be observed in all the other wars that had taken place in the intervening decades, including the Korean War and the Vietnam War, where the enemy was defined as a representative of communism. Thus the wars in the 1990s overtly signify a change in U.S. interventionism. Weber stresses that in the 1990s, there can be no clear evil because "the enemy keeps changing."[26] Burnett's words vividly illustrate this predicament: "Well, today is Tuesday—I think we're helping these people. No, no, now it's switched around. Now we're helping . . ." Barnett's indignation, however, also aptly underscores the complex nature of the Balkan War itself, a conflict that made it absolutely impossible to understand who were the "bad guys," who the "good guys." The absence of such a clear moral differentiation apparently caused any external intervention to be postponed and eventually made the mission very difficult to carry out, for commanders and soldiers alike.

In the next scene Barnett confesses to Admiral Reigart his dissatisfaction with their idleness: "If we're at war, why doesn't somebody act like we're at war. Cause as far as I can tell, we go out, we fly around, and we come back. Now, maybe we're pretending we're in the middle of the fight, but that's all we're doing is pretending cause we're not fighting. We're watching." The situation echoes the action, or rather its lack, in *Jarhead*, when Swofford, narrating the marines' daily routine, singles out the soldiers' main task: to wait. After the First Gulf War, an American soldier, now stationed in an Eastern European conflict zone, faces the same problem experienced by his comrades at war not long ago in the Middle East: first, he does not understand why one would need military forces if there is "no war," and second, he cannot comprehend the purpose of the sort of intervention he is involved in, when omission is the only choice given. Yet the scene also unambiguously reflects the hesitation of the United States to intervene in the Balkan region to help stop the fighting and the country's preference for waiting during the war years of the 1990s.

In the film's second half, Burnett gets the chance to directly participate in war after Serbs bring down his plane when it enters a no-fly zone. The Serbs are trying to avoid having any Western soldiers in their territory, for they would see that the Serbs were violating the peace agreement. Stackhouse is eventually executed by one of the Serbs, whereas Burnett—who tries to hide—is discovered. For the rest of the film, Burnett is running from a group of Serbs who are hunting him. He manages to contact headquarters in the U.S., and Admiral Reigart informs him that an American rescue plane will be sent for him and gives him the rendezvous location. However, Burnett has changed uniforms with a dead local soldier in order to disguise himself from his pursuers. This leads to a fatal misunderstanding on the part of headquarters: the rescue plane is commanded to return, as Burnett is reported to be dead. Burnett manages to send another signal to headquarters, and Reigart organizes another rescue mission. The audience watches a scene in which U.S. soldiers and their commanders prepare to set off, to serve their country, to help their comrade, to "get [their] boy back." The mission proves successful: Burnett is saved. Admiral Reigart is eventually dismissed from his post.

The film's ending is what reveals the actions of Americans in the war to be humanitarian. Burnett manages to photograph mass graves of Bosnian Muslims (civilians) as evidence of the peace agreement's violation, and the pictures are eventually made public. The intervention is justified because, as Weber puts it, "all [U.S. soldiers] need to do is ensure that they fight on the side of right. What is right is to defend humanity by preventing genocide: this was part of what justified US actions in Europe in WWII, and it is what justifies many 1990s US military interventions."[27] Burnett proves to be a "real" soldier, even if this only happens toward the end of the narrative. Indeed the viewer witnesses Burnett's transformation from the man who has questioned the U.S. military to the man who serves in that military to fight for the just cause, to protect the innocent, and to be proudly referred to as a soldier. In this respect, Burnett turns into a rather conventional, idealized image of a U.S. soldier from the past, specifically from World War II—the warrior who fights for a better life for future generations without sparing his own life.

The Religious Side of the War and U.S. Reaction
to It in Predrag Antonijević's *Savior* (1998)

Savior applies a different approach to define the role of an American soldier in the Balkan War and, consequently, to characterize U.S. intervention. The film is a unique example among those analyzed in this project because it is the only one to show an American soldier, in this case the mercenary Guy (Dennis Quaid), fighting on the Serbian side. Some scholars have argued that in the Balkan War, the Serbs were the most violent, whereas Bosnian Muslims were the "least guilty"; such claims have no clear proof, and the accusation of greater Serb brutality can be explained by their "more visible" actions being documented by various media.[28] Hence, while it is somewhat inaccurate to display Bosnian Muslims as the "good guys," this tendency is evident in film representations, where the Serbs are most often depicted as the enemy. Unlike in the actual conflict, the films about it do not seem to pull any punches about who the enemy is, although they raise this question. For example, in *Behind Enemy Lines*, Burnett's attitude concerning the soldiers' lack of awareness of who the enemy is seems to be correct: the soldiers never know which side they will be fighting on or supporting the next day. *Savior* takes a similar stance, presenting an American who fights for the Serbs, thus questioning the view that the Serbs were the only ethnic group who were murdering innocent people and violating the peace (and other) agreements.

Savior provides a clear explanation for why Guy is fighting against the Bosnians: he is figuratively taking revenge on Muslims (whom he considers terrorists). At the beginning of the film, the audience sees Guy's wife and son killed in an explosion planned by Islamic terrorists. Hence his mission in the Balkans turns into a struggle against Bosnians that is grounded in religious hatred. He fights his *personal* war—a war against Muslims. In one scene he shoots a Bosnian boy who is only trying to get a goat over a fence and poses no danger at all, then inhales, takes out a massive cross that he wears on his chest, and looks at it. This impulse characterizes his actions as a struggle against non-Christians, specifically Muslims. The scene is very provocative and disturbing. Guy obviously believes that his actions are just because he is fighting against terrorists. Yet his mistake is to equate terrorism with Islam: he considers every Muslim, including the boy he killed, a terrorist.

Later, the viewer notices significant changes in Guy's attitude toward the war as he realizes that the extermination of Bosnian Muslims will not bring back his wife and son. He starts to understand that innocent Muslims are also suffering and dying in this merciless war. His trans-formation is vividly illustrated in the scene where he and the Serbian soldier Goran (Sergej Trifunović) get into the house of an old Muslim woman, who sits on the bed, delusional, twirling an apple in her hands, and mumbling something in Bosnian. Next to her, on the floor, Guy finds an executed man and a woman (obviously one of them is the woman's son or daughter), and there is a crying baby hidden in the wardrobe. Realizing that Goran will not let the baby live if discovered, Guy puts a pacifier into its mouth and closes the wardrobe. Goran makes some nasty jokes about the old woman and Guy; Goran adds that he himself likes younger women, pointing at the dead woman on the floor. The Serbian soldier expresses his regret that the woman is already dead, implying that had she been alive, he would have raped her. Next, Goran chops off a finger of the old woman so as to steal her ring. "She's just an old Muslim bitch. Let her bleed to death," says Goran. At this moment Guy starts to doubt whether he has joined the "right" side. He realizes that it is simply wrong to kill children, old women, and all those people whom Goran mercilessly murders for the same reason that Guy used to: because they are Muslims.

Later Guy and Goran drive the pregnant and formerly imprisoned Serbian woman Vera (Nataša Ninković), who has just been freed in exchange for a captured Muslim, back home. The audience finds out that the woman became pregnant in a Bosnian camp, which implies that she was raped by the enemy. The child she bears has clearly been fathered by a Bosnian Muslim. Guy saves Vera from Goran—who punches her stomach multiple times before aiming his rifle between her legs to kill "the Muslim bastard"—and he later protects her from her own family, who cannot put up with the shame and disgrace Vera and her newborn girl personify for them. Guy tries to bring Vera and the baby to a safe zone in Croatia, but Vera is killed by Croatian soldiers. Upon reaching the safe zone, Guy leaves the baby in a Red Cross car. After he throws his weapons into the sea, a woman comes to him with the deserted baby, asking if she is Guy's, and he says that the girl is his. He takes responsibility for the life of this infant child of a Bosnian Muslim father; she is his redemption for all the Bosnian Muslims he has killed and the realization that his mission to take revenge on Muslims is unfair, unjust, and simply wrong.

While *Savior* does not display U.S. intervention in the Balkan War per se since the only American soldier shown in the film is a mercenary, it does reveal a new perspective on the intervention, a viewpoint that was also represented by single soldiers who chose to fight for various purposes, including financial gain. The film thus shows another type of Western and U.S. intervention in the war. It also comments on the fact that chaos and murder reigned in the country and the world did not bother to prevent the carnage and suffering. The viewer does not see any international military troops, even though detention camps existed in former Yugoslavian territory; women were brutally raped; men, women, children, and old people were executed. *Savior* focuses on the deterioration in the Balkan region to implicitly censure the inaction of the world. And whereas the film somewhat fails to provide an overview of U.S. intervention in the Balkan War, it does implicitly comment on American involvement through its representation of Guy. Guy's participation in the war—although very provocative in the beginning—eventually becomes a humanitarian mission, as he helps the civilian and her baby to stay alive. It is very symbolic that the film is called *Savior*, which is an unequivocal reference to Guy, who indeed has *saved* the innocent baby. The portrayal of the American as a savior (which obscures his actions directed against innocent Muslims at the beginning of the film) rehabilitates the main character, turning him into a hero; it also imposes a view of the Western—specifically American—soldier as a savior, claiming that the Balkan region needed a whole army of such saviors to stop the war and the genocide. This portrays the (potential) actions of American soldiers as good, humanitarian efforts.

Switching Roles in Mimi Leder's *The Peacemaker* (1997)

The last film in this analysis of the representation of U.S. intervention in the Balkan War deals with the issue from a different perspective. *The Peacemaker* stands out for two reasons. First, it both promotes and criticizes the idea that a serious conflict can be solved only if the United States interferes. The main plot follows the theft of nine nuclear warheads stolen from a train traveling through Russia. The U.S. government decides to step in to investigate. Its aim is to find the warheads and those who are privy to the theft. In the end, the U.S. succeeds: eight warheads are found, and the explosion of the ninth in New York is prevented.

Second, the film is conspicuous for its Bosnian subplot, which does not directly focus on U.S. intervention in the Balkans but, on the contrary, envisions an intervention in the U.S. undertaken by a vengeful Bosnian. Dusan Gavrich (Marcel Iureş), the Bosnian, possesses the ninth warhead and arrives in the U.S. to take revenge for Western intervention in the Balkan region. In the guise of a Bosnian diplomat, he intends to bomb UN headquarters. In a flashback, the viewer witnesses Gavrich looking for his wife and daughter amid sniper fire in Sarajevo; he finds both of them dead. Gavrich takes his daughter in his arms and starts to scream in English, "Help me! Help me! Help my child!" but nobody responds.

Before coming to the U.S., Gavrich records a video for Americans, explaining why he is planning to commit a terrorist attack:

> You will look at what I have done and say, "Of course, why not? They are all animals. They have slaughtered each other for centuries." But the truth is, I am not the monster. I'm a human man. I'm just like you,

whether you like it or not. For years, we have tried to live together until a war was waged on us. On all of us. A war waged by our own leaders. And who supplied the Serb cluster bombs, the Croatian tanks, the Muslim artillery shells that killed our sons and daughters? It was the governments of the West who drew the boundaries of our countries. Sometimes in ink, sometimes in blood. The blood of our people. And now, you dispatch your peacekeepers to write our destiny again. We can never accept this peace that leaves us with nothing but pain. Pain the peacemakers must be made to feel. Their wives, their children, their houses, and churches. So now you know. Now you must understand. Leave us to find our own destiny. May God have mercy on us all.

Gavrich blames the West for its involvement that, he believes, consisted supplying arms for a peace that it tried to impose, which eventually led to the death of his family as well as many other innocent civilians. The film sees the Western intervention not as a form of humanitarian aid but rather as a humanitarian tragedy. While Gavrich's speech is primarily addressed to the UN and makes no clear reference to the U.S. and its role in the Balkan War, it is significant that the Bosnian has chosen the U.S. as the place to mount his attack. He is taking aim at the status of the U.S. as a superpower, which presupposes the country's inevitable involvement in the resolution of the Balkan War. This involvement—which Gavrich sees as purely negative—makes the U.S. privy to the military operations in the Balkans. Yet the man's mission is to make the UN—but not exactly the United States—experience the same pain and emptiness he went through during the sniper attack in Sarajevo. This is an important turn because, at this point, the film judges the failure of the peace-seeking world body to maintain peace in former Yugoslavian territories, avoiding the problem of U.S. intervention and, ultimately, focusing on the role of the West in general. *The Peacemaker* offers the view that Western involvement exerted a negative influence, which stimulated rather than prevented the war. It reverses course, as it were: Gavrich is now, as the title suggests, the *peacemaker* who will bring the sort of "peace" visited upon the former Yugoslavia by Western governments and organizations—a "peace" that killed thousands of civilians.

Gavrich is shot and wounded by Lt. Col. Thomas Devoe (George Clooney); unable to continue running, he enters the nearest church that he comes across. Lying in pain on the floor, he is found by Devoe and the nuclear expert Dr. Julia Kelly (Nicole Kidman), who try to find out more about the bomb's mechanism so that the explosion can be averted. Gavrich is unwilling to reveal any information, as he does not want people to be saved—just as his daughter and his wife were not rescued. He explains that he wants everything "to be like it was," whereas Devoe remarks, "Sir, it's not our war." "It is now," replies Gavrich, and shoots himself in the head. Devoe's response explicitly reveals that American civilians, who did not carry out war actions in the Balkans, cannot be held responsible for the deaths caused by the war. Despite the largely negative focus on the Western role in the Balkan War, the film's ending, in which the bomb is successfully disarmed, portrays the U.S. in a positive light, as the country that is capable of saving people in such "war situations." The film contends that if the United States had intervened in the Balkan region to stop the war, its mission would have been successful from the very beginning. And whereas *The Peacemaker* criticizes the inaction of the U.S. in the former Yugoslavia, it somewhat rehabilitates the image of the country as a strong military power that does stick to the ideals of humanitarianism, as the main characters save millions of New Yorkers, thus performing a humanitarian mission. And although this mission takes place on American soil, it nonetheless helps construct the image of American humanitarianism in the Balkan War because the danger of an explosion in New York is explicitly revealed as part (or perhaps the result) of the Balkan War.

The Role of the UN in the Balkan War

Although the analysis of the UN's role in the Balkan War is not a primary purpose of this book, I would like to briefly address this issue and investigate the way it is reflected in film, because some of my cinematic examples articulate the problem of Western intervention, which involves not only U.S. forces but also UN peacekeepers.

Humanitarian aid provided during the Balkan War was substantial. For example, during the winter of 1992–93, it helped stave off famine and death by starvation in Sarajevo.[29] Apart from that, U.S. aircraft delivered medicine to Sarajevo.[30] The UN's humanitarian help was the result of the unwillingness of the U.S. to send military forces into the territory. Since the UN financially depends on the U.S. and depends on the Security Council and on member states for peacekeepers,[31] its strategy had to follow that of the United States. While the humanitarian aid provided by the UN was indeed helpful, films about the conflict tend to criticize the UN presence in the Balkans, displaying negative aspects of that involvement: the organization's inability to perform its mission and even its complicity in organized sex trafficking, as represented in Danis Tanović's *No Man's Land* (2001) and Larysa Kondracki's *The Whistleblower* (2010), respectively.

The Corruption of the UN in Danis Tanović's *No Man's Land* (2001)

No Man's Land raises two important issues: the absurdity of the Balkan conflict, and UN corruption. The war's essential absurdity is revealed in the clash of ethnic groups who had lived together for centuries. Tanović intentionally builds the film's plot on the confrontation between two Bosnians and one Serb, which would not be unique if it were not for the conditions the men find themselves in. The soldiers are trapped in a trench in a neutral zone. One is Bosnian, another is Serbian, and there is one more—a Bosnian who is lying on a mine. A tragicomic dialogue between the Bosnian Ciki (Branko Đurić) and the Serbian Nino (Rene Bitorajac) reveals that the soldiers themselves are not sure who started the war, or why. When Ciki asks Nino why the Serbians decided to destroy such a great country as Yugoslavia, Nino explains that it was the fault of Bosnians because they decided to separate, whereas Ciki replies that it was their only choice, since the Serbs had started the war. Shifting the responsibility from one to the other, they argue in vain because each is both right and wrong at the same time (which only underscores the complexity of the Balkan War as an ethnic conflict). To put an end to their wrangling, Ciki aims his rifle at Nino and makes him say that the Serbs started the war. But when Nino grabs the rifle, he addresses the same question to Ciki, who now has to admit that the Bosnians began the war.

When UN troops appear, *No Man's Land* "reaches a new level of absurdity."[32] Two important questions arise during the second half of the film, namely what the UN will do with the "human time bomb" and how international journalists will interpret and report the situation.[33] The film overtly demonstrates the helplessness of the UN and the failure of peacekeeping troops to perform their main task, which is to establish peace. The only man willing to help the Bosnian lying on a mine is a French peacekeeper. Yet he fails to influence the situation because his commander, Colonel Soft (Simon Callow), prefers to play chess with his young secretary instead of taking any measures to address the situation. The only solution the French peacekeeper sees is to cooperate with the journalist, Jane Livingstone (Katrin Cartlidge), who threatens Soft that she will file a report within half an hour and tell the whole world that the UN force is not doing its job. This, of course, prompts Soft to take action.

The ending of the film is dramatic not only because a German sapper is not able to defuse the mine and thus the Bosnian soldier remains lying on it, but also because the journalists and the UN leave the place as if their mission has been accomplished. Colonel Soft even makes the comment that he is satisfied with the work and hints that it may help procure promotions for the UN soldiers who took part in the operation. The journalist, happy to have her scoop, does not even want to check the trench because it does not interest her. As she leaves she is unaware that the Bosnian soldier is still lying on the mine. Interestingly, the journalist's departure seems to be more important to the UN than the fulfillment of their direct responsibilities; the prospect that her unflattering story would be revealed to the world and the UN's reputation would be sullied is more worrying than the plight of a human being left to die alone.

Rape and the War: Larysa Kondracki's *The Whistleblower* (2010)

The Whistleblower occupies its own distinct niche in the cinema of war crimes, as its plot is fully devoted to the problem of criminal offenses committed during the Balkan War. Police officer Kathryn Bolkovac (Rachel Weisz) arrives in Bosnia in search of those who are implicated in sex trafficking. The audience sees Bosnia right after the war. The country has been plunged into chaos. Once she has found Raya (Roxana Condurache), a beaten-up Ukrainian girl who has just finished school, Kathryn becomes aware of the existence of the Florida Bar, where young girls waitress and work as prostitutes. Kathryn realizes that the Bosnian police are involved in the illicit business. She is even more shocked to discover that her colleagues from the UN also have a hand in these activities. The spectator is immersed in the criminal world of postwar Bosnia, where nobody can be trusted and nearly everybody is guilty of some offense.

When the information Kathryn possesses becomes a threat to the UN's very existence, the executive tries to get immunity, explaining that "the UN is too fragile, too important." His words are sarcastically corrected by Madeleine Rees (Vanessa Redgrave), who underlines that he is asking not for "immunity" but for "impunity." Both implicitly and explicitly, the film criticizes the importance of the UN, some of whose representatives rape and sell people instead of protecting them. The same problem is briefly addressed in Isabel Coixet's *The Secret Life of Words* (2005), another film that narrates the tragedy of the Balkan War. Telling about her experience during the war, the heroine, Hanna (Sarah Polley), mentions that once UN troops arrived in the women's camp where she was being held, she and the other women thought that the soldiers would free them. However, the women remained prisoners. More than that, some UN soldiers participated in rape themselves: "I remember that one of them apologized all the time. He would apologize while smiling. If you can imagine that they rape you time and again, and they whisper in your ears, so that only you can hear, 'I'm sorry, I'm so sorry. Forgive me.'"

Although Kathryn manages to get on TV with the story about sex trafficking in Bosnia, she is dismissed. The other UN officers (those privy to the trafficking and those who are not) are sent back to their respective countries, but nobody is put on trial. *The Whistleblower* and the other two films briefly discussed here obviously do not label all UN peacekeepers criminals and rapists. Yet they make an important claim by discussing the corruption within the UN and its operations, thus arguing that the Western intervention in the Balkans had its drawbacks and tragic ramifications. The Balkan War, according to *No Man's Land*, *The Whistleblower*, and *The Secret Life of Words*, was the war where the Bosnian and Croatian peoples could rely only on the help of the international community—but this community apparently included, along with the people who tried to stop the war and help the locals, individuals who preferred to profit from the Balkan tragedy. Those people constituted yet another menace to the unprotected peoples of the former Yugoslavia. Thus, while the films do not fully undermine the humanitarianism of the Western intervention, they demonstrate that those who provided humanitarian aid and were eager to help stop the war and chaos in the country (consider the French peacekeeper from *No Man's Land* or Kathryn from *The Whistleblower*) were joined by those who saw the war as a chance to exploit the situation.

Literature and U.S. Intervention in the Balkan War

There are very few literary works that deal with U.S. intervention in the Balkan War. This lack can be explained by the initial unwillingness of the U.S. to get involved, which created a misconception that the U.S. fought no real war in the Balkans. Additionally—one can presume—the war's rather complex nature has made it difficult for literary authors to create plots that would help explain or at least provide a portrayal of the American role. The U.S. participation in the Balkan War cannot be compared to the country's participation in either the wars analyzed in this work or its earlier major wars, including World War II and the Vietnam War. Its hesitation to intervene in the Balkan region explains why there is little exploration of the role of the U.S. in most of the Balkan War novels. As a rule, these novels tend to narrate the war as, first and foremost, a regional tragedy that consisted of a civil war, ethnic hatred, and genocide. To my knowledge, the only novels that focus specifically on the role of the United States are Douglas Cavanaugh's *Into Hell's Fire* (2007) and Tom Foley's *This Way to Heaven* (2000). This section provides an analysis of these novels and claims that the main truth about the Balkan War that these texts overtly present is the hesitation of the United States to get involved in the conflict and prevent the genocide. Both narratives explicitly deal with the issue of murder, vividly portraying the sufferings of women (most of whom were raped multiple times), children, and elderly people. The novels censure the inaction of the West, arguing, just like the films did, that the Balkan War lasted so long because the West did nothing to stop the conflict at the very beginning.

From Vietnam to the Balkans: Douglas Cavanaugh's *Into Hell's Fire* (2007)

Cavanaugh's novel does not deal with the direct intervention of U.S. troops in the territory of the former Yugoslavia, yet its focus on the events that preceded U.S. involvement and somewhat help explain that involvement allows its classification as a novel about U.S. interventionism. The use of a third-person omniscient narrator only underlines the intention of the novel to elucidate the reasons for the intervention, making the narrative more reliable and unbiased. The events that unfold in *Into Hell's Fire* can be considered a preamble to U.S. involvement: at the book's core is the story of Lucas Martin, a Vietnam War veteran and a retired agent of the U.S. government, who is sent by his former colleagues into the heart of the escalating Balkan War, to Sarajevo, to collect information about atrocities and prove the existence of detention camps. Confirmation of these offenses would allow the West, and in particular the U.S., the justification to immediately intervene and stop the genocide. Lucas is sent to Bosnia as "a freelance photographer for various news agencies," which places this novel in the genre of surveillance or spy fiction.[34] Yet *Into Hell's Fire* can be analyzed as a war novel, and a novel about American interventionism, for two reasons. First, the war veteran status of the main character and his involvement with the government brings his sole intervention close to a regular military intervention that is orchestrated by politicians and decision makers and conducted by soldiers. Second, Lucas's mission can be characterized as representing an initial phase of U.S. intervention in the Balkan War; as in any other war, the U.S. needs a solid basis for military involvement—in this case, crimes against humanity.

Although the novel focuses on the war in the Balkans that eventually led to the collapse of Yugoslavia, it also meditates on the history of the region, going as far back as the rule of the Byzantine and Ottoman empires. It swiftly moves forward to the World War I era, mentioning the murder of Archduke Franz Ferdinand by a Serbian assassin, which led to the First World War. The main story, however, starts during World War II, when the Croatian boy Luka Martinović, having saved an injured American pilot, is guaranteed safety and eventual immigration to the United States for his mother and himself. Later, the boy's name is Americanized as Lucas Martin. As an adult, Lucas returns to the Balkans several times. During one of his visits in the 1980s, he is disappointed not to find evidence of the death of his father, who had disappeared and was then imprisoned during World War II. Lucas then "vowed never to return" (247) but nonetheless comes back in the 1990s.

In this respect, one should examine the relevance of Lucas's nationality to the analysis of his actions, which in themselves constitute an intervention. Lucas is always referred to as an American or a Croatian American, although he is obviously an immigrated Croat. Therefore his arrival in the Balkans can, at first sight, be erroneously considered not as a form of international involvement but as a result of his interest and willingness to help due to his ethnic belonging. Yet his long life in the U.S., his service in Vietnam as an American soldier, and his relationship with the U.S. government obviously allow one to claim that his participation in a U.S. spying operation is not only relevant to U.S. intervention but, in fact, *is* an intervention undertaken by an American in the territory of the former Yugoslavia, aimed at collecting information for the United States that will eventually define the extent of American military help in the Balkans. But no less important is the fact that Lucas is being very well paid by the U.S. government for his work, and were it not for the money, he would probably not involve himself in the war. This, in turn, corroborates the idea that the reader should not consider Lucas's participation to be motivated exclusively by his patriotic Croatian feelings. However, the novel makes it clear that Lucas wants the U.S. government to carefully examine the situation and eventually help resolve the conflict because this war is "a direct crisis within his culture of birth" (33). Lucas may be portrayed as a cold-hearted spy, but his personal national interest in seeing the war stop is not negligible.

The absence of American intervention for a considerable time after the outbreak of the war is as ambiguous in the novel as the actual political situation in the Balkans at the beginning of the 1990s. The novel skillfully reflects the American hesitation to use military force in the region without sufficient proof that external involvement is needed. The facts that should be proved, according to the novel: "ethnic cleansing, mass graves, and the forced relocation of civilians from areas in Slavonia and in northern Bosnia. In addition . . . the existence of concentration camps throughout the whole of Bosnia and Herzegovina" (67). Just as the United States had been reluctant, for various reasons, to send troops to the Balkans, in the novel the accent on Western uncertainty is very strong. Committing unimaginable atrocities, the Serbian government is sure that "Western intervention would be slow to come" (9). The U.S. government understands that due to the significant role of the U.S. in the world arena, the country will inevitably have to mount some response to the war. To fully justify a military intervention, the U.S. government needs to be certain that atrocities are taking place. Thus one of its representatives, Morton Riggs, calls Lucas to ask him to perform this mission: "It seems as though all hell has broken loose in Bosnia and Herzegovina, and the administration is more than a little perplexed about how best to proceed. Public outcry is mounting and the U.N. Security Council is breathing down our necks. The Croatian and Slovenian-American populations are pushing hard for U.S. intervention. Those populations represent millions of voters and the president wants this bag of shit to appear as being under control before the election gets any closer" (19). Describing growing dissatisfaction in its domestic arena, the novel later turns to speculations about the role of the U.S. in the international arena. The dialogue between Lucas and Morton accentuates the complex nature of the conflict and the upcoming intervention, stating that the war emerged "in a country where the United States has few 'special interests'" (21). This statement unambiguously characterizes the interventionist policy of the U.S. as one aimed at the countries that, to various degrees, concern specific national interests of the United States; Bosnia is obviously not one of them. Perhaps that is why the U.S. tried to place the burden of that war on the European Union; at least geographically, the EU seems to bear greater responsibility for helping resolve the conflict. Yet Europe is not willing to act either: "It is unbelievable how they [Europe] turn to us [the U.S.] and piss and moan about how something should be done about a tragedy occurring in their own backyard" (22). The novel, however, seems to blame neither Europe nor the U.S. for their lack of military support, referring instead to the region's complexity and its rather bloody history, which seems to suggest that peace is only a temporary state and that military action is the more natural atmosphere of the Balkans. Still, the narrative intensely focuses on the political situation in the 1990s, when Yugoslavia became a ball that the U.S. and Europe kept batting back to each other, neither being willing to deal with the war, its ramifications, or its ethnic hatreds.

In the novel the U.S. eventually decides to analyze the situation in greater depth to see if there is indeed a humanitarian crisis in Bosnia. Morton says, "What we now need most of all is concrete information about what is really happening on the ground. We are being bombarded with conflicting reports on a daily basis. We are never sure who is fighting whom, which side is committing atrocities, which side deserves the West's full support, and most important, which side we would like to have as the dominating power in the region when the fighting ends" (25). Morton vividly demonstrates that the United States is willing to make its involvement as transparent as possible, which would display the eventual intervention as a necessity, an action that had to be taken in order to save lives. Yet he also discloses the imperialist attitude of the U.S. toward the situation: the country is willing to help, but it needs guarantees that the war's winner will become a U.S. ally. The postwar countries from the former Yugoslavia would scarcely be able to become superpowers, so the quote can be understood as showing the U.S. desire to be sure that the political elite in the Balkans will cause no trouble for the U.S. but will become submissive agents in the world arena.

The novel seems to be very strongly concerned with U.S. policy with regard to interventionism as well as the country's general position in the world as a decision maker. *Into Hell's Fire* takes a very firm stance, censuring the methods the U.S. has always applied when dealing with international crises, chiefly the imposition of its own views while largely neglecting the cultural and national interests of the affected territory:

Instead, Lucas felt, U.S. policy was in line with the current American culture, applying timid, politically correct guidelines in an area of the world where political correctness could doom thousands of innocent people. Lucas had seen it countless times in the past. He had almost learned to expect it. It seemed to him to be ingrained in U.S. diplomatic policy. The refusal to understand that people in other parts of the world think, act, and desire to be different than America had led to countless poor decisions and generated substantial ill will with foreign nations. . . . He was continually amazed at the stance his adopted government endorsed, regardless of the cultures these policies would affect. . . . The political faces were always changing, but the misguided rhetoric remained the same. (33)

On the one hand, the main character believes that the U.S. should use more resolute methods when dealing with the Balkan crisis, claiming that adhering to political correctness and attempting to solve the problem in a democratic way will not work in this case. Lucas seems to blame the United States for being too soft with those countries where force should be applied to guarantee eventual peace. On the other hand, Lucas tends to make equivalent all U.S. interventions and thus compares the Balkan War to all the other wars involving the U.S., which is rather superficial. The Balkan War was undoubtedly one of the strategically most complex wars the United States has ever been involved in due to the nature of the conflict. The novel raises the question "So, exactly who is fighting whom today?" (124), echoing the problem that *Behind Enemy Lines* has already explicitly raised. Ethnic hatred made it impossible to determine who was enemy and who was friend, as works of film and literature, as well as examples drawn from the actual events, reveal. Even Morton exclaims, "In all my years, I've never encountered such a goddamn mess as this" (25). *Into Hell's Fire* seems to suggest that the nature of every war the U.S. has fought is the same, which is largely inaccurate. Yet the long passage quoted above very aptly underlines the cultural differences between the East and the West, which would eventually complicate the decision making and the intervention in the Balkans. All these issues notwithstanding, Lucas concludes, "Military intervention is very likely the only solution if this thing worsens" (69), and as history proved, that "thing" indeed "worsen[ed]."

Into Hell's Fire ponders why UN soldiers were not armed well enough, which eventually caused the loss of any degree of control and order in the Balkans and freed the hands of the criminals. At the same time, the novel creates suspense by implying that as soon as the atrocities are documented, help will be sent right away. Lucas is supposed to provide the impatient Americans with "evidence that could give his superiors a justifiable reason to intervene," yet it is also made clear that, "for the moment, there was none" (180). Despite not intervening, the United States is not considered out of the game. Its opinion remains as important as that of Europe, and the reader is informed about "the pressure the Americans are applying" (217), even without having U.S. military troops on the ground, which hints at the multiple solutions to the peace negotiations that the United States and the European Community were trying, vainly, to impose on the former Yugoslavia. Morton's lament earlier in the novel that "things aren't going the way we want them" (69) underscores the large amount of political work done by the U.S. to stop the war. At the same time, the book unequivocally foregrounds the U.S. desire to have the situation in the Balkan region under control, thus preventing it from undermining the position of the U.S. as a superpower.

Lucas's mission ends well, and he provides enough evidence for the U.S. to act and "allow NATO military intervention in order to stop the fighting in Bosnia" (312). The intervention is carried out too late to save thousands of innocent lives, although, as the novel claims, military involvement was inevitable: "Everyone knows that the West will intervene eventually" (277). Nevertheless one should analyze Lucas's actions in the territory, which I define as a solo intervention. Lucas's status as a spy undermines, to a certain degree, the whole project of pre-intervention simply because it makes such action illegal. Lucas himself thinks over what might happen if he is murdered during his mission: "If I had been killed, what would have been the position of the U.S. government after having been implicated in the conspiracy?" (280). He understands that military intervention will be postponed, which will lead to the continuation of violence and murder in the Balkans. Yet he—and, first and foremost, the U.S. government—takes that risk and professionally accomplishes the mission that, importantly, is meant to be a humanitarian effort. All of Lucas's killings over the course of the novel are justified, and the reader obviously takes Lucas's side; in contrast to the evil, corrupt, and avid Serbs, Lucas is the good guy. During his stay in Bosnia he meets his old Bosnian friend Edis, who eventually joins him on his mission. Lucas himself evaluates their actions: "*Besides*, he thought to himself, *we're the good guys here. Right is on our side*" (284). The illegality of Lucas's presence in the Balkans is obscured and his presence is justified by his mission to disclose the atrocities and to save innocent people from violence and death.

However, the humanitarian mission of the United States moves to the background at the end of the novel, when Lucas is again contacted by Morton. This time Morton offers him work on "an extremely important project with a very lucrative contract" connected to missile defense (313). Enthusiastic about the project, Morton feverishly tries to convince Lucas to accept: "Listen, if what I've learnt is true, once this technology has been mastered, the United States will dominate the world . . . or at least those segments that it doesn't already control" (315). Does the ending hint at the imperialist desire of the United States? Absolutely. Does it undermine the humanitarianism of U.S. intervention in the Balkans? Perhaps not, because, first, it is not connected to the intervention in the Balkans and, second, Lucas ultimately rejects the offer, which allows him to remain a positive character to the book's very end. He refuses out of a belief that the project might lead to an environmental catastrophe; the political reasons are not discussed (although they are slightly touched upon). One can speculate that by ending with this scene, the novel is not refuting the humanitarianism of U.S. intervention in the Balkans. Nonetheless it overtly declares that while the U.S. does accomplish humanitarian missions, the country does not exclude those policies that would support its master plan of being the dominant power.

Tom Foley's *This Way to Heaven* (2000) as an Allegory of Western Inaction

Foley's novel focuses on the story of an American soldier, Robert Jackson, who joins UN peacekeeping troops in the former Yugoslavia. As an eyewitness to unfolding events—the initial stage of the genocide—Jackson realizes that the peacekeeping force is not capable of regulating the conflict. Serbs clearly have more arms than Muslim Bosnians, and the arms embargo eventually leaves the Muslims defenseless before their nationalistic Serb foes. In this respect, the novel questions the actions of the West: "Why does the West blockade us [Bosnians] and prevent us from obtaining guns and tanks and rockets so that we can defend ourselves?" The answer: "There are people in America who think that if we [Americans] arm the Muslims, it'll lead to more killing."[35] The conflict seems to be largely neglected by a world that appears sure that the UN will be able to put an end to it. Jackson, however, realizes that the conflict is just beginning. Slaughter is unavoidable unless the oppressed have at least the same chance to protect themselves as their opponents have to do harm, and this logic compels him to supply arms to Bosnian Muslims. Doing so immediately makes a war criminal out of Jackson, who understands that as soon as he returns to the United States, he will be tried and ultimately imprisoned because there "it's a serious crime to help Bosnia" (67). That is why, to escape this fate, he decides to stay in Bosnia and help his friends in that unjust fight. The plot eventually conveys the story of the adventurous fight of Jackson and his local friends against the Serbs.

As is clear from the plot, *This Way to Heaven* is not primarily a novel about U.S. intervention in the Balkans. In fact it does not focus on any actions of American troops in the territory. Nonetheless *This Way to Heaven* can be considered a novel about interventionism; introducing a character who figuratively represents the United States, the book is a unique literary example that deals with the problem of (non)intervention, indirectly discussing the role of the U.S. in the Balkan War. The use of a third-person omniscient narrator can stand for the author's intention to present the story as unbiased and allow readers to draw their own conclusions concerning U.S. participation in the war.

This Way to Heaven harshly criticizes the inaction of the West while the war (including the genocide) was unfolding at top speed. Notably, the novel makes a reference to the First Gulf War, when the Bosnian Emir says, "How terrible of Hussein to try to take over a peace-loving nation. It was right of the United States to help Kuwait get their country back" (143). The issue of U.S. intervention in the Middle East during the First Gulf War is mentioned on purpose: it serves to compare Bosnia to Kuwait, suggesting that both Muslim countries eventually shared a similar fate, that of being oppressed by their neighboring countries; revealing similarities between the two wars, the line also censures U.S. inaction in the Balkans, questioning the motives behind the interventionist policy of the U.S. It comes as no surprise that during the dialogue between Emir and Jackson, the Bosnian says, "When you get back to America, you tell your people that we have *oil* here" (144; my italics). Emir succinctly underlines the fact that only national interest would prompt the U.S. to help the Bosnians. In other words, the Bosnians have to offer something to the Americans in return for military help. Unlike Kuwait, however, Bosnia had nothing to offer. *That*, according to Emir, was the reason the U.S. was unwilling to send military troops or, at least, to arm the Bosnians.

Earlier in the novel, when Jackson catches a Bosnian man stealing medical supplies from Jackson's convoy, the thief exclaims with bitter anger, "Maybe they taught you other things to say in our language, too? [Jackson has said to the man 'You're under arrest' in Serbo-Croatian.] Did they teach you how to say, 'Yes, we know you're defenseless, but we will give you no guns'? And did they teach you how to say, 'Yes, we know you're starving, but we will give you no food'? Or did they teach you to say, 'We know you're sick, but we can give you no medicine'?" (14). Jackson eventually follows the Bosnian, Alexandar, to meet a large group of Muslim refugees—women and children—who have lost their homes. Their situation is neglected by the UN: "The UN wouldn't protect them. The UN wouldn't restore them to their homes. Now they have no village to live in, no village for your UN trucks and your life-saving supplies to be delivered to" (15). The American obviously hears bitter sarcasm in the words of the Bosnian, who realizes that neither the

West nor the UN is going to help them fight the Serbs' oppression. And although UN troops are deployed to the Balkan region, their presence does not guarantee stability or safety: thousands of people continue to be harassed, beaten, raped, humiliated, and brutally murdered.

The heavy censure of U.S. nonintervention notwithstanding, the novel persistently attempts to rehabilitate the image of the United States from a country that does not want to get involved in the affairs of the former Yugoslavia to one that heroically rescues oppressed people. This transformation is effected through the presence and eventual juxtaposition of the only two American characters in the novel: Robert Jackson and Samuel West.

Jackson, as mentioned, chooses to act while the whole world turns a blind eye to the peoples of the former Yugoslavia. Whereas "nobody in America seemed to understand what was happening in Bosnia" (194), Jackson tries to change the situation. His desire to be useful and perhaps facilitate an end to the war and the people's suffering earns him the title of exceptional American and eventually hero (87). Zarko, frequently called a Gypsy (although eventually the reader finds out that he is a Serb who, ashamed of the actions committed by his nation, prefers to keep his nationality secret), says to Jackson, "I am a false Gypsy, and you are a false *Amerikanac* . . . because *you* are here" (18; italics in original). He continues, "Alexandar once said you were not like other *Amerikanacs*. Most *Amerikanacs*, he said, always do whatever is in their own best interests. But Alexandar says that it is not so with you. He says you're a rare *Amerikanac*" (18; italics in original). Jackson's exceptionalism is later pinpointed by a Bosnian woman named Zinna: "[Alexandar] says you're the only American he's ever met who he couldn't figure out. He says that most Americans—" Jackson interrupts her: "That most Americans always do what's in their own self-interest" (51). Over the course of the novel, one can observe Jackson develop into an overwhelmingly positive character; he is a good American soldier who, at the cost of his own well-being, stays in the Balkans: "I know what's happening here and I want to change it" (33). He loses his good reputation and becomes a criminal; he is deprived of the opportunity to go back to the U.S. and reunite with his family and partner; he sacrifices his own (successful and happy) life to fight in the war for those who are being exterminated. His help is appreciated: "He was just beginning to become one of them— the *Amerikanac* arms merchant who came to help fight the Serbs—and everywhere he went the people of the city waved to him or clapped him on the back and called him friend, or even better, *simpatican*—a man of quality. He was like an adopted brother" (31; italics in original). It is interesting that when criticizing the U.S. for its inaction, the Bosnian Muslim Emir mentions Lafayette and his participation in the American War of Independence. The Frenchman played a significant role in that war; as Lloyd S. Kramer writes, he was "a European nobleman who left family and fortune, suffered hardships at his own expense, and joined the American forces, motivated by love of a virtuous people and a righteous cause."[36] The appearance of Lafayette in the novel serves two purposes. First, it demonstrates that during such an important war, the U.S. received outside help that, eventually, allowed it to win its war against Great Britain and become an independent state. That war parallels the situation in the former Yugoslavia in the way that Bosnia was desperately trying to become an independent state but obviously could not win without external support. Second, Jackson himself parallels Lafayette: just as the Frenchman came to America to fight for its independence, so Jackson has come to Bosnia, at exactly the same cost.

Yet Jackson's role is eventually determined to be something other than that of a soldier. He becomes friends with the Bosnians he meets on his way; he feels he needs to protect them, not because this is his responsibility as a soldier but because he cares about them as a friend. This peculiarity is shrewdly pinpointed in the novel: "*You can't worry about Aleks*, he told himself. *You have responsibilities; you have to think coldly, without emotion, the way they taught you in the army*" (59; italics in original). Although he desperately tries to be a soldier in wartime, Jackson takes his place with Bosnian civilians (particularly those who *could* defend themselves).

Another American, Samuel West, arrives in the Balkans on a special mission, left unrevealed for a long time, apart from being characterized as one that "could end the war" (19). I would argue that West is a personification of the United States. Making this contention, I rely on the character's name and on his actions. Without taking up actual politics and policies, Foley skillfully displays the image of the West in the character of Samuel West. More than that, Zarko's reference to the character as "uncle Sam" (26) allows one to conclude that West embodies the United States. Thus it is symbolic that his mission in the Balkans can put an end to the war. Here the novel refers to the power of the U.S. and implicitly claims that if the U.S. intervenes, the war will soon be over.

Beyond his name, West's attitudes toward the Balkan War strongly parallel the actual attitudes of the U.S. government toward the war. As Jackson and Zarko help West reach his final destination, overcoming multiple obstacles, West makes a telling observation: "West looked toward Dubrovnik, taken aback at the ferocity of the attack. *It was much more than he had expected from what he had mistakenly considered a small conflict amongst equally ill-equipped guerilla factions. 'We're not going anywhere near there,'* he insisted" (27–28; my italics). His stance echoes that taken by the U.S. government to not intervene, and it hints at the erroneous American characterization of the Balkan War as a local conflict that will easily resolve itself on its own over time. Later, observing the murder of a Muslim boy, West thinks, "If he had come close enough, I might have thrown him my gun. . . . Imagine what that little Muslim could do if he were armed?" (137). West's idea suggests how different the situation would have been had the U.S. not supported the embargo but had instead armed the Bosnian Muslims. "Little Muslim" extends to the Bosnian people, whose inability to defend themselves made them look like helpless children, easily intimidated by the Serbs. It is worth mentioning in this regard an incident from later in the novel, when West awakes in a detention camp after being beaten by Serbian guards and says, "My God! I can't see a damn thing!" (255). The character cannot see anything because he was severely beaten and his physical condition is bad. However, taken figuratively, these words suggest that while innocent people are held in special camps where they are systematically beaten up, raped, and killed, no one, including the United States, actually *sees* it.

West is described as a cold-hearted man, a mercenary paid by the Israeli diplomat Katz to come to the Balkans and assassinate the key military and political figures who have unleashed the war. *That*, according to West, would help end the war. He obviously would not have come were he not being paid for his services, as becomes evident from his talk with Jackson, whom he asks, "If you're not doing it for money, why would you agree to help?" (42). An even more representative scene takes place soon after this talk: a shot rings out, then the screams of a woman and a child are heard, but when Jackson rushes to help, West stops him:

> "It's none of our business," West told him.
> "Are you kidding me? I heard a woman and a child."
> "Guerrillas," West said.
> "I'm going out there."
> "What do you think *you* can do about it?" West challenged him.
> (43; italics in original)

The scene overtly demonstrates the difference between the two men, the "good" and "bad" Americans. Whereas Jackson tries to help in every situation, West prefers to stay indifferent to what is going on. One can speculate that West's unconcern stands for the way the U.S. ignored the war. As the dialogue continues, West announces his attitude several times, saying, "What do I care what these savages do to each other?" and "What the hell do I care if these goddamned savages slaughter themselves." Jackson counters, "I can't believe Katz would send *you*! You don't even care about what's happening here!" (44; italics in original). This persistent reference to the act of caring and its obvious absence allows one to conclude that the reaction of the international community to the Balkan War was strikingly peculiar; namely, the pervasive global indifference left the peoples of the former Yugoslavia trapped within the borders of their own collapsing country to experience the brutality of the war and to overcome it as best they could on their own.

The novel reflects the desperate desire of the locals to be saved by the U.S.: "Many nights," says the Bosnian girl Sabina, "I have prayed for America to come and save my people" (277). It also displays the U.S. neglect of the Balkan War; for instance, when Zarko brings an injured Bosnian boy to a local imam, he is surprised to see that the latter is burning a huge pile of teddy bears to warm himself and the other people who are hiding in the mosque. When Zarko asks where the toys are from, the imam answers, "They were a gift from the people of America for the poor children of Bosnia" (387). Zarko hopes that the Americans have also sent antibiotics, yet he finds out that those toys were the only aid given to Bosnia by the U.S.

This Way to Heaven touches upon an even more shocking issue, the UN's awareness of the existence of mass graves: "Spy satellites pinpointed these graves. We've known about them for months, but it wasn't until recently that we could get some men out here to investigate" (391–92). The novel deals with the problem accurately, pointing to the difficulty of identifying and defining the murderers; without evidence, the crimes must go unpunished.

Despite the novel's focus on the steadfast indifference of Samuel West toward the conflict (and, through him, the indifference of the U.S.), *This Way to Heaven* seems to justify international inaction, wisely accepting the view that perhaps the conflict was not so easily stopped, even with the help of external involvement: "But then Jackson realized that what had happened was over now, and West had been right. There was nothing he could do" (45). Although the quote refers specifically to the case of the woman and the child described earlier, it may well characterize the general situation. Was it possible to easily stop this war without any rules, a war predominantly based on national and ethnic hatreds?

It is important to mention that West is a Vietnam War veteran; moreover he took part in the slaughter at My Lai, one of the biggest war crimes committed by the U.S. in that conflict. The author makes the man a war criminal of such a notorious event to intensify his status as a bad character and, consequently, to blacken the reputation of the U.S., given that his character is a personification of the country. One can interpret the significance of West's status in two ways. On the one hand, because of that massacre (and other war crimes) in Vietnam, the U.S. did not want to repeat the same mistake, and perhaps was even afraid of that happening. Therefore its policy of nonintervention should be understood not as the country's cowardice or carelessness but rather as a cautionary strategy not to make the same mistakes. To ensure this could not happen, the peoples of the former Yugoslavia would be left to handle the situation on their own. That explains West's overt indifference or unwillingness to get involved in the Balkan War. On the other hand, by *not* intervening, the U.S. has allowed the war in the Balkans (clearly no less brutal in its atrocities than what happened at My Lai) to continue. In this way, the novel criticizes the noninterventionist policy, implying that by not getting involved, the U.S. has allowed more My Lais to take place, this time in Europe. The novel also compares the wars in Vietnam and the Balkans, accentuating the difficulty that Americans face with regard to the latter. The salient problem is the enemy: While "killing Vietnamese, who to a racist like West, were better dead than alive because they were an inferior race that he [West] considered barely human" was somewhat easy, it was an absolutely different story with Bosnians and Serbs, "who looked European, if not American" (118–19). The "*normal*-looking" and "civilized-looking" (119; italics in original) peoples of the former Yugoslavia were an unusual, perhaps even culturally uncomfortable enemy to fight.

West's military service in Vietnam is crucial to the analysis of *This Way to Heaven* as a novel about U.S. interventionism. The Vietnam War was America's most infamous war experience, transforming its military and interventionist policies. The novel reflects this:

He [West] still got angry when he thought about the shame of being told he could no longer serve his own country, that he could no longer

do what he knew he was born to do. He was put on earth to be a soldier, and he was a damned good one, he thought. Anyone who knew
anything about soldiering would know that. It was the bureaucrats
in Washington, the liberals from those watchdog groups who ended
it for him. Sure, he was at My Lai, and sure, he was alongside the
lieutenant [Lt. William Calley, convicted of the murder of twenty-two
civilians in the massacre] when they went in with their guns blazing
and finished off everyone in the village.

*But hell, we were told they were Viet Cong. The lieutenant was just
following orders, like every good soldier does. He was a good man, and
a damned fine officer. He knew you couldn't fuck around with the Viet
Cong. He did what any good soldier would do, but when they needed
a scapegoat, they pinned it all on the lieutenant. The poor bastard's
life was ruined. He was court-martialed.*

The lieutenant was a patriot, West thought. *He deserved a medal—
and so did I. When they came to me and wanted me to rat him out,
I wouldn't do it. When they offered to let me stay in the army if I
admitted I made a mistake, if I admitted that I followed illegal orders
to massacre everyone in that village, I refused. It was a question of
honor. I am a patriot.*

He sat in the church eating the bread and wine, certain that he
had done the right thing in Vietnam. (159–60; italics in original)

The novel meditates upon the issue of U.S. involvement in Vietnam
through the example of a particular military man, revealing his personal
experience both during the war and in its aftermath, but it also attempts
to interpret the burden of the Vietnam War on the United States. This
is most evident when considering West to be the personification of
the U.S. His experience stands for the experience of the United States
in Southeast Asia. Just as West, not suspecting anything bad, became
a war criminal while following orders (which were derived from the
principle that the U.S. was freeing Vietnam from communist oppressors), so did the United States endure a terrible transformation: no

longer the potential savior, it became the enemy. The novel by no means tries to justify the criminal actions of U.S. soldiers in Vietnam; rather it attempts to tackle the problems raised by Vietnam from a different perspective, and instead of blaming the U.S. for getting involved in the war, it interprets its experience as the one that, first and foremost, made the American people feel ashamed of their country's actions, which eventually led to its cautious attitude toward war and military intervention in general. Having said that, the novel uses the Vietnam War experience as an excuse for delayed intervention in the Balkans, implicitly claiming that the U.S. was not willing to repeat a failure it had made once before.

Building his novel on the contrast between Jackson and West, Foley deals with the hesitation of the United States to get involved in the Balkan War. On the one hand, the country had to get involved—just as Jackson did. On the other hand, history had obviously taught the U.S. to be cautious in such serious matters as war and intervention. Presenting these two perspectives on the issue, the novel does not seem to be taking either side. It does not fully support West, presenting him as a rather negative character, yet it does not fully support Jackson either (although the reader most probably identifies with Jackson, since he is presented as a more positive character). At one point, West thinks of Jackson this way: "[West] knew plenty of men like Jackson. They would back any cause and could even sound sincere, as if they truly cared. But they were such hypocrites. When things got tough, when it was time to fight, to pay with blood and the lives of young men, they were gone. America was filled with men like Jackson. *I am a man of honor,* Samuel West thought. He placed himself well above Jackson and his phony ideals" (196; italics in original). Whereas one might claim that this quote underscores West's selfish nature, I would argue that the passage also adequately describes Jackson. Specifically, despite Jackson's help and his devotion to the Bosnian people, it is striking that he is the only character in the novel who cannot kill anyone (even though he is the only real soldier, excluding West). On the other hand, the fact that he does not kill can stand in this case not for U.S. inaction but for the idealism of that intervention, especially when compared to the intervention in Vietnam (epitomized by the infamous slaughter in My Lai). This only illustrates the fact mentioned earlier, that the actual U.S. involvement in the Balkans "was quickly successful and with no loss of American life."[37]

It is crucial that West eventually dies in the novel, whereas Jackson stays alive: symbolically the reputation of the United States is restored. The country's past experiences thus remain in the past, while the present opens up a new trajectory. By keeping Jackson alive, the novel reveals a positive perspective on the future of the United States. It is also significant that the character's name coincides with that of a celebrated U.S. Supreme Court justice who was also the chief U.S. prosecutor at the Nuremberg Trials. This coincidence is noticed in the novel by a UN officer. Thus Jackson's role in *This Way to Heaven* is symbolically determined as one that brings justice to the Balkans by finding the criminals and punishing them. Introducing the man who played a crucial role in the aftermath of World War II, the novel makes an implicit comparison between the Balkan War and that larger, historical conflict. *This Way to Heaven* not only refers to the Bosnian genocide, comparing it with the actions committed by the Nazis (the UN officer's words, "I guess we all need a history refresher course now and again, don't we?" [398], as he explains to Jackson who the prosecutor Robert Jackson was, are perhaps the most evident hint of that), but it also underlines that U.S. intervention in the Balkans would be as important, at least in moral terms, as the country's intervention in World War II.

Given this positive depiction of U.S. intervention, the murder of West does not seem problematic. As Jackson tries to escape the camp with Sabina, he understands he will not be able to take West with him because the man is too weak. He wants to suffocate West with a pillow, but cannot; instead Sabina commits the murder. One can speculate that while the U.S. has not forgotten its past failures (metaphorically expressed through Jackson's inability to kill West), the country's image is restored in the minds of those who do not think of U.S. interventionism only in terms of its debacle in Vietnam. (Sabina kills West and thus, symbolically, erases the disgrace of Vietnam.)

The positive image of Jackson is also supported by his multiple acts of communication with and prayers to God. As he observes the war in the Balkans firsthand, he seems to turn away from God, blaming Him for allowing the suffering of the innocent and for not stopping the injustice and endless killing. However, when the war is over and Jackson must remain in the Balkans (as he is considered a criminal in the U.S.), he turns back to God. He comes to a special place where people claim to see the Virgin Mary and prays for the well-being of his friends and, most important, his partner. Her name, Maria, is also significant, as the relationship with her figuratively brings Jackson closer to God, especially considering the novel's last scene, when Jackson, waiting for the appearance of the Virgin Mary, sees his Maria coming to him; she gave up her life in the U.S. to come to the Balkans to be with him. Finally, Jackson's role as a soldier and missionary seems very obscure throughout the novel, especially because of his multiple rejections of faith; still, the frequent references to God along with the final description of Jackson rather overtly position Jackson in the role of a pilgrim, a missionary of God, who came to the Balkans to fulfill a significant task—a role that is obviously derived from the ideology of American exceptionalism: "[The religious pilgrims] always assumed he was like them—a true believer who had made the long pilgrimage to pray at the spot where Virgin Mary had appeared" (418).

The final important issue to address in the analysis of the novel is its depiction of Muslims. As Serbs terrorize the Muslim population, a Bosnian Muslim joins a group of Muslims who have come from the Middle East—from Iran, Libya, and Syria—to "carry on the jihad in Bosnia" (363). While Bosnian Muslims are considered Europeans and their religion is not treated as a threat, the emergence of these men from the Middle East provokes the opposite reaction. Jackson, for example, asks them, "You're real Muslims?" (363), which suggests that "real"

Muslims are only those who come from the Middle East. In the novel they are obviously considered to be more dangerous than European Muslims. Jackson calls the Muslims who came to support the Bosnians "mujahideen" (364), which in fact they are, and their brutality is vividly illustrated when they kill a baby elephant being transported to Italy. These men openly call themselves "America's enemy," and they justify their mission by saying, "The Bosnian people have turned to us because the Western world to which they were seduced for decades has turned its back on them. But we come. We will liberate Bosnia, or we will die trying" (363–64). In the end, the Bosnian who joined the mujahideen turns out not to be a religious fanatic, and thus his example illustrates Jackson's belief that European Muslims differ from those who live in the Middle East.

The American decision not to send military troops to Bosnia is explained by the country's unwillingness to help Muslims. "How can the president send American boys to die for Muslims in a place called Bosnia, a place they never knew existed?" asks Jackson, to which a Bosnian responds, "It's hard for Americans to look at Muslims as the good guys, because they don't understand the situation here. But when the people of America and Europe find out the true story, they'll demand that we do something" (401). Although the novel was published in 2000, and so one cannot connect the U.S. attitude toward Muslims it portrays to 9/11 and argue that the novel belongs to the era of the War on Terror (although it does read like such a novel), it is still possible to claim that *This Way to Heaven* vividly illustrates the situation in the Middle East, specifically the aggressive attitude of particular groups toward Western countries, especially toward the U.S., that eventually led to 9/11. This issue will be examined in greater detail in the next chapter.

4

The War on Terror, Part I

THE AFGHANISTAN WAR

Introducing the New War

The terrorist attacks of September 11, 2001, as well as their dreadful consequences—which Stephen Prince calls "the biggest structural failure of buildings in the nation's history" and "the largest loss of life in an attack by a foreign power" on American soil—changed "the world, America, and the Bush presidency" and initiated a new, global war.[1] Discussing the new type of war characteristic of the twenty-first century, Matt Carr pinpoints the issue of "military futurism," explaining that traditional, regional war has been replaced by war fought in a "global 'battlespace.'" The change in war's military interface has taken place because of the new type of enemy confronting the U.S. and, for that matter, the whole world. So who *is* the "global" enemy in the twenty-first century? Carr identifies these opponents as those who resort to "'asymmetric' warfare, terrorism and insurgency."[2] Robert W. Merry describes the situation that has unfolded as follows: "The enemy is Islam, particularly its Middle Eastern core."[3] Geographically, the main task of the United States is to be fulfilled on Middle Eastern territory. Yet Merry's speculation reveals how superficial are the views of some on the war because the aim of the War on Terror was not to fight Islam or

Muslims but to punish those responsible for 9/11 as well as to prevent further terrorist attacks. The goal was to eradicate Osama bin Laden and fight against his global terrorist organization al Qaeda, as well as their strong supporters in Afghanistan, the Taliban. The first stage of the War on Terror was the U.S. intervention in Afghanistan that began on October 7, 2001, and is known as Operation Enduring Freedom; the second stage was the U.S. invasion of Iraq on March 20, 2003, known as Operation Iraqi Freedom.

The main problem facing the two interventions was that the enemy was without a face or single nationality. The strategically and tactically complicated task was undertaken out of a desire to avenge the murders of innocent Americans and out of zeal to prove that nothing could shake the United States as the world's sole superpower. Additionally both Gambone and Prince stress the emergence of new threats in the form of biological, chemical, and nuclear weapons that could be used against the West and the United States in particular.[4] Thus another reason for the U.S. to start the War on Terror was to prevent possible future attacks from the outside.

The War on Terror is usually portrayed as a chain of small wars, each of which involves a particular task or operation. One can arrive at this conclusion from an analysis of the tactics used by U.S. soldiers during the wars in Afghanistan and Iraq, as well as the very sharp and narrow focus of their operations, as depicted in film and literature. One such example that illustrates the War on Terror (not specifically the intervention in Afghanistan or Iraq) as a complicated intellectual and military operation consisting of multiple wars is Kathryn Bigelow's *Zero Dark Thirty* (2012), a film that for more than two and a half hours focuses on the U.S. Army Special Forces' operation aimed at catching and killing Osama bin Laden. The time period of the events in the film is identified from the beginning, as the audience first reads the inscription "September 11, 2001" that appears on the opening black screen, soon to be accompanied by the voices of people who became part of that horrifying tragedy. Bigelow also informs the viewer that "the following motion picture is based on firsthand accounts of actual events," revealing that she is working in a mode related to documentary. The film then moves to events that took place two years after the terrorist attacks. Embittered by the tragedy the United States had to live through, the CIA intelligence analyst Maya (Jessica Chastain) gives up ten years of her life to find the terrorist responsible for 9/11. *Zero Dark Thirty* accentuates the main stages of the operation, revealing its large scale: starting from the time spent on the search for the terrorist and concluding with actions taken specifically for this operation, like designing top-secret helicopters—indispensable for entry into bin Laden's compound—and destroying them in the end. The raid was conducted by U.S. Army Special Forces on May 2, 2011. The novelty of the intervention can be distinctly observed toward the end of the film, in the scene showing the raid. The helicopters, almost indistinguishable from the landscape, are practically noiseless; the soldiers have special equipment, and quite frequently the spectator is forced to view the scene through a green filter, that is, through the eyes of the soldiers who are wearing night-vision goggles. As the helicopter lands and the soldiers jump out, the audience hardly hears them; because their rifles are equipped with silencers, the shooting sounds like simple clicking. For more than twenty minutes the viewer witnesses a meticulously designed operation, where every step is planned, every movement is predicted, and every action is justified. The soldiers do not incur losses, they do not shoot into nowhere, nor do they randomly throw bombs. They do not kill the women and children they find in the house. The operation that was designed to catch and kill bin Laden is a carefully planned mission, revealing the preparedness of the U.S. to fight this important war—at least against the person responsible for 9/11.

The end of the operation is also the logical ending of the film. Maya's mission is now completed—bin Laden has been killed. The final scene shows Maya on a plane, tears running down her face. The scene is reminiscent of the film's opening, filled with screams, despair, and fear, framing the film. Crying Maya symbolically stands for the mourning people of the United States, the nation that will never forget September 11, 2001, the nation that will never be as it was before the attacks. One might also argue that Maya cathartically weeps because she realizes that the goal of assassinating bin Laden, to which she has devoted a decade of her life, was achieved only with horrific human rights abuses. Yet the film, despite its tragic implication, shows a triumphant United States: although it took quite a long time, the U.S. accomplished its mission of killing the number-one terrorist and thus proved its legitimacy as a global, though not an invulnerable, power.

Besides killing bin Laden, the U.S. set other important goals, most importantly to free the world from terrorism—a purely humanitarian aim, it would seem. This country mounted two military interventions, in Afghanistan and Iraq. It is therefore important to examine how these two interventions are represented culturally and to what extent these "fictional" representations are docu-fictions of war that visualize and narrate the culture and history of the War on Terror to their viewers and readers.

The History of the War

The U.S. government's reaction to the terrorist attacks of September 11, 2001, which killed nearly three thousand people, was shock and anger: shock because of the realization that national security measures did not prevent the attacks, and anger mainly due to the national loss and the physical and mental trauma caused by the attacks, which at the same time spread fear among the American people. The Bush administration's decision to wage war in Afghanistan was an immediate response to such a cruel offense. Importantly, U.S. actions taken after 9/11 were not the first time the country had responded militarily to terrorist attacks. Barak Mendelsohn cites the examples of U.S. bombings in Libya (1986), Iraq (1993), and Afghanistan and Sudan (1998) as military reactions to earlier terrorist actions. However, he underscores that unlike those bombings, the U.S. military response to terrorism after 9/11 was considered fully legitimate because at that time states were already legally allowed by the UN Security Council to protect themselves from specific terrorist attacks. And whereas before 9/11 retaliatory bombings were questioned by the public worldwide, often provoking censure and criticism, after 9/11 actions taken against terrorists were mainly approved. The support that almost eighty countries provided to the United States in the fight against terrorism proves this.[5]

Yet the Afghanistan War became one of the most complicated and controversial military experiences in American history. From a political perspective, the war's chief problem was the U.S.'s wrong course in relation to Afghanistan prior to 9/11. Bert writes about the financial support that the United States (together with Pakistan) provided the mujahideen during the Soviet-Afghan War in 1979–89, ignoring the Geneva Convention.[6] U.S. Defense Secretary Robert Gates has revealed his own participation in helping the mujahideen defeat the Soviets and the government of Afghanistan: "I was pumping arms across the border to some of the same guys" the U.S. ended up fighting. He admitted that the U.S. made a big mistake by "turning [their] backs on Afghanistan" after the Soviet-Afghan War was over. Gates concludes that 9/11 was the "price" the U.S. had to pay for these mistakes.[7] Wendy Kozol reports that the U.S. supported the Taliban government up to 2001.[8] The U.S. government was obviously unaware of al Qaeda's plans concerning the U.S. The terrorists were certain they would be able to destroy the U.S. because of the Taliban's success against the Soviet Union—the other superpower—in the 1980s.[9]

After 9/11 it did not take the United States much time to determine that al Qaeda was responsible for the attacks.[10] Yet al Qaeda was not an easy enemy to fight or even catch. The U.S. managed to identify only some of its leaders, including bin Laden, who was held responsible for 9/11. The U.S. also found out that the Taliban—the ruling group in Afghanistan—were strong supporters of al Qaeda. Therefore Afghanistan "became an obvious, nearly unquestioned target for U.S. wrath."[11] Although President Bush thought that Iraq too hosted terrorists and was involved in organizing the 9/11 attacks, he lacked evidence of this in 2001 and could not order an invasion of the country based just on these assumptions. Afghanistan became the number-one target in the immediate aftermath of 9/11. Scholars suggest that the United States did not realize that when fighting terrorism, it was wrong to "revert to thinking in terms of states."[12] Yet it is hard to blame the U.S. for thinking that the war against terrorists was like any other war the country had fought; the global war against terrorists was being fought for the first time and nobody could predict that regular means would not suffice to conquer the enemy. Another problem, of course, was that there was no *specific* enemy. The enemy remained unclear both to the U.S. government and to U.S. soldiers.

"The absence of meaningful military targets in Afghanistan" made U.S. intervention a long and confusing action. Bert says it is more important to ask what he calls a "basic" but what I would argue is a crucial question: "[Is al Qaeda] driven only by religious motivation or, as one might surmise, by both religious and political objectives?"[13] In this respect, Viotti writes that "the presence at the time of American military bases in Saudi Arabia—home to sacred shrines in Mecca and Medina—or elsewhere in the Arab Gulf," triggered hostility toward the U.S. in the Middle East, which reveals the tight connection between the religious and political motives of the terrorists.[14] These reasons, needless to say, cannot justify the actions of terrorists who killed thousands of innocent people.

Starting the War on Terror with the invasion of Afghanistan, Bush aimed at "hurt[ing] the terrorists, not just mak[ing] Americans feel better,"[15] which, in my opinion, aptly illustrates that the U.S. was not driven by the intoxicating feeling of revenge that would eventually lead to the realization that the enemy suffered too; rather the U.S. government aimed at ridding the world of terrorism, or at least weakening it as a global menace. This goal, in turn, reveals the humanitarianism of the Afghanistan mission and allows one to argue that the intervention conducted by the U.S. government as part of the War on Terror can be called humanitarian.

Invading a country and imposing the type of order that the invader considers the only right one does not make an intervention humanitarian. This question has frequently been raised in relation to the U.S. participation in the First Gulf War. In the case of Afghanistan, however, this problem did not emerge for one simple reason: the U.S. did not plan to impose any particular regime. Bert writes that Secretary of State Colin Powell explicitly stated that the U.S. did not have the aim of suppressing and conquering Afghanistan: "Powell said propaganda and diplomatic pressure on the Taliban should be the focus. The goal at the outset should not be to change the regime, but *to get the regime do the right thing*."[16] Although most Americans did not support the military intervention, they did support the idea of "spreading democratic or liberal values" among the people who were oppressed by the terrorist regime.[17]

Having started the intervention in Afghanistan with air strikes and a ground invasion a month after 9/11, on October 7, the U.S. government obviously could not predict that the conflict would turn into one of the country's longest and most controversial wars. The enemy could not be easily identified; it was constantly escaping, which, once again, underlines the fact that terrorism was supported by several countries, including Pakistan—for whom Afghanistan, specifically the Taliban, secured "its stability" as well as provided help in "defense against India."[18] Between 2001 and 2016, 2,371 American soldiers and 31,419 Afghan civilians died in the Afghanistan War.[19] The intervention also caused chaos and fear among the civilians. While they were under the rule of the Taliban "there was a system: there was law and order. . . . One knew the rules, for they were explicit. And if one followed them, harsh and intransigent as they were, one could be relatively sure to be left in peace." But after the Taliban was defeated "there was no law."[20] This does not mean that U.S. intervention aimed at defeating the Taliban was a mistake; in fact the U.S. soon freed civilians from their oppressors. The problem was that it was only temporary; in a country that wallowed in war, "oppression was arbitrary and it struck without reason."[21]

Of course, there has also been much criticism of U.S. actions in the Middle East, specifically in Afghanistan. David L. Altheide contends that 9/11 was exploited by politicians who "pursue[d] the politics of fear" in order to "achieve certain goals." Barack Obama, for example, raised the image of Hitler in relation to terrorists, thus justifying U.S. wars in the Middle East by comparing them to the task the U.S. had to fulfill while fighting evil and freeing the oppressed from the Nazis during World War II. Another important issue that emerged was the way terrorism was presented to the public: "Terrorism has joined crime as a master narrative of fear that justifies all kinds of social actions, policies, and even wars."[22] Kozol calls "a policy of preemptive strikes through a civilizational model in which the Unites States and its European allies would rescue victims from primitive and repressive regimes" a "neo-colonial policy."[23] This significant point prompts me to return to the issue of U.S. hegemony and address a pivotal question: Can one argue that the War on Terror has become a symbolic battlefield, where one of the tasks of the U.S. is to demonstrate that even after such severe attacks it has still remained the world leader? Viotti makes the shrewd observation that "what intervention advocates tend to see as decisive leadership is viewed by its opponents as hegemony (or a new imperialism)."[24] In relation to the U.S. wars in Afghanistan and later in Iraq, this claim can be interpreted as supporting the firm will of the U.S. to demonstrate that it can protect itself and punish the offender, which turns U.S. military operations in the Middle East into a demonstration of leadership and power. At the same time, the continued presence (as of 2018) of American troops in Afghanistan, which for a long time has been a subject for discussion and criticism worldwide, makes it possible to characterize U.S. behavior as hegemonic. Yet Jane Burbank and Frederick Cooper warn that America's "repertoire of power, based on selective use of imperial strategies," along with "the use of force and occupation—in violation of norms of sovereignty," do not mean that the recent U.S. wars in Afghanistan and Iraq make their actions analogous to the case of Puerto Rico.[25] Even if one believes that U.S. imperialism continues to exist, it is important to understand that it has undergone tremendous changes and cannot be compared to the sort of imperialism that characterized U.S. policy in the late nineteenth century.

Some scholars believe that U.S. imperialism is a constituent part of the War on Terror and that "humanitarianism simply functions as [its] alibi."[26] Kozol, for example, claims that in the case of Afghanistan, Bush justified military intervention by asserting that the goal was "the humanitarian rescue" of civilians. Such an understanding of humanitarianism, according to Kozol, is very controversial, yet the response to "state violence" can "lend credibility to the ideals of humanitarian intervention."[27] The problem of the imperialism-humanitarianism nexus is best described by Anne Orford: "While much of the human rights movement has been properly appalled by the abuses carried out by US military and security forces in the war on terror, advocates of humanitarian intervention do not ask whether increased intervention by the US military under its current rules of engagement [2009] offers the best strategy for the protection of individuals in Third World states."[28] Yet it is important to remember that the war in Afghanistan was initially started by the United States because of the direct offense and threat that terrorism posed to the country. Going to war against the unknown enemy and losing its soldiers in action, the United States not only demonstrated determination in defending its own principles and avenging the deaths of American citizens, but in its efforts to prevent the spread of the terrorist menace throughout the world the country also showed its readiness to protect all the other people who might become future victims of terrorism. This cause makes the intervention in Afghanistan, at least at its initial stage, a humanitarian operation. The deaths of civilians that cannot be justified and remain the moral burden of the U.S. are, as history has cynically proved, an inevitable part of every war. Those deaths undoubtedly allow one to question the humanitarianism of the U.S. war in Afghanistan. Yet considering the eradication of terrorism to be the main purpose of U.S. involvement in Afghanistan, the intervention was probably the country's most humanitarian military effort since World War II.

The controversy surrounding U.S. involvement in Afghanistan has also been widely discussed in film and literature. Works in both media have examined the intervention from different perspectives, revealing its multifaceted nature and usually both supporting and criticizing it, mirroring the problematic history of the war. Mostly created in the genres of action and drama—as with the narratives on the Iraq War—these texts are docu-fictional narratives, successfully creating a rather realistic image of the war that contained a lot of action in the beginning but turned into a human drama in the end. While some of the texts (especially those created recently, when the general view of the war has been clearly formulated) tend to be critical of the intervention, they still do not give up on the issue of humanitarianism, eventually presenting it as a necessity and as an imposition by the U.S. military.

Film and U.S. Intervention in the Afghanistan War

Inception: Mike Nichols's *Charlie Wilson's War* (2007) and Peter MacDonald's *Rambo III* (1988)

Along with attempts to interpret recent U.S. involvement in Afghanistan, films dealing with the conflict have also tried to explain why the war came about, going back in history and analyzing the relatively long relationship between the U.S. and Afghanistan. The best-known cinematic example in this regard is Mike Nichols's spectacular but very controversial *Charlie Wilson's War* (2007), the film that, focusing on the Soviet-Afghan War of 1979–89 and the role of the U.S. in it, skillfully prophesies the U.S. war against Afghan terrorists in the twenty-first century. The film narrates the story of a roguish congressman from Texas, Charles Wilson (Tom Hanks), whose inclination for alcohol and young women almost ruins his career that is revitalized when he organizes a large financial operation aimed at supporting Afghan mujahideen fighters during the Soviet invasion of Afghanistan.

Wilson's interest in the Afghanistan War is inflamed by his friend Joanne Herring (Julia Roberts), who believes that the Soviet invasion of Afghanistan might lead to "the greatest national security threat [the United States has] faced since the Cuban Missile Crisis." Herring incites Wilson to provide help to the Afghan people against the Soviet attacks. She also convinces him to go to Pakistan to meet the president who, according to Herring, will "convince [Wilson] that it's a Christian imperative to let the Afghans rid their country of Communism." During the meeting Wilson learns that the situation at the border is disastrous, as Afghan refugees are running either to Iran or to Pakistan or remain homeless in Afghanistan, which reinforces the humanitarian tragedy of the unfolding events. More than that, thousands of the Afghan people have died. The president of Pakistan persuades Wilson to visit the refugee camps in Peshawar. That visit becomes crucial to Wilson's understanding of the war. The congressman observes people living in tents, fighting for a sack of rice; he listens to the stories told by Afghan men, describing the cruelty of Soviet soldiers; he visits children— victims of mines hidden in toys—whose limbs have been blown off. Devastated, Wilson gazes around, unable to believe the horror endured by the refugees. With his back to the camera (so the viewer is forced to see through his eyes), the camp stretches to the horizon. Having witnessed the hunger, despair, fear, and death in those camps, Wilson decides to act immediately to help the suffering civilians. He intends to make the U.S. government finance Afghan mujahideen fighters, convinced that only with strong American support will these fighters be able to defeat the Soviet forces and eventually stop the war in Afghanistan.

Wilson manages to increase financing for the fighters from five million to one billion dollars, and so Afghanistan becomes "the first country in history to defeat the mighty Soviet Union." When the war is over, Wilson tries to draw the attention of the U.S. government to the current problems in Afghanistan, the ruin and devastation that has afflicted the country, and asks for money for the building of roads, schools, and more, to develop the country's infrastructure. His solicitation is refused because the other politicians are sure that it was sufficient to kill those who had brought Afghanistan into a state of war—now the country has to solve its problems on its own. "This is what we always do," says

Wilson indignantly. "We always go in with our ideals and we change the world and then we leave. We always leave. But that ball, though, it keeps on bouncing." His words are pivotal, as they provide an interpretation of the role played by the United States in various interventions over the course of its history. It is hard to say for sure which wars Wilson is referring to here when he claims that the U.S. "always" intervenes to promote its interests. The Vietnam War, the Korean War, and World War II are likely the key events that the politician has in mind because they were the freshest conflicts in the memories of people of that era. Nonetheless the major war that most influences Wilson's understanding of the American way of fighting is the Vietnam War—a catastrophic involvement that remains one of America's biggest military failures. Proclaiming that the United States intrudes when it thinks it is time to and then leaves the country in ruin and devastation, assuming that help was needed only during wartime, Wilson raises a serious humanitarian issue: How does the U.S. decide when it is time to start and stop its involvement in armed conflicts abroad? If one considers the 1980s war in Afghanistan (and particularly American financial help) to have been a humanitarian intervention aimed at supporting, first and foremost, the civilian population of the country, does this mean that humanitarianism should have stopped when the war was over, thus leaving people in a destroyed country with no decent living conditions, chaos in the government, and no idea of how and by what means to restore their homeland? The politicians fail to understand Wilson's metaphor, and one of them bursts out, "Yeah, we're a little busy right now reorganizing Eastern Europe, don't you think?" The scene mocks the U.S. ability to interfere in global affairs, trying to "reorganize" this or that country or region in a way that the American government finds appropriate (whether for the United States or for the country it intervenes in). Wilson continues to insist that the U.S. spend one million dollars to build a school, but his colleague interrupts him: "Charlie, nobody gives a shit about a school in Pakistan." "Afghanistan," Wilson replies, realizing the incompetence and, what is even more important, the indifference of some U.S. politicians toward the actual problems of the Middle East. It is striking that the politicians who decided to support Afghanistan are not even aware of the country's name; some of them may not even be aware of its geographic location, which makes Afghanistan an indistinguishable territory in the Middle East. One interpretation of this lack of awareness or indifference is that, according to the film, the U.S. has decided to support the country simply because it would be good for its image as a financially and socially stable Western country that does care about the world and is eager to help solve the emerging problems that are destabilizing other nations.

The film's message is, however, very direct: as soon as the war was over, American politicians lost interest in the country they were purportedly so eager to help; as soon as a positive image of the U.S. as savior was created, the government was not interested in spending funds to continue helping Afghanistan. This obviously leads to the conclusion that the help that might seem disinterested was in reality provided to support the desire of the U.S. to position and display itself as the country that unselfishly tries to bring the world to order, thus gaining or maintaining the status of the world's leading country. Yet another important item should not be overlooked: because the film was released during the second involvement of the United States in Afghanistan, the viewer is compelled to compare the two wars. Dealing with the war that took place in 1979–89 today, in the twenty-first century, when the country has to fight a much more costly war (in lives and treasure) in Afghanistan, the film suggests that the current war is the result of the wrong policies adopted during the earlier war and also mutely supports the current U.S. intervention in Afghanistan, claiming that this time the U.S. has to finish its business instead of simply abandoning the country, as it did earlier.

The film concludes with Congressman Wilson receiving a government award. When the scene is over, words appear on the black screen: "These things happened. They were glorious and they changed the world . . . and then we fucked up the end game." These are the words of the real

Charlie Wilson, referring to the U.S. contribution to the destabilization of Afghanistan as well as to 9/11, the result of that destabilization. However, if one considers this to be a post-9/11 motion picture, one sees that it also serves as a critique of past American foreign policy, censuring those who participated in the financing of Afghan mujahideen fighters (known as Operation Cyclone). Indeed the supplying of arms as well as the military training of Afghan mujahideen promoted the emergence of al Qaeda,[29] which means that in the 1980s the U.S. government, of course unaware of the tragic future, sustained those who two decades later would organize the devastating terrorist attacks on the territory of the United States. That fatal mistake is implicitly discussed in the scene when, during the celebration of U.S. victory over the Soviet Union, Gust Avrakotos (Philip Seymour Hoffman) talks to Wilson on a balcony in private and, telling him a fable, warns Charlie that their celebration now is not necessarily the final victory but there is still a lot of work to be done. Gust predicts the refusal of the U.S. government to help stabilize postwar Afghanistan. The concluding lines of the dialogue are even more important and can be interpreted as a prophecy. Charlie's remark about "a hell of a job" done by the politicians receives a very apt comment from Gust: "We'll see." Obviously a film released in 2007 can criticize the role of the U.S. government in a conflict that took place from 1979 to 1989, and indeed it does, making a careful but explicit reference to September 11 and the War on Terror that followed.

It is, however, important to understand that *Charlie Wilson's War* is a very specific example, as it analyzes the events from the past from a current perspective that has inevitably been influenced by the 9/11 terrorist attacks. This reconsideration of the past obviously is not present in films on the Soviet-Afghan War that were released prior to 9/11, including Peter MacDonald's *Rambo III* (1988). The third installment in the *Rambo* series continues the story of the legendary John Rambo (Sylvester Stallone), who, some time after his service in Vietnam, now finds himself in the deserts and mountains of Afghanistan. He is there to save his friend Colonel Trautman (Richard Crenna). Juxtaposing

Charlie Wilson's War and *Rambo III*, one inevitably notices crucial differences in the films' main accents and messages. Apparently the Cold War, not yet ended when *Rambo III* was released, influenced the film's plot and preferences: Rambo's fight against Soviet soldiers provides the main action of the film. Despite the same narrative background, the war in Afghanistan, this is not the case in *Charlie Wilson's War*. The more recent film focuses on the political disagreements between the United States and the Soviet Union; the audience, however, does not see a direct fight. The action of *Rambo III* is, on the contrary, chiefly built upon the representation of the unconquerable American hero, a "fighting machine," and his personal war against the Soviet Army. In an early scene Robert Griggs (Kurtwood Smith), a field officer at the U.S. embassy in Thailand, reveals to the main character that in Afghanistan "over two million civilians . . . have been systematically slaughtered by invading Russian armies. Every new weapon, including chemical warfare, has been used to eliminate these people. And they've been very successful on many levels." This shocking information does not provoke Rambo to go and fight. He ends up in Afghanistan only when Trautman is captured by the Soviets. Rambo's mission is to save his old military friend, not to save the people of Afghanistan.

The film underscores political problems that existed at the end of the 1980s in relation to the U.S.: its ongoing confrontation with the USSR, as well as the devastating influence of the Vietnam War that at the time was still a very fresh memory. (Indeed the film makes several references to Rambo's experience in Vietnam.) *Rambo III*, unlike *Charlie Wilson's War*, neither analyzes the role of the U.S. in the Soviet-Afghan War nor speculates on the war's future ramifications. It would be illogical to expect that a film released in 1988 would refer to the possibility of a terrorist attack in the future, to something that nobody could predict in the 1980s (or later, until 9/11 actually took place). Yet examining the film from our current perspective, it is possible to claim that, in fact, it provides a clue that (we can now see) indicates that something like 9/11 could happen. Like *Charlie Wilson's War*, *Rambo III* acknowledges the help the U.S. provided to Afghanistan in the 1980s. First, Griggs tells Rambo, "After nine years of fighting, the Afghan forces are now getting shipments of Stinger missiles, and they're beginning to hold their own against the airstrikes." Although the man does not explicitly say so, the audience can clearly understand that this support is provided by the U.S. because it is a U.S. officer who shares this information and because Stinger missiles are U.S. weapons. Second, Rambo joins "mujahideen soldiers, holy warriors," in their mission to stop the Soviets (and, along with that, to save the American POW). Although Rambo does not represent the U.S. Army per se, his image does stand for that of an American soldier, the American hero of the 1980s. Third, the ending quote of *Rambo III* glorifies the Afghan nation: "This film is dedicated to the gallant people of Afghanistan." This dedication, however, appeared in the film only after 9/11. Prior to that, the film concluded with the phrase "This film is dedicated to the brave Mujahideen fighters of Afghanistan,"[30] which proves that the U.S. was on the side of the mujahideen, supporting them in the war against the Soviet Army. Clearly, after 9/11 it would be ethically perverse for the United States to have a film (even one produced thirteen years prior to the terrorist attacks) that is dedicated to those who are, although indirectly, responsible for the nation's biggest national tragedy.

It is important to note that despite the criticism of the support that the U.S. provided to those who in the future would be considered terrorists (obviously being unaware of that fact in the 1980s), both *Charlie Wilson's War* and *Rambo III* are great cinematic examples that, when read from the current perspective, provide insights into 9/11, demonstrating the flaws in American foreign policy in the 1980s. As mentioned, *Charlie Wilson's War* is a better example (because of the year of its release) in this regard: aware of the tragic future, it shrewdly and overtly underscores the fatality of the mistake made by the U.S. in the 1980s, blaming those who made the wrong political decision to help the mujahideen, which led to 9/11 and the country's next involvement in Afghanistan, in 2001.

To Be Continued: From Robert Redford's *Lions for Lambs* (2007) to Peter Berg's *Lone Survivor* (2013)

The War on Terror started with U.S. intervention in Afghanistan. The film industry responded, releasing a number of films on the Afghanistan War and the Iraq War, as well as films that deal with the problem of terrorism, 9/11, and its aftermath. There are only a few cinematic examples that specifically reflect the Afghanistan War; they deal with the issue of U.S. intervention from three different perspectives. Robert Redford's *Lions for Lambs* (2007) investigates the role of the American government and media in escalating the conflict. There are films that present the direct participation of U.S. soldiers in combat; examples include Jim Sheridan's *Brothers* (2009), Peter Berg's *Lone Survivor* (2013), and the documentaries *Restrepo* (2010) by Tim Hetherington and Sebastian Junger and *Hell and Back Again* (2011) by Danfung Dennis. Some of the latter films, namely *Brothers* and *Hell and Back Again*, also touch upon the controversial issue of the reintegration of war veterans, thus revealing the deplorable consequences of U.S. intervention for its participants.

The first perspective is best illustrated by *Lions for Lambs*. The action of the film takes place six years after the invasion, in 2007, and is built upon two main stories: first, in his office Senator Irving (Tom Cruise) gives an interview to Janine Roth (Meryl Streep) and discloses the government's plans on how they intend to proceed with the war in Afghanistan; second, Professor Malley (Robert Redford) tries to convince his smart but somewhat lost student Todd Hayes (Andrew Garfield) that education is important. Both stories eventually touch upon the problem of American participation in the Afghanistan War, although from different angles. The talk at the university is aimed at portraying the war as a personal experience, for the professor narrates the story of his students who volunteered to join the army. Another purpose of the talk is to criticize U.S. policies, since the unmotivated student does not want to attend the professor's political science classes because they do not teach him anything new. The student is annoyed with the lies that some politicians tell, and, as he admits, he would never be able to become "a doughboy who parts his hair the same style as everyone else . . . who never says anything even though he never stops talking . . . who lectures you on morality." He criticizes presidential candidates who "announce their candidacy by standing in front of a large audience and loudly saying they will not run for president."

The scenes devoted to the interview with the senator attempt to display the role of the U.S. government in the intervention. Senator Irving invites Roth to hear about a "new plan going to motion in Afghanistan" that will "win both a war and . . . the hearts and minds of the people." Roth is clearly perplexed to be encountering a politician who so openly seeks to discuss with the media a plan that has not yet proved successful and asks him why he has really decided to talk frankly with her. "This is my honest effort to keep the press better informed and to change the subject from the past to the future, acknowledge mistakes and talk openly about ways of fixing them," responds Irving. He is careful to project the image of a politician who understands the importance and complexity of the Afghanistan War and America's role in it, and to demonstrate his awareness of the intervention's flaws, which he admits, as well as the significance of a new strategy in Afghanistan in 2007. The plan is to reorganize the strategy and put more stress on military action, which Roth interprets as "kill people to help people." The senator corrects her, "I said the enemy," emphasizing that the U.S. fights against terrorists but not Afghan civilians. Roth openly questions the new plan and Irving's later reference to the strategy used by the Romans centuries before, namely that they "establish[ed] a constant presence" (because there was a state of "constant violence") that gave them "the opportunity to *preside*," gets an immediate reaction from the journalist: "So we're gonna be there for good, like Romans?" Irving, clearly unsatisfied with that interpretation, replies, "I said constant, not permanent." Importantly, the senator reveals that the U.S. has begun acting without having received a response from NATO; that is, the U.S. ignores NATO because the operation has to be launched without delay.

Roth, remaining skeptical toward this new plan, believes that the government is simply going to make another mistake. Irving's confidence that the strategy will bring them success receives an acid comment from Roth—"Says the man in the air-conditioned room"—pointing out that the interventionist policy is *decided* by politicians but ultimately *performed* by soldiers. The journalist realizes that more American soldiers are going to die in that war, particularly because of this strategy, since somebody from above has decided that the plan *might* work. She sees diplomacy as the key to success in Afghanistan, but Irving disagrees: "We were attacked. You do not respond to an attack with diplomacy." Irving condemns the policy that the UN has been adhering to with respect to Saddam Hussein and blames France, China, and Russia for trading with him. But as soon as Roth states that the U.S. "also arm[ed] Saddam in the eighties," Irving immediately shifts the topic to the present-day situation. The journalist tries to make the senator think about how the U.S. came to its current predicament, obviously meaning its foreign policy failures prior to 9/11, but Irving refuses to consider the matter: "How and why is not the issue now."

When Roth continues insisting that the best strategy would be "to bring the troops home," she gets a shrewd and very convincing response from Irving: if they withdraw the troops now, it will mean that they have lost. The Taliban would then turn into "something infinitely more vicious and potent because they are now two to nothing versus superpowers." Irving is, of course, referring to the Soviet-Afghan War in 1979–89, in which the mujahideen were victors over the Soviets. The pressure on the U.S. to win the current war is therefore incredibly strong, not only because the country has to take revenge for the 9/11 attacks, and not only because the U.S. has promised to free the whole world from terrorism, but also because its status as a superpower means it cannot allow itself to lose, since a failure would put American leadership in question. The senator claims that millions of Afghans will suffer at the hands of the Taliban if the U.S. leaves the country now; such a decision will lead to "the end of American credibility, the end of America as a force for righteousness in the world." The ideology of American exceptionalism obviously comes through in this phrase and can be questioned; Roth herself starts to ask, "When did America become . . ." but fails to finish the question, as Irving continues speaking. Irving is determined that his plan will work and America will win the war. "We do whatever it takes," he says, showing a willingness to bear any financial or human cost that this intervention (or this particular strategy) will demand. Yet the journalist, tackling the problem from another angle, asks, "Why do we send a hundred and fifty thousand troops to a country that did not attack us?" Roth's confusion is understandable because, as has been noted, neither Afghanistan nor the Taliban attacked the U.S. on September 11, 2001. Therefore a certain perplexity that U.S. involvement in Afghanistan might have caused among the American public (and throughout the world) is intelligible here. The public's unwillingness to put up with the deaths of American soldiers in Afghanistan results from the confusion provoked by U.S. involvement in a country that technically had nothing to do with 9/11. Yet, as was also mentioned, the task of the U.S. in Afghanistan was to overthrow the Taliban *because* they were partners with al Qaeda, the group that actually was responsible for 9/11. The U.S. government, however, obviously failed to explain this to the public. (Neither did it demonstrate a clear policy even as it kept U.S. troops in Afghanistan for years.) Roth's question therefore provokes nothing but anger in Irving. Yet the woman stresses that the question will be asked "till we get the answer." The American failure in Afghanistan happened, according to Irving, because of faulty or insufficient military intelligence or because people who gave orders had never been in war themselves but also because of "bad PR." That is, the case of Abu Ghraib in Iraq was given so much media attention it worsened the image of U.S. intervention. (Irving later blames the television channel Roth is working for, which had already broadcast incorrect information just because it made for a good story.)

The senator seems to be very convincing, explaining how hard this war against "little tribal ragtag gangs" is for the American nation. And he would seem to have won the audience with his concluding sentence, said with tears in his eyes: "God knows, it breaks my heart to ask the men and women in uniform to risk their lives for this victory." But when he shifts to discussing other issues, such as "tax internet transactions," at the end of the interview, one senses the hypocrisy and insincerity of the senator's whole speech about the war in Afghanistan. Roth leaves his office with the realization that Irving only wanted to sell a good story to the press that would help him "get . . . into the White House." The film director's sarcasm is patent now, for Irving is portrayed as exactly one of those "presidential candidates" described by Todd Hayes, who say they will not run for president (this is what Irving tells Roth too) but eventually show they are seeking their own self-promotion. Thus the film suggests that U.S. intervention in Afghanistan can be exploited for selfish careerist purposes by certain politicians who do not care about the lives of the thousands of soldiers who have been sent to the Middle East. And it clearly does not "break [Irving's] heart" to see all those people deployed to Afghanistan.

The film's final scene is, in this respect, very symbolic. The audience observes Roth in a car, passing the World War II memorial on the Mall in Washington, looking at one of the monuments whose full inscription reads, "Americans Came to Liberate, not to Conquer, to Restore Freedom and to End Tyranny." Significantly, however, the only words Roth and the audience can read from the inscription as the car passes the memorial (they are inscribed around the monument and the camera cannot film the whole phrase in one shot) are "Tyranny" and "Americans Came to." My contention is that the director made this choice on purpose, as he obviously could have focused on "Liberate" or "Restore Freedom"; instead he has equated tyranny with Americans. This, of course, should not be understood as the director's questioning of American participation in World War II because in this context the words are meant to refer to U.S. involvement in Afghanistan. This is how Roth perceives this war, which has already killed thousands of soldiers and civilians but has brought no positive results or any hope for its end. She then passes the White House, the political heart of the United States, the residence of the U.S. president, the commander in chief, the decisive policymaker concerning U.S. participation in any of its wars. That shot recalls the moment in the senator's interview when, with determination and patriotism, he claims that the war is a tragedy for the U.S. but there is no other way to solve the conflict. And the U.S. has to continue losing its soldiers in a war that, as the film articulates, has not been thoroughly planned or thought through.

Finally, right after passing the White House, the film shows Roth looking out from the car as it passes Arlington National Cemetery, the nation's most prominent military cemetery, which seems to have neither beginning nor end. The scene serves to demonstrate how many brave soldiers the U.S. has already lost fighting numerous wars. There are tears in Roth's eyes: she understands that these deaths have been the result of political decisions, and that hundreds of the men and women deployed in Afghanistan are already buried there and God knows how many more will join them in the future, partly because of U.S. political ambitions. Deep criticism, frustration, and disappointment—this is the reaction of *Lions for Lambs* to U.S. intervention in Afghanistan. The film disapproves of those who, like Irving, promote achieving goals by any means. To illustrate, consider a scene in which the camera focuses on the notebook Roth uses during the interview with Irving. The line written in the biggest letters is "Whatever it takes!" The action is then transferred to Afghanistan, where two soldiers (Malley's ex-students) are surrounded by members of the Taliban. Some scenes later they are shot. The camera lingers on their dead bodies for a moment, giving time for the audience to remember Irving's words, now so cynical and terrifying. The soldiers become "little more than ciphers of nationalistic pride—they enlist in post-9/11 patriotic fervor—sacrificed in a war that cannot be won."[31] Yet while the intervention—which in the film seems driven mostly by the patriotism of Americans who want revenge for 9/11 and to spread their democratic values to oppressed Afghanistan—is largely criticized, the initial aims of the war, to fight the Taliban and thus terrorism, as well as to liberate the Afghan nation, are not undermined and remain purely humanitarian even in such a cynical and politically depressing film as *Lions for Lambs*.

The role of the soldier in war is a more popular topic in war films, including the ones on the Afghanistan War. With an analysis of the soldier's role as it is represented in film, it is possible to understand another perspective on the intervention. While *Lions for Lambs* does not devote much of its plot to soldiers' experience, documentaries like *Hell and Back Again* and *Restrepo*, along with the war action film *Lone Survivor*, explicitly do, and they also explore the reaction of the locals to the intervention.

Both *Hell and Back Again* and *Restrepo* center their plots on the stories of war veterans. The first film focuses on Nathan Harris, who, after he is severely wounded, comes back home and suffers through a long and torturous healing process. *Restrepo* presents a group of war veterans who, in the mode of the HBO World War II miniseries *Band of Brothers* (2001), tell about their service in Afghanistan. Both films provide two major perspectives: soldiers' experience in Afghanistan and their reintegration into society after their military service is over.

For the sake of this analysis, I have not moved the examination of *Hell and Back Again* and *Restrepo* into a separate section (as I did with documentary films in the section on the Iraq War). Yet it is important to make it explicit that the two films, unlike all the others analyzed in this section, are documentaries. While being aware of the complex and at times biased nature of documentary films, I include these examples not to complement the analysis of the genre of docu-fiction but rather to provide a broader *documentary* perspective on the history of U.S. involvement in the Afghanistan War. *Hell and Back Again* and *Restrepo* raise similar issues as *Lone Survivor* (a docu-fictional account), which reinforces the docu-fictional status of the latter. While the three films are examined together, the difference in the genre and style are kept in mind.

As for the war experience, both documentaries aptly demonstrate a significant but frequently neglected side of any intervention: the reaction of the locals to these armed newcomers. Both films make it apparent that the American soldiers have good intentions. They are ready to sacrifice their lives so that the Afghans can enjoy the democratic freedoms so integral to American society; they are going to fight evil, and though they incur personal losses (their brave comrades, their war brothers), they understand that these were necessary to bring peace to Afghanistan. The soldiers' mission is, therefore, made explicitly humanitarian in these two films.

Both films also demonstrate that the Afghan locals are not happy that the Americans are there, and they do not understand how *war* (or, for that matter, the intervention in its other manifestations) can be a positive action that will lead to *peace* in their land. The American soldiers do try to be friendly toward the locals—they always apologize when they accidentally destroy something during an operation—but such friendliness is not what the Afghan people need. The locals openly tell the Americans that as soon as they leave, the lives of the Afghan people will return to normal (which they think will be good). For instance, in *Hell and Back Again*, the soldiers accidentally spill a bag of wheat that is "a matter of life and death for [one local man's] children." The soldiers say they are sorry and promise to compensate the loss, but the man is obviously upset, perhaps because he does not believe the soldiers or maybe simply because that wheat was the only food he had, a real treasure for him and his family that these U.S. soldiers, who came without his invitation, do not care about. A similar scene takes place in *Restrepo*, when the American soldiers have to kill a villager's cow, provoking indignation among old Afghan men, who complain that the soldiers have killed their food source. The soldiers are ready to offer sugar, rice, and other food as compensation for the dead cow. But the Afghans consider it unacceptable that these soldiers can so easily destroy something so important to the local populace. Such actions only worsen the attitude of the local Afghans toward the intruders.

The dissatisfaction and even anger that the Afghans feel toward the American soldiers are understandable because, as the films make explicit, the intruders brought not only military help but also disaster. Thus in *Hell and Back Again*, one Afghan man says, "Last time, they burned eighteen shops in the bazaar!" This is what it costs to "provide security," one of the soldiers replies when asked by an Afghan man, "We are here to ask you if you can leave the area so we can bring our children back. What we are saying is that there are sixty homes here. What alternative do we have? Leave this area to us and go so we can bring our children back to our homes." Another man adds, "This is the fifth night we've had to live by the river. All of our children are sick. They all have diarrhea and there is no doctor. There's no pharmacy, no shops, no medicine. All of them are closed! . . . Why have we been brought into this? We can't resist against you or the Taliban. Give us a solution. Or we will leave the entire area forever." Another man shares his fears and frustrations: "The Taliban can come anytime—morning, afternoon, or evening. They fire, then leave. Then you arrive and keep shooting at the whole village. And there are children. Certainly, two or three children will be killed, at least." The locals consider the intervention that the U.S. has carried out to be just another act of violence. U.S. goals may be just, but by the time they will have been achieved, too many innocent civilians, including children, will have suffered or died. The local men ask the U.S. Army to leave because the losses they experience at the hands of the Taliban are large enough, and they do not want to double those losses by having a group of U.S. military men in their village. The response from the Americans is that the villagers can, of course, return home, "but we are gonna be here also." The words underscore the true nature of any military intervention: a forceful intrusion into someone else's territory (in this case, the village itself as well as the houses of the locals).

The soldiers question the Afghans roughly when they try to get information about the Taliban; this too sickens the civilians, as we see in *Hell and Back Again*. "I don't care about you [the American soldier] or any Talib," remarks an old man, obviously tired of the war between the Taliban and the Americans that has affected him and other innocents against their will. The soldier explains ("from the bottom of [his] heart") that they are there not to harm the people of Afghanistan but "to help" them, at which the confused Afghan man responds, "If you have come here to help us, then why are you doing this to us?" referring to the injuries and deaths of civilians, the destroyed houses, and the absence of food and medical care.

Restrepo shows a similar attitude of the local population toward U.S. intervention. Early in the film, an Afghan man tells some American soldiers, "You kill the enemy, that's okay. But our concern is that you're shooting ordinary people on their land." The problem is reinforced in Captain Kearny's response: "Remember last week when we said that everything that happened in the past when Captain McKnight was here—we're kind of, like, wiping the slate clean. Captain Kearney's got a new slate. Let's put it behind us, and let's get on with what we've got to do now." The war that the U.S. is fighting in Afghanistan, according to this perspective, is entirely lacking in ethics, as the civilian deaths that occurred when the region was under the command of another officer can be neglected and forgotten by the soldiers who are "kind of, like, wiping the slate clean" and starting over. For the locals, who obviously knew the dead, such an attitude is shocking and unacceptable; more than that, they may simply be afraid that a similar situation will happen when another officer is in charge. There is another controversial scene later in the film, when the soldiers, attacking a group of civilians, kill and injure some of them, including women and children. An Afghan man angrily reacts: "Show me which of them is the Taliban. There is no Taliban." Captain Kearney responds, "Damn it! You know? I need to know better. I need to figure this stuff out better so that I can do this, so that I'm not killing these people and not making them mad. I mean, first impressions are the lasting impression. That's the first time anybody's been in Yaka China, and what do I do? I kill a bunch of bad guys, but in the same instance, I'm killing five locals that may not have been the ones that have pulled the trigger, but in some way, shape, or form were connected to them." Kearney reveals not the evil or excessive brutality of American military men but rather the complexity of the war that, first, has not been well planned and, second, is hard to fight because the enemy is disguised. The latter reality obviously does much to explain the former deficiency, as it is impossible to plan a war when the enemy is not clearly defined.

In *Restrepo* the locals do not accept U.S. intervention; they do not welcome intruders on the land that for centuries has belonged to the people of Afghanistan. That is why they do not want to get along with the soldiers: they perceive Americans to be the *enemy* who has come to their territory. The soldiers, however, believe that their presence is needed; the locals may not understand this now, but they will later on, and they will be thankful when (or *if*) the U.S. frees them from the Taliban. At the same time, the military men realize how hard it is for them to accomplish this mission, because, as has been stated, the enemy is elusive, but also because of the civilians who complicate the situation. For example, "the elders basically want jihad down here in the Korengal." The U.S. mission to bring democracy and freedom therefore comes to a dead end, as the locals themselves do not realize that, speaking in plain terms, terrorism is bad. Hence the sacrifice that U.S. soldiers make becomes absolutely pointless because they are fighting to bring the locals something that these people do not want. Andrea Greenbaum's comment on the soldiers' mission is very apt: "The Korengal is No Man's Land, and the platoon often wonders, amongst each other, and with questioning by the filmmakers, what they're doing here in this remote valley, in this faraway land, and how their particular mission fits into the scheme of the war in Afghanistan, and whether or not their presence will, ultimately, make any difference in the war."[32]

Both *Restrepo* and *Hell and Back Again* reveal the hardships of the intervention for the American soldiers who have become trapped by American policy in the Middle East and must endure the skepticism of the locals, the hatred of the Taliban, and their own struggle to believe in the righteousness of their mission. The intervention turns into a war where each of them has to fight for their own lives. The psychological and physical damage the war rewards them with is colossal. This is what both films present to the viewers. Hollywood films too reflect on these struggles. The salient examples can be classified into action and drama genres and include *Lone Survivor* and *Brothers*.

Based on a true story, *Lone Survivor* focuses on Operation Red Wings, which was conducted in 2005 by a group of four U.S. Navy SEALs: Marcus Luttrell (Mark Wahlberg), Michael Murphy (Taylor Kitsch), Danny Dietz (Emile Hirsch), and Matt "Axe" Axelson (Ben Foster). The aim of the mission is to kill Ahmad Shah, a Taliban commander who organized the killings of U.S. marines in East Afghanistan, and his henchman "Taraq."

The SEALs are thrown into the rough terrain of the mountains of Afghanistan. Soon after reconnaissance is carried out, they realize that the number of the Taliban fighters nearby is larger than had been estimated. The operation seems to have failed when the soldiers, lying in ambush, are discovered by a group of Afghans who are tending to their grazing goats. The Americans capture them and there ensues a considerably long scene showing the SEALs deliberating about what to do with the captives. Murphy suggests three possible solutions: let them go; tie them up and leave, which will probably cause their deaths from cold or from a wild animal attack; or kill them and bury their bodies. Luttrell immediately responds that killing the captured Afghans (two of whom are children, one an old man) is wrong and the soldiers would have serious problems when the world found out that they had killed civilians. The real Luttrell later explained that he was being pragmatic—he simply did not want to be imprisoned for the killing; but he also had a humane perspective: "They just seemed like—people. I'm not a murderer."[33] The audience anticipates that it would be wrong to set the captives free when Murphy finds a walkie-talkie in the old man's clothes and suspects that the man could be speaking with the Taliban, and later, when the older boy, whom Axelson orders to look down, defiantly spits and keeps his eyes glued on the soldier. Luttrell insists on letting the Afghans go, while Axelson and Dietz believe that they should kill them. Finally, Murphy concludes that since the mission has failed, their task now is to go up to the mountain peak and catch a signal so as to contact headquarters and have a rescue plane sent for them. The SEALs agree on that, but after climbing a considerable distance realize that the peak will not be high enough for them to capture a signal and make the call. Simultaneously the older Afghan boy is shown in slow motion, determinedly running to the Taliban. The scene is accompanied by monotonous but tense music that serves as another foreshadowing of the tragic outcome. The SEALs have to return to the forest zone, where they become an easy target for the alerted Taliban fighters. Luttrell realizes now that his decision to let the captives go was wrong; it will prove fatal for three of the soldiers.

The fight between the Taliban and the SEALs is filmed in an extremely severe yet realistic manner. The director does not prettify the scenes; on the contrary, the audience sees blood and wounds on both the Taliban fighters and the Americans. The fight is a challenge for the U.S. soldiers not only because they are outnumbered but also because of the mountainous landscape, in which they cannot move as fast as the Afghans do. Although they confront the enemy with all their strength, it is not enough. The most horrific scene comes later, when the American soldiers, exhausted and with multiple wounds, jump down the rock, which they believe to be their last chance to escape death. In slow motion, all four of them jump, while the audience witnesses an explosion in the background. At once the pace is radically changed—for one minute, the camera focuses on each soldier in turn, showing them clumsily rolling down, hitting their faces against rocks and stones and blundering into trees. We can clearly hear the crunches and crackles mixed with the dull sounds made by the soldiers' bodies and the trees and stones they make contact with. The scene is later repeated even more brutally because the next slope to traverse downward is steeper and the soldiers are already severely wounded. Dietz is killed first, his corpse left up on the rock above.

That the soldiers, trying to save themselves from the Taliban, desperately seek to come to Dietz's rescue or otherwise help him—as the man appears to be in the worst condition compared to the others— when each can barely move, is inconceivably striking. They remain a group, a brotherhood, till the very end. When it seems that none of them have any strength left, they manage to stand up and continue to fight. Murphy gets up to the top of the peak and succeeds in calling headquarters for help. While the audience hears the voice in the walkie-talkie asking the soldier for their coordinates, Murphy is shot in the back by the Taliban fighters. He dies kneeling on the peak, his back to the camera, which is focused on the opening view of an endless chain of mountains. While Jeong Lee describes the "mawkish dramatization" of the scene,[34] I would note that this is the only sequence in the film that seems unrealistic, demonstrating the heroism that one sees in a blockbuster instead of a true-life sacrifice. Yet such a scene is a necessity rather than a drawback for a film in the action genre.

Axelson is the third to die. The scene of his execution is accompanied by the sound of his heavy breathing. When he is already dead, a final bullet pierces his forehead. Luttrell continues his way through the mountains alone and later runs up against a group of Afghan civilians. After what has happened, he cannot trust the locals. However, one of the men, Gulab (Ali Suliman), stretches out his hand to help the soldier, and the skeptical Luttrell eventually takes it. The civilians bring him into Gulab's house. The Taliban, whom Gulab hates, learns of Luttrell's rescue, but because of the tribe's hospitality traditions they cannot take him from Gulab. Luttrell stays safe in the village; he is later rescued by U.S. soldiers and returned to his country. The soldier leaves the village tremendously thankful to Gulab, who, risking his own life, stood up to Taliban to protect him. The real Luttrell later commented that he came to Afghanistan without any "respect for these people"; then Gulab's actions made him realize that "in the middle of everything evil, in an evil place, you can find goodness. Goodness . . . godliness." Interestingly, the real Luttrell went to fight in Afghanistan driven by a feeling of revenge. He carried with him a photograph of a man who had died in the attacks on September 11, 2001, which he had cut out of a magazine. In Afghanistan, Luttrell "killed in the man's unknown name." His personal aim in that intervention was to "double the number of people [the terrorists had] killed."[35] The intervention in Afghanistan, as illustrated by this particular soldier, was therefore humanitarian in the way that its ultimate goal was to stop terrorism—not only in the form in which it can be brought to Western countries but also its daily existence in Afghanistan, as exhibited in the everyday oppression and intimidation of the locals.

The savagery of the Taliban is briefly but strikingly reflected in *Brothers*, as the audience observes two soldiers who are captives of the Taliban being repeatedly tortured. Eventually one of them "gives up" and agrees to record a video message that is directed to the United States: "My name is Private Joe Willis. I'm with the United States Marine Corps. I was told I was coming here to fight for my country but now I realize that Afghanistan belongs to its people and we have no business being here. I love you, Cassie. Joe Jr., your daddy always loves you." Both Willis (Patrick Flueger) and his comrade, Capt. Sam Cahill (Tobey Maguire), realize that this is the end for the private. (The last lines, addressed to his family, illustrate the soldier's understanding that he is never going to see them again.) The Taliban surround the captives and, telling Sam that they no longer need Willis, give Sam a choice: either he kills Willis or they kill Sam. Probably realizing that Willis is slated to die anyway, Sam takes the metal pipe offered to him and beats Willis to death. Luckily for Sam, the Taliban group is soon discovered and eradicated by U.S. troops, and Sam is saved and returned home. But not safe and sound. The murder drives him crazy, and he starts tormenting his own family.

The film thus moves to another level, and from that moment on deals with the problem of the social and mental adaptation of the war veteran back into his family life, into his social surroundings before the war. Sam's confession to his wife that he killed Willis, which the film concludes with, is supposed to explain his unstable behavior and the hatred he has been expressing toward everyone. As his wife hugs him, we hear Sam's voice-over: "I don't know who said only the dead have seen the end of war. I have seen the end of war. The question is: Can I live again?" With the help of these lines, the film asks a more fundamental question, namely whether those who took part in war can continue living afterward, whether it is Sam with his psychological problems, or Luttrell from *Lone Survivor* who miraculously survives a savage operation, or Nathan Harris from *Hell and Back Again* who almost lost his leg during one of the operations, or thousands of other soldiers who fought for their country, defending the interests of the U.S., but who are now doomed to live with their personal war forever. The intervention in Afghanistan is represented in the analyzed docu-fictional films as a brutal mission that, due to its political complexity, has done more physical and mental harm to U.S. soldiers than any other war before 2001. Yet none of the films seems to reject the fundamental—humanitarian—reason for the intervention: to fight against terrorism.

Literature and U.S. Intervention in the Afghanistan War

American Cowboys and Afghan Terrorists: Aaron Gwyn's *Wynne's War* (2014) as a War Western

The involvement of the United States in Afghanistan was widely reflected in literary fiction or, as this project proposes, docu-fiction. The portrayal of the war in Aaron Gwyn's novel *Wynne's War* repeats, to some extent, consideration of the issues raised in other novels about the Afghanistan and Iraq Wars. Yet, apart from its narration about relationships among human beings during wartime, this novel uniquely demonstrates how animals can become part of a conflict. *Wynne's War* may not be the first novel to touch upon the problem of how nature is, inevitably, drawn into war's chaos, but this account stands out for one simple reason: not only does the novel position animals as victims of war, but it also analyzes human beings, namely American soldiers and their enemies, through the prism of their treatment of animals. It is the third-person omniscient narrator who presents the story, allowing readers to be distant observers of this docu-fictional account.

The novel's protagonist, Russell, is in Afghanistan to break horses as well as to train a group of soldiers to ride these horses in preparation for their next mission, which is to take place in the mountains of Afghanistan. Raised by his grandfather, Russell grew up loving these animals and has become a skillful rider who treats horses as clever and tender animals. Now in Afghanistan he understands that the mission's success, indeed the riders' very lives will depend to a great extent on the horses. Therefore Russell is patient: "If the horse did what he wanted her to do, he'd pet and rub on her, and if the horse didn't, he'd work her until she could do it."[36] He treats the horse not as a soulless object that has to be taught to obey a soldier's orders but as a helpless child who should not be hurt, offended, or betrayed; Russell's "swinging the horse on the end of the rope" is touchingly compared to "a father swing[ing] his child by the arms" (54). In response to one of his comrades asking, "You can put that horse's feet anywhere you want, can't you?" Russell assures him, "They're my feet" (58), thus suggesting the ideal unity between the soldier and the horse he rides. The horse becomes a continuation of the soldier and inevitably a direct participant in the war.

At the same time, *Wynne's War* depicts horses as the soldiers' comrades. Russell worries about their fate in war, speculating about what would happen if he or other soldiers were killed: "If they were killed out here, these animals would likely be found and taken by the very men whose compound they were about to assault. Russell thought about that. He told his horse that everything was going to be alright" (125). The thought of the animals being taken by the enemy is as unbearable as the thought of American soldiers being taken by the Taliban as POWs. Significantly, while the POWs would most probably be severely tortured and killed by the enemy, this would not happen to horses. However, Russell cannot endure the thought that terrorists would use these kind animals for their evil purposes. He also demonstrates his care for the horses when the squad comes across two mutilated corpses, suggesting "hood[ing]" the horses and then "talking to Fella [Russell's horse] the entire time, telling her she'd be all right" (180). Although it is clear that Russell shows such an attitude partially for practical reasons—he does not want the horses to get scared and become uncontrollable—it is apparent that he cares for the well-being of these animals.

The blurring of boundaries between horses as a means of transport and as war comrades is especially evident toward the end of the novel, when members of the Taliban detect American soldiers and the mission seems doomed to failure. Russell is equally worried about his friends and the horses, though, significantly, he thinks of the horses first: "It occurred to him that the horses might've been killed in the exchange earlier, *and then* it occurred to him that perhaps Wheels [one of the soldiers who was involved in the mission] had been as well" (195; my italics). A similar episode happens later, when Russell, surrounded by doctors, comes to consciousness, and "the first thing he asked about was his horse, *and the next* was the body of his friend" (218; my italics). An equal degree of care and devotion is showcased when Russell tries to deliver the wounded Wheels to medics, using horses. He is sympathetic both with tired Fella and with Wheels, who is in pain, but ultimately, the horses' lives are of primary importance to him: "He didn't care whether or not he [Russell] made it, but he did care about the horses" (215). And later:

> On the evening of the fifth day, he counted rations and found he had two meals left and half of another. He'd no idea how much farther he had to ride or how much longer he'd even be able to, and the horses had six boxes of oats left between them. He'd been lucky, so far, when it came to water, but he couldn't count on his luck to hold. He made a cold camp in a high pass on the mountainside, inspected the horses' hooves. Their coats were in need of grooming and their tails had started to grow out, but other than that, they were better than could be expected. (216)

Fella becomes his closest friend during the war, and after he returns to the U.S., Russell remembers the horse with tenderness: "He couldn't think about the horse without getting emotional. You spend so many hours on an animal's back, and with every bump and bounce you are jarring some part of yourself into the horse and the horse into you, a transfer of the spirit through violent osmosis, convection by impact, collision" (241).

Apart from helping to construct and unveil a certain purity possessed by the American soldier—Russell is represented as a hero because he is a devoted soldier and friend—the presence of the horses in this novel is an important element that is bound up with the issue of U.S. intervention in Afghanistan as a whole: the horses play such a significant role in *Wynne's War* that one can contend that the novel is not only a war drama but also a western that presents U.S. intervention as a cowboy story. I dub this genre the "war western."[37]

To understand the nature of a war western and how it helps one grasp the problem of American interventionism, I draw on the definition of the western proposed by Corey K. Creekmur: "At its best, the western has been acclaimed as an ideal representation of American values, character and exceptionalism, providing a modern mythology for a nation without an ancient past by instilling frontier history with greater symbolic resonance than a relatively brief period in American history might otherwise engender. The western thus not only glowingly recalls a key period in American history, but in effect summarizes America as a whole and being American as a national identity."[38] Considering *Wynne's War* a war western, I apply this definition of the western to the novel. Given that a war western aims at "an ideal representation of American values, character and exceptionalism," *Wynne's War*, whose main aim is to portray U.S. intervention in Afghanistan, should be built on three levels of representation: first, there is a good American character; second, American values are explicitly articulated; and third, the narrative contains the elements of American exceptionalism. American values and American exceptionalism are integral parts of the novel because, raising the issue of U.S. intervention overseas, *Wynne's War* accepts and promotes the idea that the U.S. fights for what it believes in (American values), and it does so because it believes in the purity of its actions (American exceptionalism). As for the presence of a good American character, there is one such figure. It is not, however, Russell (although virtually every American soldier is represented in the novel as a positive character), but Captain Wynne, a New Yorker (with an "Ivy League education" and "experience in business") and a ranger (29). For most of the narration, the reader perceives him as a rather clear character: a tough, determined man who knows his business, a good officer who has endured a lot in his life, particularly during his military service. Only toward the end of the mission that he performs with his squad—to free American POWs—does the reader start to doubt his goodness. When investigating a cave, his group of soldiers finds a chest with treasure instead of the POWs they're searching for, and Wynne orders that they take it with them. Russell thinks that the captain is doing this for his own profit, that he is robbing the Taliban. He asks the captain and other participants in the mission to leave the chest behind and hurry outside to help a wounded soldier, yet none of them listens to Russell. Finding himself in despair—because his expectations of Wynne have now been shattered—Russell does not want to obey someone who is betraying the most basic and also most important rules of the army and the soldiers' brotherhood. Indeed it seems that Wynne is ready to sacrifice his comrade for his own material profit. "He ain't no kind of officer," says Russell later about Wynne (224). He draws that conclusion after Wynne, finding a wounded Chechen, gets all the information he needs from the man and then shoots him, to the obvious shock of the other soldiers, who had expected the captain to order that the Chechen be taken as a POW. Russell's reaction aptly describes the soldiers' confusion: "I watched him execute an unarmed prisoner. . . . I never seen anything like that. Not from an American, I haven't. Not from an officer" (142). These words stress not only how appalling it is to see an officer committing a crime but also how unbelievable it is that an *American* could do that—a somewhat naïve endorsement of the idea that Americans make up the purest nation, an assumption underpinning the ideology of American exceptionalism.

To Russell's and the reader's surprise, the novel's last pages reveal the truth about the special operation. Russell is in the hospital, having had an operation on his spine, and two men visit him to find out what really happened in the cave. They are adamant that Wynne is a war criminal and ask Russell to affirm this judgment. Russell, certain that Wynne's aim was to steal the treasure, nonetheless does not hurry to spit out his thoughts. After some time, one of the men reveals two satellite photographs of the cave. Nobody can solve the mystery of a demolished entrance in the cave evident from the second picture, made shortly after the first one. Now the whole story makes sense to Russell. With great determination, accompanied by a realization of his own stupidity and a renewed sense of respect for Wynne, Russell explains that Wynne had blown up the treasure, which is why the cave was partially destroyed. He realizes that the chest was too heavy for the soldiers to take out of the cave, and so Wynne decided to blow it up so that the treasure would not get into the hands of the Taliban. Thus the exemplary image of Captain Wynne is restored; he is now a real hero, ready to sacrifice his reputation amid the inevitable obvious questions about where he had hid "[the treasure] that belongs to the people of Afghanistan . . . [and] to their government" (231). Wynne's deed turns him into a typical positive character out of the western genre, where "the core elements of the genre [are] rooted in visceral images rather than abstract words, and *in decisive action rather than sophisticated ideas*."[39] Wynne himself claims, "I don't think in terms of chances," when, shortly before the mission starts, Russell asks him what the chances are that they will free the POWs (184). Instead of giving patriotic speeches in front of the group of soldiers, Wynne acts nobly and proves himself to be a real officer, patriot, and savior. Therefore Wynne's characterization fits another theory about the western, where "the figure of the Westerner [has] an apparent moral clarity."[40] Although the character is not represented in a plain way (which obviously helps create the climax), the ultimate discovery of the truth wholly justifies Wynne, who ends up being portrayed as the most ethically unequivocal character in the novel.

Creekmur describes another characterization of the western: "At its worst, the western has also been denounced as an artifact of and explicit justification for brutal conquest and genocide by 'superior,' 'civilized' Anglo-Saxon and Christian hegemony."[41] I contend that this interpretation of the western does not apply here for one simple reason: in a typical western, Native Americans are always there as a potential enemy group, but in a war western, exemplified by *Wynne's War*, the enemy is terrorists. Since Native Americans and terrorists are different enemies, and incomparable with each other, American intervention in the novel cannot be said simply to be "brutal conquest and genocide by 'superior,' 'civilized' Anglo-Saxon and Christian hegemony." The understanding of the western as "relentlessly racist," cited by Creekmur, cannot be applied to the novel either, though the view that the genre is sexist does have pertinence in relation to the novel. "The unrepentant celebration of assertive patriarchy, physical dominance, and masculine violence" is rather predictable in a war novel or film, where war is represented as an environment that is conventionally created by and for men.[42] The only female character in the novel, the medic Sara, is introduced to support the sexism that is inherent in war. She looks "girlish, petite"; she cannot stand looking at a burning beheaded corpse: "Her pupils were large as dimes and her expression that of someone coaxed from trance. Euphoric. Enthralled" (94). She has mental problems, and is ultimately dismissed from the army because she has concealed them. The vulnerability that characterizes Sara proves that women belong neither to the sphere of war nor, as a consequence, to that of a war western, which, according to Creekmur, is "made by, for, and about (implicitly heterosexual) men."[43] Finally, the western's predictability, with its "opposition of 'good guys' and 'bad guys,'"[44] is another apt characteristic of the novel, which contrasts American soldiers and Afghan terrorists.

What new insights does the choice of depicting U.S. involvement in Afghanistan as a story about cowboys bring to one's understanding of American interventionism? It opens a whole new perspective, supporting a general understanding of U.S. intervention as a positive and humanitarian intervention. Tasked with fighting evil, which is embodied by Afghan terrorists, the American soldiers are, according to the rules of the western genre, automatically the "good guys." Indeed it is hard to challenge or dispute this viewpoint because, the ensuing flaws of the intervention notwithstanding, its initial goal—to protect the American nation, the Afghan people, and the world in general from the actions of terrorists—was undoubtedly fair and just. Gwyn's choice to westernize the story works perfectly well since the plot of any western can be associated with the American experience of 9/11. In a western, the main character (a cowboy) faces injustice, violence, and murder, and he eventually avenges himself on the bad character(s). Metaphorically, this is exactly what 9/11 is about. Evil (terrorists) encroached upon the security of the U.S., murdering thousands of innocent people and striking terror into millions in the U.S. and worldwide; the task of the good cowboy (representing the United States and the U.S. military) is to defeat the enemy, thus avenging the injustice. To read the novel in this way allows one to contend that *Wynne's War* strongly justifies U.S. intervention in Afghanistan.

Yet apart from its overview of the intervention, the novel provides more specific speculations on why the U.S. invaded Afghanistan. For example, Wheels assures Russell that the U.S. military presence is because of the region's lithium resources: "What do you think all those BlackBerries run on? All those iPods and laptops? This place has the largest lithium reserves on the planet. You think we're here because of Al-Qaeda? . . . We need their lithium" (31–32). Later, however, Wheels changes his opinion, claiming they are in Afghanistan because of gold: "People say 'natural resources,' but they don't know what they're really saying. It's natural resources, all right. It's gold" (89). Russell notices the inconsistency in his friend's argumentation: "*Gold*, [Russell] thought. A few months ago it had been lithium" (89; italics in original). Yet Wheels insists, "Don't think for a second we don't want in on *that* action [digging up ancient treasure], cause since when have you ever known Americans not to be interested in gold?" (90; italics in original). The opinion of another soldier, however, reveals a different side of U.S. interventionist policy in Afghanistan: "That's who we're fighting. In this culture, women are nothing. . . . Rape, torture: these are our enemy's weapons" (146), thus showcasing a more profound, complex, and terrifying humanitarian problem faced by the country controlled by the Taliban. In this reading, U.S. intervention is aimed at saving Afghan citizens from the oppression and constant fear they have been forced to live with. Last but not least, the terrorist attacks on 9/11 are cited as triggering the U.S. action in Afghanistan. Although the novel does not focus much on 9/11, it implicitly displays the crucial importance of the tragedy and its influence on the decision to intervene. Such rare reminders as "when 9/11 happened" (24), "after the Towers came down" (142), and especially "[Russell and Sara] talked about how they'd ended up in the mountains of a country they'd not even known had existed before the Towers fell" (90) serve to reveal the actual, essential reason for U.S. involvement in the Afghanistan War. The last example also underscores the fact that if 9/11 had not happened, the U.S. would never have sent its soldiers to Afghanistan because the U.S. was not concerned with what was going on there; this is reflected in the exaggeration that U.S. citizens did not even know that there was such a country as Afghanistan.

One should not conclude, though, that the novel fully supports the military action. References to Vietnam amount to a form of criticism. There is a mention of Russell's father's service in Vietnam and of a piece of advice given to Russell by a Vietnam War veteran: "Anything worth looking at was worth pointing your gun at" (98). But most interesting in this regard is the comparison of U.S. involvements in Vietnam and Afghanistan: "[Wynne] told Russell this *was not* Vietnam. Seemed *too obvious* to even say, but it wasn't obvious to command. *They were always fighting the last war*" (67; my italics). This point is significant when examining the representation of U.S. participation in the Afghanistan War. On the one hand, the war in Afghanistan is understood to be different from the war in Vietnam: the recent intervention is a much less cruel action and therefore more easily justified. On the other hand, the passage unambiguously points up the problem of a policy of *ceaseless* U.S. military interventionism. Afghanistan, as the novel patently claims, is clearly not a second Vietnam. But *Wynne's War* adopts a tragic tone toward the military destiny of the United States, hinting that Afghanistan is not the last war that the country will fight.

Apart from the reference to Vietnam, the novel also evokes the memory of U.S. participation in World War II, which, through comparisons, helps portray the intervention in Afghanistan in a positive light. Russell's grandfather is "a war hero" (17) who fought at Normandy and was awarded two Purple Hearts. Russell was brought up by his grandparents, since his father died and his mother abandoned him, and he loves his grandparents as parents. He had an especially tight bond with his grandfather, who was also his teacher, a man whom Russell deeply loved and respected for his wisdom as well as for his service in Europe. Russell wants to be a hero too: "He believed he'd come into his grandfather's knack for soldiering, though this was never something the man had encouraged" (79). When his grandfather died, Russell enlisted and was deployed to Afghanistan. His decision to fight in this war demonstrates his wish to be a hero like his grandfather, but it also shows the tight, almost unexplainable connection between generations of war veterans. It is striking how omnipresent the image of Russell's grandfather is. The frequent references and evocations of the American participation in the "good war" to some extent help justify U.S. intervention in Afghanistan, demonstrating that just as Americans were helping save people from the Nazis in the 1940s, they are trying to free oppressed people from terrorists in the Middle East. The novel endeavors to display U.S. intervention in Afghanistan as another "good war" undertaken by the United States, and it virtually succeeds in doing so.

The tendency that one can observe in certain films to logically connect the war in Afghanistan that started in 1979 and the one that started in 2001, is present in the novel too. This connection stresses the fact that the recent U.S. war in Afghanistan is not a new involvement (despite Russell and Sara saying that if 9/11 had not happened, they would not have found themselves in the country they had never heard of or whose location they had not even known) but, to a certain extent, is a continuation of the earlier conflict. Frequent references to the Soviets and their participation in the earlier war, such as the bottles and matchboxes with Cyrillic inscriptions found by American soldiers, as well as the presence of Chechens, may even confuse the reader in terms of when precisely the action of the novel is taking place. This obviously showcases the complexity of the region and of Afghanistan in particular, where war has been a nearly permanent phenomenon, where the foreign policies of the United States and the Soviet Union (and later Russia) have long been complicated, and where the fight against terrorists has turned into chaos and destabilization and eventually resulted in deaths among the Afghan civilian population and of American and Russian soldiers.

Apart from drawing a connection between the two wars in Afghanistan, the novel also links the recent Afghanistan War to the recent U.S. invasion of Iraq. For example, before coming to Afghanistan, Russell served in Mosul, Iraq, thus demonstrating that although, technically, the United States started the two wars in Afghanistan and Iraq, one can consider the two interventions part of a bigger war—the War on Terror—since their aims were similar and the enemy was a manifestation of the same threat.

The final issue that the novel raises is the psychological habituation that the soldiers experience, or fail to experience, in war. The novel leaves a very ambiguous impression about how soldiers feel while waging war, perhaps because the issue is essentially equivocal. There are only a few descriptions of Russell's longing to return home to live a normal civilian life, but they are very powerful. One example: "His home was seven thousand miles away in northeastern Oklahoma, and for the first time in months, he wanted to be there very badly" (13). Another example, when Russell imagines his perfect life with Sara: "Sara and a farmhouse. Sara and children and a porch. Sara at a table with steam rising from dishes and a sense that there were others and all of them were his. She was his and the children were his, and he knew this daydream was distant as the stars" (184). During the mission Russell continues thinking of Sara: "He tried to hold it down, but some things couldn't be held, and he thought, inexplicably, of Sara. The feel of her palm, cool against his head. He thought that she was the opposite of all this, the opposite of squatting inside the mouth of a tunnel in the bowels of a mountain range with your teammate's blood still wet on your cheeks and fear like an imp on your back" (191). Yet there is something in war that turns it into a kind of drug; the soldier starts to both hate and enjoy "that noise of a bullet breaking the sound barrier just beside you, the thump of the rifle's report following seconds behind" (168), along with the moments of "gripping [a] rifle so tightly [one] couldn't feel [one's] hands" (194). The soldiers seem to be fully ready to die: "[Russell] realized that by now he'd prepared himself to die a number of times, but he hadn't—not in any way that mattered—prepared himself to live" (16). Yet they clutch at their lives as tightly as they can and always hope to survive: "[Russell] had two fentanyl lollipops in his kit, but he was saving them, he didn't know for what" (214). Russell is now ready to bear the pain because he subconsciously *hopes* that this is not the end and he might need the painkillers later.

There is no explanation of why Wynne "quits a six-hundred-thousand-dollar-a-year job and takes one that pays forty-four thousand and where any given moment the odds are decent you'll be shot or shelled or blown-thefuckup" (142–43). There is no explanation of whether it is possible for Wynne to quit "soldiering" (242), as Russell does. The ending of *Wynne's War* is the novel's most ambiguous part. The narrator draws the reader's attention to a "column" of riders—"A gray company. A cavalry of ghosts" (245)—who are continuing to serve in Afghanistan. The novel uses the pronoun "they" to describe the soldiers, thus depersonalizing the group. The reader may wonder whether Russell preferred to reenlist, choosing war over a peaceful life with Sara, or whether this is a group of other men, unknown to the reader, who are continuing the endless fight. The narrative provides a very brief but striking description of one of the riders, the leader of the group, talking in particular about his "blue eyes" (245). The reference immediately recalls the photograph of Wynne that Russell found earlier: "[Wynne's] cheekbones. Square jaw. Blond hair and blond eyebrows and *very blue eyes*" (29; my italics). It is clear that the ending is not about Russell, because the unknown rider is in fact Captain Wynne—a true officer, a real patriot, a strong fighter, an exemplary American man—for whom war has become his life, the fight against evil the main purpose of his existence.

Jesse Goolsby's *I'd Walk with My Friends If I Could Find Them* (2015) and the Attempt to Understand the Nature of the Intervention in Afghanistan

Goolsby's novel, although different from *Wynne's War* in genre and subject matter, also explores the issue of American intervention in Afghanistan. Unlike *Wynne's War*, *I'd Walk with My Friends* is a pure war drama that does not employ any special techniques (such as westernizing the plot) to reflect the problem, and the ramifications, of the U.S. participation in the Afghanistan War. The novel's major aim is to reveal the hardships faced by war veterans, specifically those of the Afghanistan War, when they return home and try to reintegrate into civilian life. Although a large part of the book investigates this particular issue, the novel also includes episodes that present the experiences of U.S. soldiers in Afghanistan and their direct participation in military actions. These scenes make the novel a consideration of, among other things, intervention and thus are of particular interest to this analysis. Like many other narratives examined in this book, *I'd Walk with My Friends* has a third-person omniscient narrator, which makes this docu-fictional story more believable.

Just like *Wynne's War*, Goolsby's novel connects the tragedy of 9/11 with the U.S. intervention in Afghanistan, thus providing a reason for U.S. involvement. *I'd Walk with My Friends* is a 9/11 novel and, just like any other 9/11 novel that must, according to Birgit Däwes, provide explicit and implicit references to the events of September 11,[45] it does so too. For example, there are references to towers: the song "Tower of Power," for instance, performed by the band with the same name; a secret word used in one of the family's games is "Tower"; at the stadium during a sporting event, a war veteran and his pregnant wife sit next to "four men in turbans" and the man subconsciously perceives them as a threat to his unborn child, although "logically [he] knows that these men aren't terrorists."[46] The films that the characters occasionally watch, like *The Empire Strikes Back* (57) and *Die Hard: With a Vengeance*, where "Bruce Willis and Samuel L. Jackson . . . kill, maim, and solve logic puzzles to save New York City from pissed-off foreigners" (86), make implicit (albeit sometimes anachronistic) hints at 9/11 and U.S. interventionism. There is also an explicit mention of "the day the towers fell," along with a detailed explanation of the tragedy of those events: "This is why we despised terrorists: people dying, diving from the towers, it was dismal business to be sure" (16). The novel describes the personal 9/11 trauma of Dax, who eventually joined the army:

> After returning home to three funerals in a week, Dax stayed up late replaying television clips of people jumping from the buildings. The news had stopped running them. And he couldn't understand why. Without these clips the whole disaster was like any other demolition of steel and concrete, but these scenes showed living men and women falling through the air. This is where the pain lived, in impossible choices on a clear late-summer morning. Dax had never considered choosing between flame and gravity, but watching the people fall to their deaths, weighing which way to die, he guessed he would pick gravity. (17)

The novel thus attempts to elucidate U.S. involvement in Afghanistan as a reaction to the tragedy and as an act of revenge. It overtly articulates this rationale twice: first, in the words of Dax's father, "It's okay to feel good when you *make them pay*" (17; my italics); second, in providing an explanation for why Wintric, another American soldier and later a war veteran, was in Afghanistan: "He was there to deliver justice for attacks on American soil" (271).

Yet the novel does not proclaim that 9/11 was the only reason for the U.S. to intervene in the Middle East. On the contrary, it reflects the controversy of the issue and, it seems, tries to strike a balance between the pros and cons of the intervention and of the actions of American soldiers in Afghanistan. Was the involvement a forceful intrusion or was it a necessity? Can one perceive the actions of Americans to be humanitarian and therefore characterize the intervention as a humanitarian effort? Or was the war a huge political and military mistake? These are the questions braided through the novel as it tries to assess the nature of U.S. intervention in Afghanistan.

Having portrayed the outbreak of war as an act of American revenge—a somewhat widespread and widely accepted understanding of the presence of U.S. troops in the Middle East—the novel accentuates the paradoxes of the intervention. For example, the explanation of Wintric's enlistment as "to deliver justice for attacks on American soil" continues as follows: "But outside a few crazies, all he saw were people searching for food" (271). More than that, the reader finds out that one of the soldiers, Armando, "got in before 9/11" (119), which obviously undermines the singular importance of 9/11 for a number of soldiers who are serving in the army.

Another paradox arises in the attempt to classify the intervention. The novel convincingly portrays the involvement as humanitarian because it is aimed not only at eradicating terrorism but also at helping local Afghans. It is symbolic that *I'd Walk with My Friends* begins with the description of "a low-risk humanitarian mission" (1); since the novel obviously cannot provide an overview of all the events of the long war, the choice to start with a humanitarian mission places initial emphasis on the war's general humanitarianism. The reader learns about local people who thank soldiers for doing their job; physically disabled Afghans are happy to receive prostheses from Americans, and although "most of the arms are too long or the wrong shade of skin . . . the limbless smile, cry, hug the soldiers" (13). There are also shocking images of local kids, for whom the war has caused suffering: "Not a single child appears nourished, and as [Armando] touches their arms and hair and holds their hands and the anger inside him, he thinks of his two daughters. His mind goes to Camila, his oldest and the prettier one, who refuses to eat anything unless she has a dollop of crunchy peanut butter on her plate" (9). Such a comparison serves to demonstrate the radical difference between the living conditions in Afghanistan and the United States. U.S. intervention, according to the quote above, can be interpreted as an attempt to improve the situation for the local populace, even to save children from hunger; such descriptions characterize the intentions of the U.S. as humanitarian.

Along with the problem of food supply, the novel illustrates that there is a bigger and perhaps more dangerous threat: unexpected bombings. Indeed the novel immerses its readers in the chaotic world of Afghanistan, where there are the ubiquitous "bombs, somewhere, everywhere," where "the bombs [can be] strapped to men, women, children, dogs. Bombs the size of tennis balls, soccer balls, tackling dummies" (1). That clearly makes the war unpredictable, unexpected, and more dangerous for U.S. soldiers, not to mention the locals, who suffer attacks every day and cannot withstand them. The consequences of one such bombing on the local Afghans are very vividly described in a scene where Armando "picks a scrap of metal out of his biceps, then reaches down to drag a silent girl away, and with his rescue yank the girl's shoulder detaches, the surrounding skin separates, and her thin arm slides from her body" (14).

Complementing these shocking descriptions, which illustrate the disastrous situation in the country and therefore justify U.S. involvement, the novel also deals with American involvement in the Middle East in general (and specifically in Iraq), when in one of the scenes Colin Powell is saying on TV, "We know that Saddam Hussein is determined to keep his weapons of mass destruction; he's determined to make more" (44).[47] This reinforces the importance of the presence of the U.S. Army in territory that is controlled by terrorists. Interestingly, oil, which is often represented as one of the main reasons for U.S. intervention, is mentioned in the novel only once, when Armando's father says to his son, "It's not just oil. I also know that no one is invading Florida" (120). The novel does not deny that oil could have been a reason for U.S. military involvement; however, it explicitly articulates the view that oil was not the only factor driving the military action.

The climax of the novel, which also becomes the decisive moment in the lives of the main characters, takes place in Afghanistan and begins when the soldiers observe a girl running toward them, holding a soccer ball. Dax, Armando, and Wintric realize that the girl is going to activate a bomb, and after a long debate on what to do, having tried to stop her without violence, they decide they have to shoot her: "The girl falls down, curled, and they hear the rifles' simultaneous report and smell the gunpowder and heat. Then quiet. No wind now. No talk. Everything has been swallowed. The girl's body jolts on the road, legs kicking, the soles of her bare feet exposed in the afternoon. Her legs jolt again, then still. Her bare feet. One heel digging at the road, then still. All quiet. Quiet" (108). This episode becomes the turning point in the lives of the soldiers, who, after their service in Afghanistan, will forever remember the girl, trying to figure out whether it had been possible to avoid killing her, whether she was even wearing a belt of explosives and thus posed any danger to the men who killed her, whether the burden of the child's murder is going to haunt them forever, and whether they eventually will have to pay for that. The episode is a controversial inclusion in a relatively smooth narration. As argued above, the intervention in Afghanistan was initially portrayed as a purely humanitarian action, since American soldiers were fighting against terrorists, avenging the deaths of thousands of innocent people killed on 9/11 and working to restore peace in Afghanistan, where men, women, and children had to live in endless fear of being killed by terrorists or of dying of hunger or disease in the absence of adequate food and medical care. The American soldiers therefore became true saviors who, by means of the military intervention, attempted to help stabilize the country. However, the murder of the girl becomes a blot on the landscape, as it is obvious that she was made to wear the belt, that she was intentionally sent by terrorists; instead of saving her, the soldiers killed her. On the other hand, it is clear that had they not done so, most probably they would have died. The complexity of the war is close at hand here, yet obviously the scene is included so that the reader does not question the intervention and the actions of the U.S. Army since the shooting was an act of self-protection rather than a deliberate killing. Nevertheless it leaves a nasty taste because a humanitarian intervention is generally aimed at protecting people and is positive in all aspects. The killing of a child has nothing to do with humanitarianism. There is, of course, a second reason for the inclusion of this episode, which is of greater interest to the novel because the main issue it raises is the life of a war veteran after military service is over. The murder is the turning point that literally breaks the lives of the men into fragments, before the killing and after; it causes the characters to endure physical and psychological mutilation and practically destroys their worlds back home, as the men eventually cannot keep peace within their own families.

The novel tackles U.S. intervention in Afghanistan from a political perspective, blaming politicians for the decision to send soldiers to the Middle East and not helping them afterward. "You volunteer to serve at the whim of presidents and senators with no skin in the game. Holy shit, we just reelected Bush. You volunteered to let human beings like him make the call on how *you'll* die" (119; italics in original), says Armando's father to his son. Later, when Armando watches the presidential debate on TV between Barack Obama and John McCain, the readers are told that Obama "want[s] to make sure that we [Americans] are investing in energy in order to free ourselves from the dependence on foreign oil" (199),[48] which obviously refers to a specific U.S. interest in the Middle East. The debate continues and Obama says, speaking of Iraq:

And so John likes—John, you like to pretend like the war started in 2007. You talk about the surge. The war started in 2003, and at the time when the war started, you said it was going to be quick and easy. You said we knew where the weapons of mass destruction were. You were wrong. You said that we were going to be greeted as liberators. You were wrong. You said that there was no history of violence between Shia and Sunni. And you were wrong. And so my question is . . . of judgment, of whether or not—of whether or not—if the question is who is best equipped as the next president to make good decisions about how we use our military, how we make sure that we are prepared and ready for the next conflict, then I think we can take a look at our judgment. (201)

Obama's opinion foregrounds how badly planned were the interventions in the Middle East and Central Asia, which shows that the decisions to intervene in Afghanistan and Iraq made by the politicians led to deaths among American soldiers, Afghans, and Iraqis without any effective outcome. The struggle "for Iraqi freedom and American freedom" (201) that McCain talks about was made in vain because the soldiers were sent to the Middle East without their mission being clearly defined. And although U.S. soldiers expressed their eagerness to end the war—"They said, let us win. They said, let us win. We don't want our kids coming back here" (201–2)—this quote from McCain hardly demonstrates anything positive about the intervention, apart from its hardships and the obvious desire of military men and women to end the mess, chaos, and murder in the Middle East so that future generations of Americans would not be commanded by their government to fight there, suffer, and die. Armando's reaction to McCain's words vividly supports this argument: "*Oh, McCain,* [Armando] thinks. Then, out loud to the television, to a close-up of McCain's face, mocking, 'Let us win, they said. Please John, let us stay here forever and win. We love it here! We're winners! Fuck you'" (202; italics in original).

The last issue raised in the novel that is crucial to one's understanding of U.S. intervention in Afghanistan is that some regarded the U.S. mission—to borrow from the ideology of American exceptionalism—as being blessed by God. For example, although Armando believes in God and prays from time to time, he is "unsure if God wanted him to join the military" and thinks that "God is mostly hands-off" (122). Yet in the minds of soldiers, as depicted in the novel, the war in Afghanistan becomes something of a religious war, as Armando "often contemplates who's going to win in the end, Allah or God" (126), demonstrating the cultural and religious differences of the rivals and suggesting that while Americans are being guided by their Christian God, terrorists are being led by Allah. Armando's wife, Anna, believes that "America is blowing it because there are not enough real Christians, that the Muslims have nothing against Christianity, that if Christians actually practiced their faith, were as devout as the Muslims were, most would get along fine" (126). Her opinion underlines the fact that the actions of the American soldiers are not dictated by God, which, in turn, shatters the idea of American exceptionalism as it pertains to the Afghanistan War. "Some of the blame is ours. . . . America's. We're strong in all the wrong ways. We call ourselves Christians, but we're something else" (126), says Anna, censuring the intervention and the actions of Americans in the Middle East. Whereas Armando continues to insist, "Muslims can't even get along with other Muslims" (126), overtly stating that all the problems in the region come from Islam, that aggression is in the very blood of Muslims, and that if they cannot regulate the conflict among themselves (a clear reference to the split between Shia and Sunni) but continue to kill fellow Muslims, it comes as no surprise that they treat Americans, and Christians in general, as infidels.

The novel, however, does not condemn Islam while praising Christianity. On the contrary, it questions Christian attitudes toward God and the idea of "prais[ing] God only for the good things in life" (176). Dax says, "What the hell is up with cancer and dropped touchdown passes? . . . No one points to the sky and pounds their chest during chemo or when a pass slips through their fingers" (176). Later Dax raises a pointed question: "Do we praise Jesus if Sim [the brother of Dax's wife] impales himself on a mile marker?" (191). Dax does not understand the hypocritical attitude of Christians toward their God when they *selectively* praise

Him for something that *they* find good for themselves. Doubting the religion that most Americans profess to believe in, Dax also implicitly questions the ideology of American exceptionalism, which allows one to conclude that he most probably does not treat U.S. intervention in Afghanistan as an action that is guided by God.

All the cinematic and literary representations of the Afghanistan War analyzed here help one understand not only the nature of U.S. intervention but also the War on Terror in general, through the various cultural interpretations they have provided in the documentary and docu-fictional modes. These representations of the Afghanistan War unveil the political, historical, and cultural elements that have surrounded the recent U.S. involvement in the Middle East, yet they are only part of the puzzle and should be examined in combination with the representations of the Iraq War in film and literature in order to construct a full picture of U.S. interventionism in the twenty-first century.

5

The War on Terror, Part II

THE IRAQ WAR

The History of the War

Soon after it intervened in Afghanistan, the U.S. realized that another country in the Middle East could, for various reasons, pose a threat to the U.S. and arguably the whole world, namely Iraq. To ward off any danger that might come from Iraq, the U.S. invaded the country in 2003. This was the second war fought by the United States in Iraq, yet although its involvement in the First Gulf War seemed justified (particularly from a humanitarian perspective), this was not the case for the Iraq War. The invasion had the following goals: to remove Saddam Hussein from power (which was not done during the First Gulf War) and thus free the people of Iraq from their leader's tyranny; to help secure Israel's position in the region, at least so that it would need not to fear military attacks from Iraq; to build a model democratic state in the Arab world that could become an example for other Arab countries; to create a lasting peace in Iraq that would allow the U.S. to withdraw its troops from Saudi Arabia and thus stop the spread of anti-American ideology in the Middle East;[1] to get access to oil. However, none of these aims can account for why the U.S. felt such urgency to invade Iraq in 2003. The U.S. government eventually listed two other, weightier reasons for starting the war: it claimed that Saddam's regime possessed weapons of mass destruction (WMDs) and that Iraq, acting with al Qaeda, was involved in the spread of terrorism. These assumptions turned out to be untrue.[2] Moreover, "only after occupying Iraq" did President George W. Bush admit that Iraq had not been linked to 9/11.[3] However, because 9/11 was considered too large an attack to have been planned and carried out by a limited group of terrorists, many in the U.S. administration were sure that Iraq was involved: "Just because FBI and CIA have failed to find the linkages [with Iraq] does not mean they don't exist."[4] Following this view, U.S. intervention in Iraq was an act of "preemptive self-defense"—a measure taken to prevent possible future attacks and thus guarantee the security of U.S. citizens.[5] Yet while the official term used in relation to the new policy was "preemption," it was rather a policy of "prevention." Barak Mendelsohn provides an important distinction between the two terms: "A preemptive strike takes place when a state has information about an imminent enemy attack. Once violent conflict has become inevitable, the role of a preemptive strike is to give the defender the initiative. On the other hand, prevention implies a case of general hostility between states that makes a violent conflict likely. Since it has no information on a specific plan to attack, the initiator of a preventive strike relies on the existence—or often, on his perception—of hostile intentions."[6] Not having provided a convincing justification for the intervention, the Bush administration adhered to "a new rule long favored by the United States," according to which the country could carry out "attacks on countries that harbor terrorists."[7] As Bush formulated the policy, "If we wait for threats to fully materialize, we will have waited too long."[8] The U.S. considered Iraq its greatest threat and thus initiated one of its most senseless wars. To borrow from Bert: "The risk to go to war without pausing to investigate . . . was one of the key landmarks in the long list of mistakes in Washington's Iraq policy."[9]

The American public widely supported the invasion of Iraq for one reason: the trauma that 9/11 had caused the nation, as well as fear of future attacks, was so immense that the American people largely approved of the government's decision to send troops to the Middle East to eradicate terrorists. One can therefore argue that the government simply took advantage of the situation and, as Bert puts it, "played this advantage to the maximum."[10] Moreover George H. W. Bush's comparison of Saddam to Hitler in 1991 had only reinforced the image of the Iraqi president as evil, so the goal to free the oppressed from Saddam's tyranny found wide support.[11] George W. Bush proclaimed that the aim of the U.S. was to spread democracy throughout the world, eventually "ending tyranny."[12] But writers like Jacob Weisberg have argued that the president's repeated references to the spread of American values throughout the world did not correspond to his actions: "His eight-year administration hardly showed excessive concern with parsing and enhancing those values domestically." The same applies to the president's references to religion and America's religious (specifically Christian) imperative to help the world: both "Bush's faith and his liberal democratic values are part of a 'constructed persona' rather than a framework through which he looks at the world."[13]

Despite the disbelief of some concerning "the ability to transform Iraq into a democracy in any realistic period of time,"[14] the invasion took place. Yet even when Baghdad was occupied, "the United States was not sure what it wanted to do there." Instead of discovering WMDs, U.S. soldiers found "violent and widespread opposition to the US presence."[15] The war became incomprehensible both to the invaders and the locals; whereas U.S. soldiers saw their aim only as freeing the country from oppression, the Iraqis considered the Americans to be intruders who wanted to impose their views and way of life and extract profits from their country. And while the liberation of the oppressed was, to borrow Kennan Ferguson's phrase, "a gift" because the United States did not demand anything in return, the Iraqi people remained generally negative toward the presence of Americans in their territory. They obviously did not want Saddam to be their leader anymore, but neither did they want their American "saviors" to be in Iraq.[16]

At the beginning of the intervention, the Iraqi population was "approximately evenly divided on whether the United States was an invader or a liberator," but after only half a year a mere 15 percent of Iraqis considered the U.S. a liberator.[17] And the American public reconsidered its enthusiasm for U.S. involvement in Iraq; while the war was widely supported at its beginning, five years later 63 percent of Americans were calling the war a "mistake"—the "highest recorded opposition in an active war in American history."[18] The British were also very skeptical toward U.S. actions: "By 2006 a poll found that 69 per cent of British respondents believed US policies since 2001 had made the world less safe, 75 per cent considered President Bush a threat to world peace and 71 per cent stated that the war in Iraq was unjustified."[19] Unlike the Afghanistan War, the war in Iraq was understood by many "as producing not a public good but a major public bad."[20] And it seems plausible to argue that the unjustified involvement in Iraq not only was bad for the direct participants, that is, the U.S. soldiers and Iraqi civilians who were either killed in the war or were physically and psychologically mutilated by it; it also inflamed hatred toward the United States as well as contributed to the spread of anti-Americanism among those who had suffered in the war that was, as they viewed it, provoked by the Americans.

It is possible to contend that the invasion of Iraq was a humanitarian intervention, especially if one bears in mind such goals as the fight against terrorism and the prevention of the use of WMDs, but the fact that none of the stated violations were proven ultimately points to the war's being little else than a reckless invasion. Alex Bellamy remarks, "Rightly or wrongly, a large majority of the world's states believe that the coalition abused humanitarian justifications to suit their own purposes. This will set back attempts to galvanize a global consensus on the necessity of action when basic human rights are violated on a massive scale."[21] And whereas some scholars consider the war in Iraq a humanitarian intervention because, even though no WMDs were found, the population was liberated from Saddam's oppression, others shrewdly point out that a political regime change has nothing to do with human-itarian intervention.[22]

It is worth noting that the war, which ended in 2011, after almost nine years, inevitably caused many Iraqis to migrate; millions were forced to seek refuge in other countries. Such factors as the lack of food and medical help as well as economic instability caused people's health to deteriorate and ultimately provoked the deaths of many.[23] It is impossible to provide an exact number of Iraqis who died in the war. *BBC News* reports an estimate of 461,000 people.[24] According to the *Huffington Post*, 4,486 American soldiers died in the war.[25] The war turned into one of the greatest traumas of the twenty-first century. It undoubtedly became one of the largest military failures of the United States. And although the intervention was aimed at doing good, the only result it produced was disapproval, global and domestic. The intervention in Iraq, unsurprisingly, became one of the most preoccupying themes for many film directors and writers and thus generated a wide cultural response, best described as a protest against it.

Film and U.S. Intervention in the Iraq War

The absence of specific goals made U.S. involvement in Iraq perplex-ing to people around the world and at home in America, as well as to the direct participants, the soldiers. Hardly any film on the Iraq War neglects this issue. Before proceeding to the film analyses, however, it is important to mention that the War on Terror has been widely reflected in fiction and documentary film. Yet when one compares the coverage of the two major American interventions in the Middle East in the twenty-first century, it is the Iraq War that has received much more attention. This is due, one can speculate, to the general disapproval of the war—the widespread protest against the war that had more flaws than virtues. Terence McSweeney writes that the U.S. administration sought generally to "help market the war on terror through the medium of film" and had announced this intention to some of the key figures in Hollywood. A similar action had been taken during World War II, when President Roosevelt attempted to "mobilize" Hollywood, and it obviously was at work again, as Hollywood agreed to display the War on Terror extensively: "We are willing to volunteer to become advocates for the American message."[26] For the U.S. government it was important that the war not be seen as a military operation; the administration wanted to win the support of Afghans and Iraqis, of course, but also of Americans.[27] Yet, as my analysis will demonstrate, the plan did not work out exactly as it was supposed to. Of course, the films that deal with the War on Terror censure terrorism and attempt to justify U.S. military actions as necessary steps that had to be taken to eradicate terrorism and prevent future attacks from "evil" organizations. However, most of the films also overtly question the intervention, showcasing that its aims are not clear, the sought-after results hardly reachable, the casualties too heavy, and the war trauma simply intolerable. One can conclude that while the government had hoped that Hollywood would have been able to help win the support of every American citizen, it eventually turned out that the films on the Iraq War only reinforced the American public's general bewilderment toward the military intervention. Finally, while the U.S. administration planned that the War on Terror would be reflected in film, one can argue that the Iraq War has attracted more attention from film directors than the Afghanistan War, which again can be explained by the puzzling nature of the intervention in Iraq and the general desire to understand that war.

Another interesting peculiarity of the Iraq War (as well as the Afghanistan War) films is that most of them were released around 2006–7, when the war was still going on. Scholars have observed the tendency of those films to be unpopular among viewers; this was not because the films are bad or the audience was not interested, but because both wars were not even close to conclusion: "Disorientation, ambivalence, a lack of clarity—these are surely part of the collective experience [these films] are trying to examine. How can you bring an individual story to a satisfactory conclusion when nobody has any idea what the end of the larger story will look like?"[28] The situation that these films' directors found themselves in perhaps can serve to explain the issues they preferred to raise in their works: perplexed themselves, witnessing the general bewilderment, and (like everybody else) not really having a plausible guess about when and how the war would end, they created films that depict American involvement in Iraq as an operation that is equivocal in every sense.

Documentary Accounts: Soldiers' Firsthand Experiences

Perhaps the most famous documentary accounts of the Iraq War are James Longley's *Iraq in Fragments* (2006) and Deborah Scranton's *The War Tapes* (2006).[29] These films are interesting to analyze together because they present opinions from the two very different sides: Iraqis and Americans, respectively.

Iraq in Fragments is stylistically somewhat reminiscent of Werner Herzog's *Lessons of Darkness*, on the First Gulf War. Longley's film also demonstrates how destructive war is, opening with scenes of an occupied city that, once peaceful, has become a dangerous environment. The viewer observes collapsed buildings, destroyed roads, fresh smoke coming from bombings, and soldiers—the intruders who, as the film suggests, forced this undesired change on the local Iraqis. The cityscape is filled with helicopters, tanks, weapons, and other attributes of war that submerge the audience into a horrifying yet mesmerizing, artificially created environment of modern war. It is also significant that the main character in the film is a child—a local boy—who is living through the occupation. On the one hand, the boy personifies the innocence of the Iraqi nation, whose territory is now occupied by the United States. On the other hand, the boy's age points to his inexperience and thus unawareness of what is going on and why; symbolically the Iraqi people—just like a small child—have to learn the reasons for their involvement in this war. The viewer witnesses how unprotected the people are, as they now consider death to be an everyday part of their lives. In addition, the war has caused a significant economic decline: poverty eats up the country, and no one seems to care. All the U.S.

thinks of, according to the local Iraqis, is oil. They believe the American soldiers may kill anyone who seems suspicious to them, including children. The local population therefore perceives the war not as an act of help but as a grab for financial gain (oil), and thus the intervention is not an act of liberation for them but purely an occupation. The main problem in this war, as the local Iraqis see it, is that the U.S. applies force but is not willing to understand what the local people want, and this misunderstanding comes, first and foremost, from a lack of cultural knowledge and the language barrier. In Iraqi eyes, the U.S. has shed its role as a liberator and now is Iraq's greatest enemy, a tyrant that has symbolically substituted for Saddam.

The War Tapes, on the contrary, provides the viewer primarily with the occupying soldiers' viewpoint on the war. Although the film also briefly touches upon the impact of the war on Iraqis, particularly in the scene when two elementary school children are returning home from school, walking along a road controlled by U.S. soldiers. War is part of their everyday reality, and what would normally seem to be polar-opposite themes, such as childhood and violence, coexist in war-torn Iraq. Yet the film's main concern is the American soldier. *The War Tapes* reveals how for some soldiers—specifically one of the main characters—participation in the Iraq War was unquestionable after 9/11, since they took the terrorist attacks to be personal tragedies.

In the midst of the war, U.S. soldiers wonder why they cannot improve their tactics and ultimately win the war, having "the most technological army in the world." In addition to the Americans' bad planning, the film foregrounds the problem of "the language barrier" as one of the chief obstacles in this war, since there is practically no communication between Americans and Iraqis. Dealing with the problems faced by the soldiers in Iraq, *The War Tapes* also provides two reasons for American involvement. The first one is oil. (When one of the soldiers says they could "build a wall around the country and leave," he then laments: how can they "leave" if there is still oil that the U.S. cares for so much?) The second reason is "safety in the U.S." With respect to the question of safety, it is symbolic that one of the key episodes in the film involves an accident on the road, when soldiers do not notice a local woman and run her over. The accident serves to censure U.S. involvement, which, as the scene shows, caused many random deaths. The U.S. presence in Iraq is also criticized in an earlier scene, when trucks carrying waste are emptied and one of the soldiers comments, "We are bringing democracy and good vegetation to Iraq." The soldier's sarcastic tone clearly indicates that while the goal of the intervention, as explained by the U.S. government, is to turn Iraq into a democratic state—a decent enough rationale—in reality, what the soldiers do is worse, and the human feces emptied by the truck figuratively stand for all the damage that the U.S. has caused Iraq. The words "It will be a better country . . . in twenty years . . . because we were there" seem more like a cry of hope than a statement: the soldiers cannot really believe it, no matter how much they may want to. It is also significant that the film concludes with scenes wherein Iraq War veterans speculate about the reasons for U.S. involvement in Iraq. One claims that oil was not the only reason for the invasion and occupation, or even the primary aim; the other soldier is determined that it is:

> Why the fuck are we there? We better get that oil, right? The U.S. army is not the fucking Peace Corps! The marines are not the Peace Corps! That's not why we're in Iraq! We're in Iraq for money and oil! Look at any other war in the history of the world and tell me it's not about money. This better be about money. And if we don't get that oil and that money then all the lives that are gone right now—What's it? Eighteen hundred? Something around there?—they are all in vain. Boy, you don't put a hundred and fifteen thousand troops from all over the country in there and say we are there to create democracy. Man, you create money, yeah! They're making money for us, you know. Somebody other than Dick Cheney better be getting their hands on it pretty soon.

The documentary does not provide an optimistic message—and that is not its aim. It intends instead to search for a possible explanation for U.S. intervention, and though it occasionally tries to refute the idea that oil was not the key factor motivating the political decision to go to war, the film ultimately seems to suggest that it is, as there is hardly any other reason. Or at least *The War Tapes* provides no other plausible rationale. It mocks the idea of bringing democracy to Iraq, and it presents the pursuit of material gain as the only explanation for the intervention.

Docu-Fictional Accounts: Abundance of Texts, Sameness of Stories

Nondocumentary—though not purely fictional either—examples that deal with the Iraq War are numerous. Among the most famous: Peter Markle's *Saving Jessica Lynch* (2003), Brian De Palma's *Redacted* (2007), Peter Berg's *The Kingdom* (2007), Paul Haggis's *In the Valley of Elah* (2007), James C. Strouse's *Grace Is Gone* (2007), Kathryn Bigelow's *The Hurt Locker* (2008), Kimberly Peirce's *Stop-Loss* (2008), Ridley Scott's *Body of Lies* (2008), Luke Moran's *Boys of Abu Ghraib* (2014), Clint Eastwood's *American Sniper* (2014), Susanna White and Simon Cellan Jones's miniseries *Generation Kill* (2008), and the television series *Homeland* (2011–), directed by, among others, Lesli Linka Glatter. I consider these examples to be docu-fictions because they largely base their plots on a war that indeed took place, focusing on its specific events, policies, and ramifications. Whereas one cannot precisely determine to what extent the events described in the films and series authentically reflect what actually occurred, I argue that by entwining the political, historical, and moral aspects of the Iraq War and U.S. participation in it, these examples do reflect some truth about the intervention.

LaRocca argues that we can consider a miniseries "a long film." Comparing miniseries to a "true television 'series,'" or a "maxiseries," the scholar posits that unlike the usual serial structure, which is "webby, diffuse" and "reaches out to a range of subplots and subcharacters," a miniseries "merely elongates and enriches a linear three-act structure": "A television show, or maxiseries, is capable of following obscure narrative routes and digressions and pursuing the development of secondary and tertiary characters and themes, as well as experimenting with the presence of guest stars, engaging with social commentary, and even allowing for false paths."[30] This characteristic can never be applied to a miniseries due to its limited duration. The precision, compactness, and straightforwardness in its plot development make the miniseries a cinematic form akin to film. In line with LaRocca, I consider a miniseries a longer film, and, in the section that follows, I examine *Generation Kill* as a docu-fictional narrative akin to a docu-fictional film.

The series *Homeland* is only briefly cited in this work because it primarily deals with the War on Terror and the problem of terrorism in general. The genre of a series (and not of a film or miniseries) aptly underlines the endless war that the U.S. and its allies fight against their elusive enemy throughout the world. *Homeland* inevitably comments on the problem of U.S. military interventions in the Middle East, providing the audience with its own view on the wars in Afghanistan and Iraq. Because of this, the series can be considered a docu-fictional account on the two interventions. Its longer duration (compared to that of a film or miniseries) should not be viewed as a disadvantage since the story itself moves at a very fast pace. The truth about the interventions that the series has to say is never hidden behind a convoluted or protracted plot but is always made explicit to the audience.

Discussing the issue of truth in the cinematic examples that follow, I again refer to Lacan's theory of truth, according to which there is no unified truth but only multiple truths. The competing representations of the war (from the portrayals created by numerous media to the soldiers' stories and the interpretations made by scholars and politicians) and views on the war (varying, for instance, from one political party to another, from one country to another) reinforce Lacan's theory of truth, on the one hand, and Baudrillard's concept of simulacrum and Barthes's notion of myth, on the other hand.

For example, *Redacted* uses an interesting technique: the film starts with an inscription; part of the larger text reads, "This film is entirely fiction, inspired by an incident widely reported to have occurred in Iraq."

Already the first line of the film complicates the genre of the narrative, overtly questioning the fictional status of what is claimed to be "entirely fiction." What this line means to say is that through a fictional story, the film attempts to tell its audience the truth about the Iraq War; this truth is indeed only a fragment of a larger picture, yet this should not lessen the cultural and historical significance of what is presented in *Redacted*. The film's central story is the brutal rape of an Iraqi girl by American soldiers. And whereas the film's initial remark does not allow the viewer to fully believe that what is shown on screen is truthful, it is exactly the addition of real pictures at the end of *Redacted* that depict bombings, child murder, and war violence that makes one realize that even if the characters in this film are fictional and some of the events did not take place in *exactly* the way they are described, war violence, and particularly soldiers' violence, is a phenomenon in the Iraq War that no one can refute. *Saving Jessica Lynch* "is based on a true story." *Boys of Abu Ghraib* "is inspired by true events." In *In the Valley of Elah*, also "inspired by actual events," it is impossible to say whether the story that is narrated in the film took place or whether the "actual events" are the Iraq War, the problems experienced by war veterans, and soldiers' violence, but it is clear that whether by raising each of these issues or by stressing only particular ones, the film deals with U.S. involvement in Iraq, attempting to understand the intervention and vividly re-create a sense of it. An even more interesting tactic is used in *American Sniper*, as the audience finds out only in the end that the film is based on real events. Thus, while one watches the film as a fictional story, the concluding realization that the characters and some of the plot lines are true makes one reconsider what one has seen and understand that the brutality of war shown in the film is an authentic face of the conflict. Many of the analyzed examples incorporate various video recordings that serve to suggest that these films are "real life," in contrast to the recorded materials created in the film by the characters. Stacey Peebles speculates that the inclusion of videos creates "a more personal, and therefore more realistic and effecting, representation of war."[31] Despite the richness of the material, all the films about the Iraq War touch upon similar issues: they attempt to demonstrate that the intervention was a humanitarian mission aimed at ridding the world of terrorism, yet they also call into question the humanitarianism of the war, focusing on the damage—whether physical, moral, or economic—that it caused.

Thus, in *Stop-Loss*, a soldier suggests that the U.S. "drop a ten-thousand-pound bomb on one of those cities every time they hit us. No more this urban-combat-bullshit. I'm tired of going, killing hajji in his kitchen and his bedroom." Although this is drunk-talk, and most of the people listening seem to be skeptical about his proposition, the soldier's words reveal an important fact: the difficulty, if not the impossibility, of catching the enemy, for U.S. soldiers in Iraq cannot easily identify who is a civilian and who is a terrorist. Because of this, they have to die in action, performing countless missions. This is later supported by the protagonist, Brandon King (Ryan Phillippe), who explains to his friend how dangerous yet perplexing the war is, because "nobody knows who is who." Whereas the soldiers in *Stop-Loss* joined the army because they wanted to "protect [their] country, [their] family" as well as to "pay back for 9/11," as soon as they were in Iraq, they realized that "the war wasn't even about any of that." Not that the film is trying to make a larger point, proposing that imperialist or economic interests brought the U.S. to the Middle East; the only thing the film suggests is that the U.S. got involved in a war that it did not fully understand and had no plans on how to win it.

The motif of 9/11 and the revenge that American citizens wanted to take on terrorists is present in practically every film about the Iraq War. The titular character of *American Sniper*, Chris Kyle (Bradley Cooper), first watches a news report about the 1998 attacks on the U.S. embassies in Tanzania and Kenya, then decides to join the SEALs; later, having watched the breaking news on CNN about 9/11, he joins other American soldiers fighting in Iraq. *Boys of Abu Ghraib* opens with a voice-over in which the main character explains that 9/11 made him join the army and fight in Iraq. Symbolically the film opens with a party devoted to the celebration of the Fourth of July—Independence Day—and the main character's send-off to Iraq. The combination of the two events suggests that just as Independence Day was the result of a national achievement, so the Iraq War represents the will of the American people to help the oppressed and to fight against terrorism so that Iraq (and eventually the world) can have its own Independence Day, that is, freedom from oppressors.

Grace Is Gone—a film that tells the story of Stanley Phillips (John Cusack), whose wife dies while serving in Iraq and leaves him with two daughters—attempts to explain why American soldiers are fighting in Iraq through the conversation between Stanley and his teenage daughter Heidi (Shélan O'Keefe):

HEIDI: Do you ever think that mom should've stayed home?

STANLEY: All the time.

HEIDI: Why did she have to go?

STANLEY: She was doing her duty, Heidi, you know that.

HEIDI: I know. But what exactly does that mean?

STANLEY: We talked about this. We have people all over the world looking out for our safety. When they discover a threat, they have to act on it. That's the way the world is.

HEIDI: On the news they're saying that we went to war with the wrong people, that it was all a lie.

STANLEY: Well, you can't always believe everything you hear on television, can you? Sometimes you just got to trust that you're doing the right thing. We got to believe . . .

HEIDI: Well, what if you can't?

STANLEY: Then we're all lost.

The scene touches on the problem of soldiers' deaths, particularly underlining the fact that many American families lost their relatives and friends in the Iraq War; the war has given rise to thousands of personal problems that play out painfully in many American homes. But the scene also implicitly raises the question: What if what the Americans are doing in Iraq is wrong? It is significant that the film was released in 2007; the doubts that many Americans started to have about the intervention and its ultimate goal were very real at that time and offered the unsettling thought that if the war was for nothing and the U.S. was unable to win it, then all the soldiers' deaths were for nothing. In 2007 these questions were raised only as doubts, but later, in 2015, the series *Homeland* was more certain about the fallacy underlying U.S. policy: "We are supposed to build a functioning society in the middle of that. What don't they get in Washington: you can't shove democracy down people's throats." These words are from a conversation between two CIA agents in Baghdad in 2005, yet the understanding of the problem, and particularly of the U.S. attempt to democratize Iraqi society, sounds fresh, as if emerging only toward the end of U.S. occupation.

The films also tend to depict the tactical tradition that took shape in the new war. This is especially apparent in Kathryn Bigelow's *The Hurt Locker* and HBO's miniseries *Generation Kill*, directed by Susanna White and Simon Cellan Jones. My contention is that in *The Hurt Locker*, just as in *Zero Dark Thirty* (released four years later, in 2012), Bigelow accurately outlines and visually constructs the concept of a new type of war. In turn, *Generation Kill*, released like *The Hurt Locker* in 2008, views the U.S. role in Iraq from another angle, persistently emphasizing the futility and groundlessness of U.S. intervention. At the same time, *The Hurt Locker* and *Generation Kill* both communicate similar emotional messages; each intends to make the spectator meditate upon the savagery of the war.

The Hurt Locker slowly but firmly plunges its audience into the monotonous but deadly dangerous events that took place in Baghdad in 2004. The film's first scene, when Staff Sergeant Matt Thompson (Guy Pearce) has to defuse a bomb, is one of the key scenes in the whole film. The robot assigned to disarm the explosive gets broken on its way to the site, so the task is passed on to Thompson. What is surprising about the scene is that the audience does not yet expect anything bad to happen. Thompson obviously has a wealth of experience and his playful mood makes one think that this is just another bomb that will be defused in a few minutes. Sergeant J. T. Sanborn (Anthony Mackie) and Specialist Owen Elbridge (Brian Geraghty), who supervise Thompson's actions, seem not to take the assignment as particularly dangerous either, until Elbridge notices an Iraqi bystander with a phone in his hand. The soldiers sense a threat and order the Iraqi man to put down the phone, to no avail. Thompson hears their shouting and tries to run away from the bomb. The Iraqi presses buttons on the phone, and the bomb explodes. Thompson is killed by the blast wave.

The scene does not illustrate combat and the heavy casualties that result from large-scale military actions. Rather it focuses on a quiet street in Baghdad with no Iraqi soldiers and only three U.S. soldiers, where the only possible danger comes from the bomb. However, the setting leads to the emergence of two important elements salient to the Iraq War. First, as I have argued above in several instances, the War on Terror is characterized by a depersonalization of the enemy; in this scene, the soldiers cannot fully control the so-called battlefield simply because they do not know who exactly will set off the bomb. Additionally, the Iraqis observing the defusing are civilians and the U.S. Army does not expect any threat from them (although the soldiers have to observe everyone, since they suspect there is a disguised enemy among the civilians). Second, the scene succeeds in transmitting, as Caetlin Benson-Allott puts it, "the horror of military violence."[32] Significantly, this is done not with the help of countless dead bodies but rather with a precise and detailed demonstration of the explosion. Whereas the soldiers rush to prevent the bomb's activation, the explosion is depicted in slow motion. And while a moment before the explosion the audience can hardly cope with the speed of the action as the camera quickly switches from one character to another, thus increasing the tension, the explosion itself minutely focuses on the stones lifted from the ground because of the blast wave, and then on the dust and rust coming off an old car. Only after that does the camera focus on Thompson, who falls down; the stones lifted by the explosion smash down to the ground too.

In Thompson's place comes Sergeant First Class William James (Jeremy Renner), who becomes the central character in the film. He stands out due to his fearless attitude, even though he is in Iraq to defuse bombs. He refuses to communicate with Sgt. Sanborn during an operation, and once does not wear a protective suit while defusing a bomb. James does everything to make the audience think that he is either a highly skilled professional or simply does not care about his life. His behavior is clarified at the end of the film, when he is back in the United States. With his family in a supermarket, he is asked by his wife to get cereal. At first he seems to be unsure where the cereal aisle is, but as soon as he finds it, he is overwhelmed: there are too many kinds of cereal. He desperately stares at the boxes, trying to choose one, and finally grabs the closest box. The scene suggests James can more easily defuse a bomb than choose a box of cereal;[33] the war provided a more comfortable environment for James than his civilian life in the U.S. Indeed James Naremore writes, "[James's] hometown Walmart looks more surreal than Baghdad."[34] Later, James removes dead leaves from the gutter of his house and helps his wife in the kitchen while telling her about his experience in Iraq and explaining that the U.S. Army needs soldiers like him. His wife does not display much interest in his stories and smilingly asks him to chop carrots. Later, while playing with their baby, he tells the child that when people get older, there are only a couple of things left that they still love. James, though, clearly articulates that there is only one thing that *he* personally still loves. After these words, the action is transferred back to Iraq, where the audience sees James wearing his protective suit and determinedly walking toward another bomb that needs to be defused. Guy Westwell makes the interesting observation that James's return to war can be explained by the fact that the Iraq War had still been going on when *The Hurt Locker* was released, so the director did not have a possible way out for James. Westwell stresses the difference between the journey back portrayed in *The Hurt Locker* and those in films about earlier wars, specifically in Francis Ford Coppola's Vietnam War drama, *Apocalypse*

Now (1979), arguing that whereas *Apocalypse Now* demonstrates "the neurotic journeying . . . that marked the continued irreconcilability of the experience of Vietnam," *The Hurt Locker* focuses on the soldier's eagerness to return to his military duty to "finish what has been started."[35] One can perhaps explain this difference as the emergence of a new soldier in the twenty-first century, driven by the feelings of patriotism and deep love for his nation that were strongly intensified after 9/11. The new soldier wants to get back to war not because he craves the perverse pleasures of violence and danger but because he perceives war to be obligatory work. In case of James, one might also speculate that he is seduced by war. Bomb disposal brings James a kind of existential clarity—he can cut the right wire and live or the wrong one and die—as well as an escape from the messiness of relationships.

The final important point to address here is the way *The Hurt Locker* portrays U.S. intervention in Iraq. Although the film does not tell its audience why the U.S. military has intruded into Iraq, why there are so many bombs that U.S. soldiers must defuse, and why one can witness Iraqis fighting not only against Americans but also against other Iraqis,[36] it focuses on a significant difficulty that accompanied U.S. intervention in Iraq: the inability to define the enemy. Over the course of the film, the viewer observes James's friendship toward a local boy, called Beckham (Christopher Sayegh). They play football together and James buys DVDs from Beckham. Later, when U.S. soldiers find the body of an Iraqi boy stuffed with explosives, James incorrectly thinks that the boy is Beckham. It falls to James to defuse the bomb in the dead body. This seems to be his first emotionally difficult mission. The scene is important for several reasons. As McSweeney claims, the brutal murder of the boy "becomes a symbol of the need for American intervention." But the tight emotional bond that grows between the soldier and the Iraqi boy, and the ultimate death of the boy, put *the American* into the position of a victim and do not develop the narrative in a direction that would demonstrate that the Iraqi people are those who are suffering. Thus, whereas the intervention is depicted "as a distinctly humanitarian, even altruistic" action, the focus is distorted. Specifically, the intervention and the fight against terrorists are needed in order to avenge James's loss (i.e., the death of the Iraqi boy) but not the Iraqi deaths that result from the actions of terrorists. McSweeney comments on the image of the boy stuffed with explosives: "The fact that there is no recorded evidence of such a scheme ever being used reveals more about the film's desire to imagine monstrosities that continue to demonise Iraqi insurgents while at the same time glorifying James's singular humanity and heroism."[37] One can speculate that the film's desire to exaggerate the violence of the Iraq War is due to its eagerness to justify U.S. intervention as a necessary action to help stop innocent deaths, yet Iraqi violence is employed to justify or perhaps even minimize the violence that Americans committed: compared to what some Iraqi people do—stuffing a boy's corpse with explosives, for example—American war violence is no longer so horrifying.

When the bomb is defused, James covers the boy and gives him to nearby Iraqis to bury. Meanwhile Sanborn and Elbridge discuss whether the dead boy is Beckham. Sanborn at first says that it is definitely Beckham, and then adds with hesitation that he is not sure, because "[Iraqis] all look the same." These words are included in the scene not to demonstrate the arrogance of the Western soldiers who have come to an East populated by indistinguishable people, but rather to underline the inability of the soldiers to distinguish between enemy and nonenemy—the problem that is central to the film's plot. The mission in Iraq concludes with a scene in which James and Sanborn are driving on a Baghdad street and a group of children starts to throw stones at their car. Although the kids can harm neither the soldiers nor their car, they symbolically represent the enemy, thus revealing the friendship between James and Beckham as illegitimate because, as Robert Sklar argues, Beckham belongs to "Iraqi youth," which is defined in this scene as "the Enemy."[38]

The chaos and obscurity of the Iraq War is a common issue raised by films that deal with it. The miniseries *Generation Kill*, defined as a war drama and characterized by a "failure of plot," very vividly considers the problem of the "unnarratability of the Iraq adventure."[39] The first episode starts with a scene showing a group of U.S. marines training before a mission. Over the course of the first four episodes, the audience watches soldiers discussing tactics, complaining about their lack of batteries, singing songs, pestering one another, and chiefly not participating in any military actions at all. At that moment, the only distinct reason for the American presence in the Middle East given to the viewer is to fight terrorists. One understands this justification from the letters that the marines receive from schoolchildren in the first episode. Cpl. Josh Ray Person (James Ransone) reads one of the letters out loud:

Dear Mr. Army Man,
I am proud that you are being brave in defending our country against the terrorists. They are bad and I am glad that you are going to catch them and punish them. I am glad that you are so brave and I pray for you.

The soldiers react rather inadequately to the text, being mainly interested in how the letters smell, and how "hot" the young schoolgirl looks in the photograph she attached to the letter. Another reference to the soldiers' mission to exterminate terrorists can be grasped later, in a scene where a soldier trims his moustache according to army regulations. Another soldier declares that to be sure the size of the moustache is correct it is better to trim it the way he did—Hitler-style. This scene accentuates the brutality of the actions that U.S. soldiers will take against terrorists, metaphorically claiming that the marines will be as merciless toward terrorists as Hitler was against those he declared to be his enemies during World War II.

Yet the audience does not witness many scenes in which soldiers murder terrorists. Instead the miniseries stresses the great number of casualties that are occurring among the civilian population. In the second episode a group of U.S. marines are driving through Iraq, agitated about filming their surroundings, when the driver points at the "dude right there," a mutilated corpse on the roadside, and the soldier with the camera responds, "It's not a dude." The driver becomes serious and asks the soldier to switch off the camera, but the audience sees the mutilated corpse of an Iraqi girl. In the third episode, an Iraqi woman brings her son, with gunshot wounds, to a U.S. military doctor, who ascertains that a U.S. marine has shot the boy. When Evan "Scribe" Wright (Lee Tergesen), a journalist embedded with the soldiers to report on their attack on Baghdad, asks the translator, "Why aren't [the locals] angry?" the translator explains, "They are grateful to be liberated and welcome the Americans as friends." That the main goal of American involvement differs strikingly from the Iraqis' understanding of the U.S. role in the war is articulated in the sixth episode by Lance Cpl. Harold James Trombley (Billy Lush), who discredits Wright's beliefs in the rightness and solidity of the U.S. mission. Wright questions the intervention, saying, "If we're not in our MOPP suits [Mission Oriented Protective Posture equipment used in toxic environments], that means there's no WMDs. If there's no WMDs, then why are we here in the first place?" To which Trombley replies firmly, "The point is we get to kill people." Significantly, who the U.S. soldiers have to kill is not clarified, and one assumes that both terrorist and civilian casualties are part of the normality of this war. The soldiers do not seem to differentiate between the casualties either, which is why the war in Iraq, as it is represented in *Generation Kill*, is a senseless ongoing massacre covered with the soldiers' obsessive desire to exact revenge and install democracy. This argument is vividly illustrated in the seventh episode, when Wright tells Cpl. Gabe Garza (Rey Valentin) that an Iraqi man was shot. He gets this cynical response: "It's too bad. He probably would have liked democracy."

The attitude of the local Iraqis toward the U.S. soldiers is another controversial theme in the miniseries, given that the episodes are filled with killed and mutilated children. Toward the end of the fourth episode, the viewer witnesses U.S. soldiers staring in shock at the backseat of a car, where they have found a dead girl, around five years old. The girl was killed because the soldiers opened fire after the car's driver did not stop after a warning shot. Eventually the father of the dead girl apologizes for not stopping; the soldiers do not even apologize for killing his child. The soldiers come to understand, though they hardly ever articulate it, that their actions in this war are mostly wrong. In the sixth episode, Sgt. Antonio Espera (Jon Huertas) confesses his anxiety to Sgt. Brad "Iceman" Colbert (Alexander Skarsgård): "You realize the shit that we've done here? People we've killed? Back in the civilian world, Dog, if we did this, we would go to prison." Colbert responds, "Poke, you're thinking like a Mexican again. Think like a white man. Over there they'll be laying on medals for what we did." The attitude portrays the intervention as the right thing to do by the white West toward the inferior East, echoing the perspective of the colonial era.

The tragedy of the war is further underlined in the last episode, when a U.S. military doctor comforts an Iraqi boy, whereas no Iraqi is interested in the child. Instead, the Iraqis steal candy from the sick children. Later in the same episode, Brad tries to remove ordnance near where children are playing, though he understands this might cost him his life. The apotheosis of military savagery and intellectual vacancy is an incident narrated by the soldiers, in which "some newly arrived grunts slaughtered some Iraqi kids who were playing on blown tanks." The killing is justified by the children being "on top of the tanks," which made them appear "technically armed." The miniseries persistently emphasizes that Iraqi children are the main victims of the war, as they suffer at the hands of both the marauding locals and the U.S. soldiers.

The civilian population, however, reacts mostly positively to the presence of U.S. troops over the course of the miniseries; they treat Americans as their saviors. It seems that the Iraqis are ready to cope with the deaths of their own children because this is an integral part of war—collateral damage. Yet in the sixth episode, when a group of U.S. soldiers let a group of Iraqi people pass through their block, one of the women from the crowd speaks: "Thank you, soldier. Thank you for letting me pass on my own road in my own country. . . . Why are you Americans here? . . . You know I come from Baghdad. It is a beautiful city and you are bombing it. This is to make my life better? . . . You know, this is a very beautiful county and our president is very stupid. Maybe you are here for liberation, I don't know, but because of oil, it feel like war of aggression." The woman's lamentation is already the second time the reference to the hidden cause of U.S. involvement in Iraq is made in the miniseries. The Iraq War, or the Second Gulf War, is linked to the First Gulf War as early as the first episode, when a marine says to Sergeant Espera, "You believe this shit? These people still haven't picked up the trash from the last war." Espera does not seem concerned with the sorrow and loss that the ongoing war in Iraq has caused the local people: "People've been fighting over this bitch since ancient times, Dog. How many graves we're standing on?" At this phrase, the camera focuses on the ground that the soldier is urinating on, signifying the disrespect and indifference he feels toward the Iraqis who have died (and will die) in war. Espera continues, "Think about all the wisdom and science and money and civilization it took to build these machines, and the courage of all the men who came here, and the love of their wives and children that was in their hearts. And all that hate, Dog. All the hate it took to blow these motherfuckers away. It's destiny, Dog. White man's gonna rule the world." Not only are the soldier's words full of racism (which is characteristic of Espera, who endlessly complains about the dominance and rule of the white man and the oppression of other races), but they also transmit ideas about American patriotism combined with good intentions to liberate the territory that began in the early 1990s. Now it is the "destiny" of the United States to fight this war all over again, to win it and thus demonstrate American might. Later, in the second episode, Espera "elucidate[s] on the white man's burden": "The U.S. should just go into all these fucked up countries—Iraq, Africa—set up American government and infrastructure—McDonald's, Starbucks, MTV—then just hand it all over. I mean, how else we gonna make these hungry motherfuckers want to stop killing everybody? Put a

McDonald's on every fucking corner. If we gotta blow up the corner, then build the McDonald's—so be it." All these failures in U.S. policy and, consequently, in the intervention shown throughout the miniseries are important to consider in relation to the main aim of the U.S. mission in Iraq, articulated in the first episode by Sgt. Maj. John Sixta (Neal Jones) in his appeal to the soldiers: "Your president is watching! America is watching! But more important, Godfather is watching! Make no mistake! There . . . will . . . be . . . no . . . fuck-ups!" Toward the end of the miniseries, these words echo in mockery of the short-sightedness of U.S. intervention, the unsuccessful operations, and the overall improvidence of the American military actions.

The fifth episode of *Generation Kill* is crucial, because this is the first time the miniseries focuses on real combat. Right before the combat is shown, the audience hears a dialogue between Lt. Nathaniel Fick (Stark Sands) and Sergeant Espera. Fick encourages the group: "We all know we've killed a lot of bad guys already." Espera remarks, "Sure. Must be some bad guys in all those women and children we've been stacking along the roads." The scene once again underlines the problem of civilian casualties that result from insufficiently planned operations. Soon after the attack, another important scene takes place, when the soldiers find out that one of the men they killed in combat is of Syrian origin and, as it is stated in his passport, he was in Iraq as a jihadi. Capt. Craig "Encino Man" Schwetje (Brian Wade) comments, "They're coming here to fight us. I wonder if President Bush will ever find out about this. This is what the president's been talking about with the war on terrorists. This is why we're here." With respect to this incident, Fick makes a very controversial observation: "Those jihadists who attacked us? Isn't this the exact opposite of what we want to have happen here? It's all on that guy's passport. Two weeks ago he was still a student in Syria. He wasn't a jihadi until we came to Iraq." This pivotal remark in *Generation Kill* foregrounds a suspicion that U.S. intervention—though frequently considered an act of liberation—could be the main reason for the growing violence, aggressiveness, and savagery in Iraq, which clearly undermines the humanitarianism of the U.S. mission, especially in the eyes of some of the inhabitants of the Middle East.

The miniseries also draws parallels with the war in Afghanistan, when in the fifth episode Sgt. Eric Kocher (Owain Yeoman) says that the bombing of villages in Iraq was never something that took place in Afghanistan. Earlier, in the third episode, staking out a village full of children and women, the soldiers recollect how in Afghanistan they had children running *toward* them. All in all, U.S. involvement in Afghanistan is characterized in the miniseries as a better planned and strategically more accurate operation than the Iraq occupation, an intervention that incurred many fewer casualties among civilians than in Iraq.

The ending of *Generation Kill* makes quite a prominent statement, as soldiers watch a video they shot during their military service in Iraq.[40] They are excited, riled up, commenting happily on what they see on the screen. But as the video goes on, showing casualties and devastation, the soldiers realize how horrifying their actions were and how terrible the intervention was. The consequences of the U.S. failure in the Iraq War become most apparent in the video, which offers a comprehensive summary of the mistakes made by the U.S. soldiers. The soldiers slowly start to leave, unwilling to see the video through to the end: only Trombley (the soldier who shot the Iraqi boy and showed no remorse about it) remains, smiling and clearly enjoying the video, then maliciously looking around when he realizes he is alone in the room. He takes his rifle and determinedly leaves. He appears to be the only soldier in *Generation Kill* who has not come to understand the folly of U.S. intervention.

All the films that deal with the Iraq War reveal the general confusion of the intervention and ultimately show disapproval. *In the Valley of Elah*, for example, opens with an image of the American flag flying upside down. It is put into its proper position by the military police veteran Hank Deerfield (Tommy Lee Jones), who worries that somebody will see the upside-down flag and correctly interpret it as "an international distress signal": "It means we're in a whole lot of trouble, so come save our ass cause we don't have a prayer in hell of saving ourselves." At the end of the film, however, having found out that his son was brutally murdered in Iraq by his own comrades, Deerfield returns to the flag, and this time turns it upside down, suggesting that the United States is sinking in the quicksand of war violence and needs somebody to help it get out.

Some films contend that the circle of violence cannot be stopped because whenever the U.S. avenges 9/11 and tries to prevent further attacks, the terrorists will consider any retaliatory or preemptive intervention to be an assault and will seek their own revenge. This complex issue is a primary focus in *Body of Lies*, as terrorists openly announce, "We will avenge American wars on the Muslim world. We will come at them. Everywhere. We will strike at random, across Europe and then America, continually. We have bled. And now . . . they will bleed." In *The Kingdom* the opening scene narrates a brief history of U.S. relations with the Middle East, openly suggesting that U.S. involvement in the Arab (Muslim) world is precisely what made the terrorists turn against the U.S. Of course, none of these films supports terrorists; none creates a good image of them or depicts them as the victims of the U.S. Army. Rather, in showing both sides of the conflict, the films' main concern is to reveal the amount of violence that the war has generated as well as the complexity of the problem that provides no easy solution. Yet these films also make the viewer think about the violence committed by some American soldiers; instead of taking 9/11 as the start of the war, they demonstrate a broader view of the problem, suggesting that the U.S. made mistakes that led to 9/11 and has continued making them during the War on Terror. In this respect, *Boys of Abu Ghraib* is a vivid example of American violence in Iraq, where the actions of particular soldiers are overtly compared to those of Saddam Hussein: both the Iraqi dictator's men and the American soldiers tortured their captives who were against the "regime"—whether that took the form of Saddam's tyranny or fledgling democracy in the American style—in the prison Abu Ghraib.

Literature and U.S. Intervention in the Iraq War

"We Were Bred to Protect": Matt Gallagher's *Kaboom: Embracing the Suck in a Savage Little War* (2010)

Matt Gallagher's *Kaboom*—a novel that is based on the blog that Gallagher wrote during his military service (which explains the choice of the first-person point of view), describes what he and his comrades had to go through while in Iraq: from the everyday routine on the military base to their actual missions and combat actions. This docufictional narrative raises a large number of poignant issues that have become inseparable from the war in Iraq. From the discussion of the instability in Iraq that is mainly grounded on the ongoing confrontations between Shias and Sunnis, it moves to describe the experience of U.S. soldiers, whose aim in Iraq is to stabilize the region. Working in cooperation with the local forces, the soldiers aim to bring peace and democracy to this country so that Iraqi children can enjoy their lives without being scared that they might die any moment and, thus, can have a future.

Like many other narratives of the twenty-first-century U.S. interventions in the Middle East, *Kaboom* explicitly states that the main character volunteered to fight in Iraq because of 9/11. The attacks have changed every American: "Something had happened. Something new. Something historic. Something profound. And it hadn't been created in a Hollywood studio, either. America had been attacked, innocent people had died, and there was going to be a reckoning my children and grandchildren would read about some day."[41] For the protagonist—and arguably for thousands of other American soldiers—it was important to become "a part of" that "reckoning" (372). Yet while the actions of American military men and women were aimed at freeing the country from terrorism—and also avenging the deaths of innocent Americans—and helping to develop Iraq, the plan did not work out smoothly for one simple reason: Iraqis did not want such help. This is the key message that the novel tries to transmit to readers. There were, of course, cases of collaboration: many Iraqis risked their lives working as interpreters or informing soldiers about suspicious activities. Nevertheless many other Iraqis wanted the Americans out of their country. In short, most local Iraqis were "either unable or unwilling" (15) to aid the Americans. One reason, observes the protagonist, was that the Iraqis believed that the Americans had come for oil, whereas—and this is what *Kaboom* articulates most explicitly—the aim of the soldiers was, in fact, to bring democracy to and improve the lives of the local population. Pivotal lines in the book declare, "Goddamn it. Remember why you're here, I thought to myself. It isn't for *your* dreams. It's for *theirs*. Stay sharp" (115; my italics). The desire to build a peaceful future for the Iraqi children most horribly victimized by the war—"They didn't even know what they didn't have, but they did know they didn't have it" (391; italics in original)—is one of the premises of the intervention.

However, the plan to liberate the Iraqi people and eventually bring democracy did not work out: "Telling them we knew what was best and that they needed to start relying on their own government and police so we could leave, that everyone would win that way and any help we could and did provide in the meantime at least offered a new spring in a land of endless, destitute winters, often didn't have the effect I thought it would. Or should" (103). The mission of bringing freedom and democracy turned into a morass of mutual misunderstanding and hatred because the locals did not want U.S. military patrolling the streets and checking houses, whereas the U.S. soldiers could not understand why the locals were not willing to help them and would not accept what America had to offer. "I hated being hated" (105), says the protagonist, aptly summarizing the attitudes of Iraqis toward American soldiers. At the same time, the local Iraqis never ceased demanding benefits. For example, the novel describes the "complaints" voiced by every Iraqi in the city of Saba al-Bor: "'We don't have clean water.' 'We don't have jobs.' 'We only have fifteen minutes of electricity per day because the Sunnis take it all.' But the Sunnis say the Shias take all the electricity,

I remembered. 'They Ali Babas. We think America very good. Gimme water, mistah. Gimme job, mistah. Gimme power, America.' Gimme, gimme, gimme" (112).

Unable to immediately provide the locals with all these benefits, the Americans, as the novel makes quite explicit, risked annoying Iraqis with their military presence even more and thus provoked more hatred. Indeed the part of the operation aimed at improving living conditions in Iraq failed, and the U.S. presence in the country eventually turned into a straightforward occupation, especially in the eyes of the locals. Thus only more hatred was generated. It is pivotal in this respect that the novel addresses the problem of Iraqi children, claiming that they are "future terrorists" (109). The purpose of this strong comparison is certainly not to label every Iraqi a terrorist but rather to criticize U.S. intervention that resulted in an occupation that manufactured strong resentments. This occupation is exactly what will make the future generations of Iraqis view Americans as the enemy: "They will grow up hating America! . . . And they will be wrong, but that will not change anything" (148–49). These prophetic words are aptly proved when an eight-year-old Iraqi girl refuses to collaborate with the protagonist and his Iraqi interpreter because the former is American and the latter is "American now" (186).

The novel continues to meditate upon the problem of bringing democracy and liberty to Iraq. *Kaboom* first elucidates why the U.S. had to intervene: "*We'll fight the fights not because we necessarily want to but because no one else will. We were bred to protect*" (201–2; italics in original). The words obviously go hand in hand with the ideology of American exceptionalism; they also intend to justify U.S. intervention as a humanitarian mission, whose only goal was to *protect* the people of Iraq, denying that any other material or economic benefits were sought after, as these are frequently taken to be the main reasons for U.S. involvement. Next, *Kaboom* attempts to explain the futility of the intervention:

Hurt. There's just so much of it. Especially here. It's an abyss. I can't help these people. No one can. They can't help themselves, and neither can the great American sympathy.

There it is again. The siren's song of gone. A freedom bird that doesn't land anywhere at all. It just hovers there, waiting. The ultimate escape. Enticingly empty and hollow and spotless and smooth. Oh, so smooth. (203; italics in original)

The problem of imposing democracy is one of the most persistent issues in the novel. Apart from using the metaphor of the *"freedom bird,"* the narrator compares the act of bringing democracy to Iraq to the vivid example of *"a lizard and its tail"*: *"We wanted to slice off the chaos tail without smashing in the lizard's head, hoping a democracy tail would grow in the meantime. We learned firsthand that wasn't how lizards or their tails worked"* (392; italics in original). The novel does not simply criticize the approach chosen by the U.S. to impose democracy; first and foremost, it censures the lack of any historical understanding of the region the U.S. is now dealing with. "Government? This is Iraq, not America. We are tribal society, not democracy. Don't you Americans read any history books? The sheiks *are* government in Arab culture!" (242; italics in original). The narrator laments that while the cause of the intervention was just, it was not achievable because it is impossible to change what has been the norm in that society for centuries. Hence the skeptical and, at times, hostile attitude of the locals toward the invaders took shape not because all Iraqis are terrorists but simply because they considered the intervention and intrusion from the outside a threat to their customary way of life.

For the American people at home, the war did not seem very clear either, and the novel criticizes their failure to understand the war from their domestic vantage: "Thank you for what you do; please return home safely; we'll pray for you. Empty words from an empty people— they wanted to show that they cared, but our experience was so unlike anything in their realm of understanding, only trodden clichés could fill their vacuum of confusion" (168). Can one blame the nation's people for not being able to comprehend the war, when no one was providing a clear explanation for U.S. involvement and, what is even more important, it was impossible to foresee the end of the war?[42] The Iraq War, considered a "forever war" in the novel (350), was the "war no one cared about, let alone understood" (139); thus the bewilderment of American civilians "wasn't their fault . . . something [Gallagher] didn't yet understand when [he] was still in Iraq" (168).

The novel eventually moves to a discussion of war veterans and their reintegration back into U.S. society, revealing the hardships of resuming a normal life after one has seen killings and other forms of loss and death in Iraq. Hence *Kaboom* presents a cluster of problems caused by the intervention: first, the overall failure in Iraq, which was the result of badly planned military and political strategies; second, the presence of a generation of the Iraq War veterans who, upon returning to the U.S., had trouble reintegrating into society; third, the hatred of Iraqis toward the U.S. for invading their country. Gallagher comments on that hatred toward the end of the novel: "When American forces pulled back from the cities fully in June 2009, the Iraqis celebrated with fireworks. I found their choice of festivity slightly ironic, yet fitting. A few months certainly hadn't changed their love for all things that blast and go boom" (441). This illustrates that the locals were happy when the U.S. troops withdrew and the intervention was effectively over; it also reveals that during the long years of war the Iraqis simply got used to the constant sounds of shooting and bombing; hearing fireworks explode, they were not scared but rather considered those sounds to be an integral part of their environment. On the other hand, casting the Iraqis as a people who love things that explode can be interpreted as comparing them to terrorists, which proves that the image of Iraqis as terrorists did not change even after the U.S. military ended its occupation of Iraq. The intervention, according to *Kaboom*, was a failure because it neither brought democracy to Iraq, nor did it change the American perception of people from the Middle East, whom many Americans still regard as a threat.

"We Were Fighting in Iraq Because We Were Fighting in Iraq": Phil Klay's *Redeployment* (2014)

Klay's short-story cycle *Redeployment* provides a multidimensional view of the Iraq War: it tells the reader what it means to be in war, in real combat; it describes life on a military base and the routines imposed on soldiers; it raises the issue of the veteran's reintegration into civilian life in his homeland. The problem of war veterans is most distinctly present in the cycle, but the following analysis will only briefly focus on it; my major concern here is to give an overview of the American soldiers' wartime experience, considering the issue of U.S. interventionism via the Iraq War. Just as in *Dear Mr. President*, the stories in *Redeployment* are revealed from the first-person point of view. While this makes the stories unreliable, the *I*'s turn them into the soldiers' diaries—the numerous experiences that the reader learns about from the short-story cycle that presents multiple views on the Iraq War.

Redeployment offers a very controversial view of that war, though it does not distinctly reveal whether it supports the intervention. This lack of clarity, however, illustrates the controversial nature of the war itself. The collection was published in 2014, by which time the author obviously had an overview of the conflict and the policies that informed it; nonetheless it is written by a war veteran concerned with conveying (and, therefore, reflecting) his personal experiences in Iraq and his life after his return home. His priorities were to confront the war's concrete reality and to tell the reader honestly how it was.

The stories explore various problems faced by the soldiers while in Iraq. For example, regarding the soldiers' feelings during their service, the narrator points out that:

> Somebody said combat is 99 percent sheer boredom and 1 percent pure terror. They weren't an MP in Iraq. On the roads I was scared all the time. Maybe not pure terror. That's for when the IED actually goes off. But a kind of low-grade terror that mixes with the boredom. So it's 50 percent boredom and 49 percent normal terror, which is a

general feeling that *you might die at any second* and that *everybody in this country wants to kill you.* Then, of course, there's the 1 percent pure terror, when your heart rate skyrockets and your vision closes in and your hands are white and your body is humming. *You can't think. You're just an animal, doing what you've been trained to do.* And then you go back to normal terror, and you go back to being a human, and you go back to thinking.[43]

The passage vividly describes how the soldier, placed in the midst of the Iraq War, yields his purported role as a liberator to a new role, that of a target: he is considered the enemy in this country where he is not wanted. He has to adapt to this attitude and simply do his job, perform his duties.

Another issue that the stories touch upon, linked to the previous one, is killing, which is "not easy": "Out of boot camp, Marines act like they're gonna play Rambo, but it's fucking serious, it's professional" (3). In this connection, the cycle's central killing scene, described in the story "After Action Report," occurs when one of the soldiers, Timhead, shoots an Iraqi boy. That is not a random murder: the boy posed a threat to U.S. soldiers, aiming a weapon at them. However, his being a child raises a question of ethics and, what is more, the matter of child murder in war. The soldier perceives this killing differently than he would have had the victim been an adult man. His moral struggle and guilt can be understood from his comment: "I signed up to kill hajjis" (40). Another soldier counters that Timhead came to Iraq to *replace his brother*—another marine who died in action—but it is still evident that Timhead cannot forget that he has killed a child. He wonders how old the child was, and his comrade responds, "Old enough to know it's a bad fucking idea to shoot at U.S. Marines" (40). Thus there is a significant difference in the portrayal of an Iraqi boy in *Redeployment* than in *The Hurt Locker*. The former overtly depicts the child as the enemy—a direct threat to U.S. marines. Yet both children can be perceived as innocent victims of war. The boy from *Redeployment* dies not because of the cruelty of U.S. soldiers but because the war made weapons accessible to him, and the idea of shooting at Americans was inculcated through the example of his family members and neighbors. This argument is supported later in the book, when the protagonist says that the child was not "crazy," according to "hajji standards" (44), suggesting that Iraqi children are no longer mere witnesses to the war in their country; they have become participants: they take up weapons as the primary activity of their present and future lives. When the reader finds out that the boy's sister witnessed the murder, one of the soldiers comments, "This might not even be the most fucked-up thing she's seen" (49). The reader is once again reminded that for Iraqi children, death is an everyday reality. And when *Redeployment* tries to draw parallels between the Iraqi girl and an American girl (Timhead's sister), it articulates the difference between the two, suggesting the innocence and moral purity of the latter, and the lack of these qualities in the former: "There's explosions in this city every fucking day. There's firefights in this city every fucking day. That's her home. That's in the streets where she plays. This girl is probably fucked up in ways we can't even imagine. She's not your sister. She's just not. She's seen it before" (50). Even the fact that the girl has witnessed the death of her brother but nonetheless seems fine is explained by one of the soldiers: having already witnessed too much death, she is now "numb" (50).

In "Prayer in the Furnace," there is a similar example. A small boy plants an explosive, but, as the soldiers themselves acknowledge, he "couldn't know what he was doing" (148). For that reason the soldiers do not kill the child. In the story U.S. soldiers are not plainly bad characters or child murderers. One of the soldiers describes how, when his unit was under fire once, the enemy used children as human shields, and the U.S. soldiers refused to fire back: "They [the soldiers] let themselves get shot at because they didn't want to risk hurting children" (145). There are, of course, casualties among civilians, including children, but, as the book makes clear, this is not what the U.S. soldiers were trying to do. In "Psychological Operations," for example, the main character frankly states, "Marines don't like killing children. It fucks them up in the head" (202). Instead of just censuring the deaths caused by war, *Redeployment* attempts to analyze the problem not from a position of what is good and what is bad but by placing it in the context of the war, a sphere where the soldier, apart from choosing between good and bad, also has to choose between death and life.

The intervention itself is characterized through its portrayal of U.S. soldiers and their actions. While the killing of Iraqi children undermines the role of the soldiers as liberators and makes them look instead like murderers of innocent civilians, there are also positive references to the marines. The narrator uses an interesting metaphor to describe one of the soldiers, a man who displays a "huge Superman *S* he got tattooed on his chest before deployment" (21). The man is compared to an American comics character, one who is famous for his superpowers and his desire to fight evil. The metaphor (albeit ironically) helps the reader envisage the U.S. soldiers as potentially positive characters who are in Iraq to perform the important mission of freeing the oppressed and punishing the oppressor.

Redeployment attempts to explain the intervention in Iraq through the soldiers' opinions. Yet the closest it gets are two elucidations: "We were fighting in Iraq because we were fighting in Iraq," and "Fighting the fight of good versus evil. Democracy versus Islam" (78). Not being able to provide a clear reason for the conflict, the short-story cycle compares the Iraq War to other U.S. wars: "Success was a matter of perspective. In Iraq it had to be. There was no Omaha Beach, no Vicksburg Campaign, not even an Alamo to signal a clear defeat. The closest we'd come were those toppled Saddam statues, but that was years ago" (77). One can speculate that the story's main message is that when there are no specific goals, there can be no specific actions that would make Americans feel proud of their soldiers. The story further suggests that the U.S. mission—to bring freedom and democracy—was desired only by Americans, not by Iraqis. For example, one of the cities in Iraq is called "Istalquaal," which means "freedom" or "liberation," yet Americans, not Iraqis, had given this place that name (83). The motif of imposition becomes apparent in this context: the U.S. is imposing an order it thinks Iraq should have. It comes as no surprise that Iraqis blame the Americans for their actions, claiming that the Americans "destroyed this country" (85).

One of the stories, "Psychological Operations," suggests oil as a potential reason for the intervention. A veteran comments on the opinion of his female friend that the U.S. invaded Iraq because of oil: "I was one of those people invading Iraq . . . and I didn't give a damn about oil. Neither did a single soldier I knew" (171). The woman vehemently responds, "Who cares what the soldiers believe? It doesn't matter what the pawns on a chessboard think about how and why they're being played" (171). Relying on this brief dialogue, one can speculate that the story sees oil as the main reason for the invasion and suggests that the soldier's statement expresses little more than his personal viewpoint on why he is fighting in Iraq. That is, while a soldier might consider his service to be a righteous mission because he is willing to sacrifice his life for the sake of other people's freedom, in reality he is fighting for purely economic reasons. This is a crucial moment of realization, which also explains the soldier's saying, "Talking with anybody who thought they had a clear view of Iraq tended to make me want to rub shit in their eyes" (173). It reveals his self-justification about his service in Iraq. Soldiers clearly want to believe in personal or national, just and honorable reasons for their deployment. And in the case of the Iraq War, just as in the case of the Vietnam War, veterans seek the support of the people back home to prove to themselves that their time spent in one of the most dangerous places on earth was not for nothing, and that civilians appreciate their service and consider them to be heroes and liberators. The controversial nature of the intervention and the ongoing debate on the Iraq War, however, mean that there is no single answer to whether the intervention was as right and necessary as the one that, for example, took place during World War II. The main character's motivation for joining the army, as the reader later finds out, was also influenced by his inability to afford paying college tuition, which, one can assume, was a problem faced by other soldiers too. Additionally, the main character was influenced by his over-the-top patriotic father, who, when his son was already in the army, tried to demonstrate that he was serving in the most honorable way possible: "He'd send me PowerPoints with pictures of soldiers, or jokes and speeches about 'the troops' that talked about them like they shat gold" (199). Yet the story also comments on the idea that the soldiers' understanding of the war could, indeed, be very personal and did not necessarily coincide with the government's profiteering. But that does not matter when they are back home; only national approval of their service in Iraq matters: "You risked your life for something bigger than yourself. How many people can say that? You chose to serve. Maybe you never will. But it doesn't matter. You held up your hand and said, 'I'm willing to die for these worthless civilians'" (203). Their nation's approval and appreciation for their service is what the veterans seek.

In *Redeployment*, the mission of the U.S. in the end turns into a parade of meaningless tasks: teaching the locals how to keep bees, and how to play baseball. Beekeeping is eventually mocked when the protagonist imagines "Iraqi Widow Honey in U.S. supermarkets" and a TV commercial inviting, "Try the sweet taste of Iraqi freedom" (87). Baseball is an even more ridiculous thing to do in war-torn Iraq, yet apparently there are people who think that only through baseball can Iraq be vaccinated with democracy:

> Here is the idea: The Iraqi people want democracy, but it's not taking. Why? They don't have the INSTITUTIONS to support it. You can't build anything with a rotten foundation, and Iraqi culture is, I'm sure, as rotten as it gets.
>
> I know this sounds crazy, but there are few better institutions than the institution of BASEBALL. Look at the Japanese. They went from Emperor-loving fascists to baseball-playing democracy freaks faster than you can say, Sayonara, Hirohito!
>
> What I'm saying is, you've got to change the CULTURE first. And what's more AMERICAN than baseball. (10; emphasis in original)

U.S. intervention is clearly described in this passage as an imperialist endeavor to impose a regime that the U.S. considers best. Moreover, through the ideas that Iraqi culture is dead and the nation's traditions are plainly wrong, and foregrounding the American tradition as the only correct one, the story hints at the dogmas of the ideology of American exceptionalism. Yet it is impossible to claim that the story positions this view as the only right one: the protagonist openly rejects the idea of teaching baseball to Iraqis, whose current needs are more vitally important than the American game. One can speculate that the story's main aim is to contrast the two viewpoints, chiefly to contend that there were different visions of the U.S. mission in Iraq, and, it seems, none was thoroughly thought through. Nevertheless it would be wrong to argue that the short-story cycle completely gives up on the positive side of the intervention. For instance, in "Prayer in the Furnace," "violence dropped in that city [Ramadi] like ninety-something percent" (166), thanks to the hard work of U.S. marines.

Just as the soldier strives to understand what his mission in Iraq is, so do the American people back home. When the protagonist in the story "Bodies" returns home, he is thanked for his service, yet "nobody seemed to know exactly what they were thanking [him] for" (63). Everybody seems to blindly believe that the Iraq intervention was only positive, but no one bothers much about the details. The soldier's sarcastic remark while at home—"Come on, cat, . . . I've been defending your freedom. At least let me pet you" (64)—reveals his frustration with the collective response to his service, but it also mocks the intervention, whose main aim was to defend the freedom of either the citizens of the U.S. (from terrorist attacks) or the Iraqi people (from Saddam's and the terrorists' oppression). The story "Psychological Operations" deals with this problem, too, yet does so from a different perspective: it reveals the reactions of a group of Muslim Americans to the service of their friend's son (also a Muslim). They send the man notes with supportive phrases like "Good job, thank you for your service"; "Whether this war is right or wrong, you have done an honorable thing"; and even "Whatever you go through, it is the responsibility of those who sent you" (205). While most of the other messages are "real pro-war" (205), these three clearly display the public's confusion about the war and the disagreement among citizens with regard to the decision to intervene. It is also important that the opinions of the Muslim people—some of whom, as the story suggests, no longer felt comfortable living in the U.S. after 9/11—construct an array of pros and cons, showing that the war is not about religion but, in fact, about terrorists, who should be eliminated no matter whether they are Muslims, Christians, or anyone else.

One of the concluding messages of the short-story cycle is revealed in the dialogue between two veterans in the story "Unless It's a Sucking Chest Wound," when one asks, "Iraq . . . What do you think? Did we win?," and the other responds, "Uhh . . . we did okay" (268). Even the soldiers cannot negotiate this issue and come to a firm conclusion; even those who directly participated in and witnessed the war are not sure about its result and about the ultimate fate of the Iraqi people, or the relations between the United States and the Middle East, particularly Iraq. Was the involvement in Iraq the right thing to do, or was it a brutal, meaningless fight? It seems that *Redeployment* supports the latter viewpoint. Take the following conversation from its final story, "Ten Kliks South":

"If we used a howitzer to kill somebody back in the States," I say, "I wonder what crime they'd charge us with."

"Murder," says Sergeant Deetz. "What are you, an idiot?"

"Yeah, murder, sure," I say, "but for each of us? In what degree? I mean, me and Bolander and Jewett loaded, right? If I loaded an M16 and handed it to Voorstadt and he shot somebody, I wouldn't say I'd killed anyone."

"It's a crew-served weapon," says Sergeant Deetz. "Crew. Served. Weapon. It's different."

"And I loaded, but we got the ammo from the ASP [Ammunition Supply Point]," I say. "Shouldn't they be responsible, too, the ASP Marines?"

"Yeah," says Jewett. "Why not the ASP?"

"Why not the factory workers who made the ammo?" says Sergeant Deetz. "Or the taxpayers who paid for it? You know why not? Because that's retarded."

"The lieutenant gave the order," I say. "He'd get it in the court, right?"

"Oh, you believe that? You think officers would take the hit?" Voorstadt laughs. "How long you been in the military?" (274–75)

The scene explicitly articulates that what the soldiers did in Iraq was plain murder. And although the comparison of actions taken in Iraq—a country where war is being fought—to the same sort of actions had they been committed in the peaceful U.S. seems at first sight far-fetched, the main purpose of this conversation is to show that if U.S. soldiers had taken military actions of that kind in the U.S., killing American people in ways that would have been regarded as murder, then why should U.S. intervention in Iraq, with its massive number of civilian deaths, not be considered a breeding ground for murder too? Another important issue that the conversation touches upon is guilt. Talking about the weapon, the narrator describes the whole sociopolitical system that was involved in conducting the intervention. Many tend to blame individual soldiers for their "wrong" actions in Iraq, but it is important to realize that the war was conducted with "crew-served weapon[s]": there is a chain of people who made the decision to intervene, created the plan (however poorly), and sent soldiers to perform their jobs. Thus if the intervention was a mistake, it was a mistake made primarily by the state rather than by the soldiers doing its bidding.

The Philosophy of the Iraq War in Kevin Powers's The Yellow Birds (2012)

While Powers's novel can chiefly be read as a story of an Iraq War veteran (the first-person point of view contributes to the creation of an illusion that this is a memoir) whose aim is to reflect the horror of war and to meditate upon the philosophical nature of war as a destructive force, parts of the novel also describe the U.S. participation in the Iraq War and, therefore, deal with the issue of intervention. *The Yellow Birds* provides two perspectives on the intervention in Iraq: first, it attempts to explain the rationale for intervention, both justifying and criticizing the war; and, second, discussing war as a philosophical phenomenon, the novel showcases the intervention as an inevitable military action, where American soldiers are left without any alternative but to fight.

The reasons for the involvement are provided explicitly. First, the novel starts with a narration of the events that took place in Al Tafar, Nineveh Province, on September 2004. While there is no overt reference to U.S. involvement in Iraq as a response to 9/11, the fact that the Al Tafar fighting takes place in September can be understood as a link to the 2001 attacks. Thus *The Yellow Birds*, like other novels on the War on Terror, makes reference to the tragic events on September 11, 2001, highlighting that day as a crucial point in twenty-first-century U.S. (military) history. Second, the soldiers themselves clearly realize and accept their status as an intervening force. "I was an intruder, at best a visitor," says the main character of the novel, Bartle, revealing his understanding of the intervention as a military intrusion into a foreign territory.[44] Bartle thinks of the local Iraqis as people who "waited patiently for us [American soldiers] to leave, for the enemy to leave. . . . When the battle was over they would come back and begin to sweep the shells off the roofs of their houses. . . . They would fill buckets of water and splash them over dried, coppery blood on their doorsteps" (84). The image of the soldier as an intruder only worsens over the course of the narration, and when Bartle returns to the U.S., he characterizes himself as "the murderer, the fucking accomplice, the at-bare-minimum bearer of some fucking responsibility" (145). In this characterization the intervention is a means of sanctioning murder.

Before one of the missions, a colonel addresses the soldiers under his command with the following speech: "Boys . . . you will soon be asked to do great violence in the cause of good. . . . This is the land where

Jonah is buried, where he begged for God's justice to come. . . . We are that justice" (87). The leitmotif of American warfare as waging a war of justice (importantly, this claim is made by a commanding officer) is braided through the novel, presenting the intervention as a war against evil. The monologue continues, "Now, I wish I could tell you that all of us are coming back, but I can't. Some of you will not come back with us. . . . I can't go with you boys . . . but I'll be in contact from the operation center the whole time. Give 'em hell" (87). The speech is clearly a pep talk for the upcoming fight, but the colonel is not a direct participant in this fight; he is an instructor who only gives orders, without himself taking part in combat operations on the ground. That is, while explaining to the soldiers that some of them will die performing this mission, he declares that some will return "with us," which means that he is assured of being a survivor. The novel offers an interesting insight into a problem of modern warfare, in which members of the commanding staff are usually not present on the battlefield and the soldiers under their command perform the whole of the "work." Indeed the ironic comment of the narrator—also the novel's protagonist, Bartle—on the colonel's speech reflects this situation: "The speech was the colonel's pride, his satisfaction with his own directness, his disregard for us as individuals" (87).

There is, however, another pivotal point made by the colonel in his speech: "We're counting on you, boys. The people of the United States are counting on you. You may never do anything this important again in your entire lives" (89). The colonel's words characterize the intervention as a highly significant mission, whose success lies completely on the shoulders of its participants—who, in turn, should consider this opportunity a sign of great trust because the interests of the United States are at stake, and the mission's outcome will show whether or not U.S. principles will be defended and promoted. The attitude of the soldiers—who may die in Iraq—is not so pompous, and when one of them, Murph, asks the narrator, "You think this is really the most important thing we'll ever do, Bartle?" Bartle replies, "I hope not" (90). Murph's hesitation, along with Bartle's skeptical response, illustrates the soldiers' negative attitude toward the war and suggests that the intervention and its inevitable killing cannot and should not be imposed on the soldier as the most significant thing one can do. Perhaps the achievement of such a goal as liberation can be treated as "the most important thing [one']ll ever do," yet the novel, in presenting the intervention in concrete terms as a bloody fight, does not endorse the notion that it is an event that one should feel proud to have participated in. Bartle's meditation on the mission in Iraq strongly supports this assumption:

> I thought of my grandfather's war. How they had destinations and purpose. How the next day we'd march out under a sun hanging low over the plains in the east. We'd go back into a city that had fought this battle yearly; a slow, bloody parade in fall to mark the change of season. We'd drive them out. We always had. We'd kill them. They'd shoot us and blow off our limbs and run into the hills and wadis, back into the alleys and dusty villages. Then they'd come back, and we'd start over by waving to them as they leaned against lampposts and unfurled green awnings while drinking tea in front of their shops. While we patrolled the streets, we'd throw candy to their children with whom we'd fight in the fall a few more years from now. (91)

The intervention in Iraq is a bounding routine, an endless duty that the soldier has to perform as if locked within a vicious circle. It is obviously on purpose that the novel evokes World War II, in which the narrator's grandfather fought—America's "good war" that had both a purpose and an outcome that was desired. The reference to World War II creates a striking contrast, making the war in Iraq look even less planned, less purposeful, and less justifiable. Finally, just like *Redeployment* and *Kaboom*, *The Yellow Birds* underlines the fact that the presence of U.S. soldiers in Iraq only provokes hatred in the locals and that the war will never end: the next generation of Iraqis will grow up despising the U.S. and will want to take revenge for the invasion and occupation.

Not only the soldiers but also some civilians consider the intervention to be an action that the country should not feel proud of; importantly, however, they adopt this view not because they question the war's aims or actions taken by the military but because they realize that the U.S. Army inevitably incurs losses. "I just hate that y'all have to be over there" (106), says a bartender to Bartle, referring to the fact that American soldiers have to experience savagery that could have been avoided had the country not intervened. Yet the role of the soldiers is by no means belittled when they return home. The country accepts them as "American hero[es]" (107). And although the novel obviously questions this acceptance, describing the criminal actions of the protagonist in Iraq, it is impossible to completely refute the perception of soldiers and war veterans as heroes because there is a clear sense of compassion shown to them in *The Yellow Birds*, which also respects that their actions can help solve conflicts overseas. Nevertheless, along with this compassion, there is censure of the interventionist U.S. policy, because the country has a rich history of sending "all these boys with guns out roaming the plains of almost every country in the world" (186). Eventually, too, there is the problem of "accountab[ility]" (186) for those decisions and resulting actions.

The turning point in the novel is the murder of Murph. While his death is partially explained by his temporary insanity (caused by war and the atrocities)—he walked through the streets naked and was eventually killed—the further actions committed by Bartle and Sergeant Sterling with Murph's body raise crucial questions of ethics in war. The two men dispose of Murph's body so that nobody, including Murph's mother (Bartle had promised to bring her son back home safe), would see that Murph was tortured and mutilated. This incident, important to the plot, opens pivotal perspectives on U.S. intervention. First, it undermines the intervention because such actions—and, generally, war—provoke such murders, including now the killing of Murph, "who had died and been butchered in the service of his country in an unknown corner of the world" (206). Second, it claims that the further actions taken by the two soldiers are partly caused and dictated by the unavoidable reality of war, which turns good American guys into soulless, heartless, and brutal criminals. It is no surprise, then, that the novel focuses on Bartle's life before, during, and after the war to fully demonstrate the radical changes he endures because of his military service.

But the novel by no means censures every single action taken by American soldiers in Iraq. Indeed it demonstrates that certain operations were fulfilled and some positive results—sought by the U.S. government, together with the U.S. military—were achieved. For example, the narrator describes the accomplishment of one of the missions: "Our platoon had done well [in the fight] in the orchard, minimized civilian casualties, killed a lot of hajjis and suffered only a few casualties of our own" (151). Such episodes serve an important role, demonstrating that even such a complex and controversial intervention had advantages and brought positive results. Another hint that somewhat justifies the intervention is given by an American soldier: "Sarge, it's a hundred and twenty degrees. Why don't we surrender and go home" (154). The verb "surrender" shrewdly underlines the fact that the salient point is not that the United States attacked Iraq, but rather that terrorists from the Middle East attacked the U.S. first and, therefore, the intervention became a response to this attack, which openly characterizes the United States not as a hostile intruder but as a victim, the aggrieved party.

The image of the United States, along with the nation's reaction to the intervention, occupy an important place in the novel. The country is described as "the land of the free, of reality television, outlet malls and deep vein thrombosis" (101). Such a characterization obviously serves to reveal the contrast between the democratic United States and its opposite: oppressed Iraq. Additionally, when the narrator returns home, his mother hugs him so that he "fe[els] as if [he]'d somehow been returned to the singular safety of the womb, untouched and untouchable to the world outside her arms around [his] slouching neck" (109). This description of being secure and feeling protected can also refer to Bartle's *mother country*, the United States, which, as soon as he is back, guarantees him an ordinary, safe life (in contrast to the chaos and danger of Iraq). Bartle also remembers the history of his country—the discovery and settlement of what would later became one of the leading world powers—when he imagines his mother's house "close enough to the ocean that those early English settlers took it as the farthest point they'd go upstream, the geology of the place preventing them from having any choice other than the one wherein they said, 'We are lost; therefore we will call this home'" (133). The phrase, however, is ambiguous and can be interpreted as the protagonist's dissatisfaction with his homeland, which was founded merely because the migrants were "lost." This is an interesting shift in Bartle's consciousness that takes place after his service in Iraq and, more important, after his failure at being a good man and soldier, which happened when he agreed to help Sterling dispose of Murph's body. More than that, Bartle's sarcastic tone toward the U.S. persists as he thinks about Murph's death. He underlines that Murph's mother will only receive "the thanks of a grateful nation," whereas the guy will "be buried and forgotten by all but her" (207). The mother's experience to find out the truth about the murder of her son adds a substantial portion of censure: "The army had given up on her eventually, her fight for truth and justice, to know how it was he'd gone from MIA to dead so quickly, why the explanations never fit. But they knew that if they waited long enough people would forget about her pain. . . . Everyone stopped listening to her. . . . America forgot her little story, moving as it does so quickly on to other agonies. . . . Even her friends began to smile at her with condescension, saying, 'LaDonna, you just gotta find *your* truth in all of this'" (221–22; italics in original).

The other perspective from which the novel examines the issue of intervention is that of choice. Specifically, the novel claims that for some participants, particularly for soldiers, the intervention is an obligation: there is never any "alternative" (24); one must continue an operation, start a new mission, struggle to survive, and so on. The soldiers have to face death every day; therefore the loss of a comrade is unexceptional. For example, Sterling tells a story about a dying soldier and comments,

"Bart, you're just gonna make it into something bigger than it was" (120). Trapped within war, soldiers are left to enjoy the moments when they remain alive, while their comrades die: "I was really happy it wasn't me. That's crazy, right?" (121); "And I too, though sad now, had said to myself, Thank God he died and I did not. Thank you, God" (122). The novel provides an interesting explanation for why there is such cynicism among soldiers: "Grief is a practical mechanism, and we only grieved those we knew. All others who died in Al Tafar were part of the landscape, as if something had sown seeds in that city that made bodies rise from the earth, in the dirt or up through the pavement like flowers after a frost, dried and withering under a cold, bright sun" (124).

Finally, the novel meditates upon the issue of intervention through the prism of faith, showing the intrusion to be ultimately approved by God. The problem is first raised before the soldiers are deployed to Iraq: "Our families watched as we stood in formation while the battalion commander gave a rousing, earnest speech about duty, and the chaplain injected humor into sober tales of Our Lord and Savior Jesus Christ" (43). This passage reveals the important role that religion plays in the army, how skillfully it is used there, as some believe that the actions of American soldiers are sanctioned by God, so that the soldiers become God's ministers. The idea is largely developed in the scene when Bartle, going AWOL in Kaiserslautern, Germany, enters a church and meets a priest there. During their talk, the priest demonstrates his solidarity with the soldier; when Bartle introduces himself as "Private Bartle," the priest says, "I'm sort of a private, too, in a way" (57). What the priest means is that he is a soldier of God, but one can speculate that this comparison can also be interpreted in reverse, namely that Bartle too is a soldier of God. Indeed the scene underscores that the services of both the priest and the soldier are supreme and thus are guided by the supreme power. Every soldier in the U.S. military serves God in the performance of such a high-value mission. This interpretation, however, only makes sense from the viewpoint of the ideology of American exceptionalism.

Bartle's visit to the church is perhaps the only truly peaceful moment in the novel. With awe, he looks at the icons, at the majestic and sacred place, whose "entire history [of a thousand years] . . . [took only] three pages [to describe in a pamphlet]" (59). He realizes that people are interested only in the gist, the main events and crucial points, rather than the whole story. The scene somewhat parallels his service in Iraq, which virtually nobody will be interested in or remember. People will only know about the Iraq War as a historical event, the war that took the lives of a certain number of soldiers, the figure most probably rounded up or down. However, Bartle's personal experience in the Middle East will forever remain his personal war. "I realized, as I stood there in the church, that there was a sharp distinction between what was remembered, what was told, and what was true. And I didn't think I'd ever figure out which was which" (60). This is the fictitious side of history—history that is sometimes created on purpose, for specific gain, when some facts are neglected and others invented, so that the truth and the lie blend together, creating indistinguishable, wrongly proportioned, and generalized chaos that is absorbed into collective history.

Mainly dealing with the story of one soldier, his personal fears, failures, and disappointments in and after the war, the novel inevitably touches upon the broader issues of war and a specific one: intervention. The narrative explicitly articulates that Bartle's war experience is a turning point for him: it destroys him morally, ruining his life. The character himself describes his participation in the Iraq War as follows: "Everything happened. Everything fell" (148). The intervention is not so much a political phenomenon as a psychological barrier—something that no participant in war can overcome, staying safe and sound.

The Afghanistan War and the Iraq War were largely commented on in works of film and literature, which eventually amounted to a whole body of docu-fictional narratives. While some examples tend to present a particular side of the conflict, many focus on the problems that the wars caused for both sides, intervening and intervened. They highlight the issues of civilian casualties, military service in foreign lands, the domestic reintegration of war veterans, and many others. Yet one of the key issues that virtually all the analyzed examples raise—which directly influences one's understanding of U.S. interventions in Afghanistan and Iraq—is that of the enemy. Indeed historians and political science scholars have extensively commented on the problem of a not-easily-identified enemy that the U.S. went to fight in the Middle East. While terrorism was and still is a menace to world peace, terrorists as specific persons were not determined precisely. Thus, even as many U.S. soldiers joined the military for a humanitarian purpose, to fight terror, the concept of terrorism became rather abstract: an evil that did not have a face. This is one of the main concerns of all the films, series, novels, and short-story cycles that attempt to portray U.S. interventions in Afghanistan and Iraq. Foregrounding the lack of clarity about the enemy, all the analyzed examples tend to argue that the interventions, whose main goal of eradicating terrorism was eventually reworded into a claim to bring democracy to oppressed nations, turned out mostly to be a disaster, both for the U.S. soldiers involved in them and for the locals who endured largely unwanted occupations.

The humanitarian aim of the U.S. to help rid the world of terrorists as well as to create better living conditions for current and future generations of Afghans and Iraqis should not be neglected or underestimated. And, as demonstrated by all the docu-fictional accounts examined here, certain improvements were made in the war-affected regions. However, the means by which those improvements were brought to the countries characterize the interventions mainly as acts of violence and, frequently, injustice. Yet, to stress the point once again, this happened chiefly because the fight against terrorists was not like any other war that the U.S. had ever fought, since in the twenty-first century the enemy became simply unidentifiable. Thus the military interventions and the actions of U.S. soldiers in the Middle East were frequently based on suspicions rather than clear facts. Hence casualties among civilians became unavoidable in that type of war.

As chapters 4 and 5 demonstrate, docu-fictional narratives success-fully reflect the problems of the interventions in Afghanistan and Iraq and avoid reductive characterizations, neither justifying nor criticizing them exclusively. Instead they attempt to mirror the real-life concerns that emerged in relation to the two involvements, which are now among the most controversial military interventions ever undertaken in the history of the United States.

Conclusion

AFTERTHOUGHTS ON WAR DOCU-FICTIONS AND NEW TRENDS IN U.S. WAR NARRATIVES

The problem of combining history with fiction or fiction with history is complex. As this book has demonstrated, to adopt such a technique means that one provides no easy solution for the audience of such war narratives to differentiate between truth and falsehood, the reality of war and an individual's vision of it, or the fact and fiction that are incorporated into the text as braided strands. One should clearly understand that unless a film or a novel is documentary (although nothing can be *purely* documentary), it obviously pursues aims other than to merely narrate facts. Authors and directors create these stories to attract audiences, whereas publishers and production companies release these narratives to earn money. The pursuit of fame and the problem of material profits frequently force the creators of fictional war narratives to resort to stylistic and verbal tropes that enrich their texts, make them different from the others (or contrariwise, similar to those that are trending), and thus hopefully find an appreciative response from the audience. The resurrection of cultural myths and memories regarding wars has proven to be effective in film and literature. These might be the main reasons that push the authors to appeal to their imagination and inevitably choose to present an exciting fiction rather than dry facts or a less exciting story. One can assume that for some authors it is not the fame and material profit that motivates them but rather the ability to pour out their war experiences to the public—both to free themselves and to share these experiences with those who can only guess how it was. These are war veterans who can do that. They narrate their stories in a fictional mode, although frequently their work is based on true events or at least influenced by what the authors or directors saw and the emotions provoked by war. They choose fiction to shield the reader from the violence of war as well as to be able them-selves to narrate the brutality they saw yet now find difficult to verbalize.

One might argue that in choosing fiction over fact the author or director sacrifices historical reality, depriving the reader or viewer of an authentic narration. But is the author or director responsible for presenting reliable texts to the audience? Obviously not, and particu-larly not if he or she states explicitly that the story is fictional. Fiction is a solid genre on its own, and the fact that the narrative is *invented* by the creator by no means undermines the cinematic or literary value of such a text. It is also apparent that the audience seeks to attain not only truth, history, or reality through its engagement with various cultural artifacts; the imaginative aspect is something that the reader or viewer looks for and, in specific situations and for various reasons, prefers over factual, more reliable, documentary accounts.

The problem that this work has extensively engaged with is not whether fiction is less or more valuable as a mode than documentary but rather to what extent all fictional narratives are similar, that is, fictional to the same degree. Having largely dealt with war narratives that attempt to present the history of U.S. interventions after Vietnam, I have been arguing that stories of real wars that are generally classified as fiction are not purely fictional. Having discussed more than forty narratives about U.S. interventions, whether meticulously or only briefly, I can convincingly conclude that these narratives—and, in general, other narratives based on real wars—are indeed charged with truth.

Oscillating between fact and fiction, they present more than history. But they do not exist apart from war's reality. Their incursions into history are apparent, yet, while they do attempt to transmit a historic reality, they succeed only in *re-creating* one, employing an artistic approach. In doing so, these texts cannot be classified as history, yet they do contribute to one's *understanding* of history, largely by appealing to the *emotions*, connecting experiences that are incomprehensible (either due to their brutality or simply because viewers or readers have not lived through the war themselves) and plunging the public into an *artificially re-created* war to eventually help them grasp the sweep of war's *realities*.

Although this project has focused on relatively recent wars, I would like to go back to the ideas fostered almost a century ago by the French scholar Jean Norton Cru in his groundbreaking analysis of the testimonies of World War I. One of the main concepts Cru was interested in was witnessing. Specifically, he investigated the reliability of multiple media created during and shortly after World War I to understand the extent to which they presented the truth about the war. Do these stories tell the real history of World War I? How can one prove their accuracy? While largely studying documentary accounts, which Cru shrewdly dubs "combatants'" testimony,[1] he also examines war novels and considers their reliability. Cru takes a radical stance on novels about World War I, expressing skepticism toward the ability of war novels to present history and claiming that they "have disseminated more errors, confirmed more traditional legends than they have proclaimed truths" (43). I certainly agree with Cru's viewpoint in the sense that novels are not to be treated as *reliable historical documents* that present the truth about war. Cru's further speculation that particular novels are, in fact, reliable does not, however, help support his previous claim: "We must however take note of the documentary value of the novels of Bernier, Naegelen, Escholier and Werth. They are accurate, because the authors have renounced their liberty of invention, have faithfully recorded their campaigns with all the precise data as to time and place, and have introduced a fictitious element only where it does not concern the facts and the feelings of their fighting experience. They are autobiographical novels" (43). Cru accepts the possibility that a war novel can be reliable but only if its fiction is kept at an absolute minimum. For Cru, a war novel is a "false *genre*" (42; italics in original), yet he underlines the importance of war as a theme in such narratives, claiming that in them "war is not an accessory but the principal subject" (42). And it is exactly this idea that the current project has largely adopted, contending that while various texts deal with fighting in general, those that build their plots on the events of real wars are distinct, as their so-called fictional nature differs from that of other narratives. That is why they are no longer just fictions but *docu-fictions*.

It is hard to state unequivocally whether a given narrative has a historical value when it clearly contains elements of fiction. But how does one measure this percentage of historical value? And, borrowing from Cru, "would it not be necessary to have served with the troops to be able to discover what is true and what is false in a soldier's account" (17)—and in a docu-fictional narrative as well? Even if a docu-fictional story is not a text of just history—as it obviously is not—does this mean that it has no value at all? Does it not provide an interpretation of war? Does it not help one understand war, whether in a biased or objective way? It is impossible to claim which of these narratives are more "helpful," which less. One might argue that if a docu-fictional story is created by a soldier or a war veteran, it is more reliable because it is the work of someone who was an eyewitness of certain military events. This is, however, inaccurate because those who serve in the military can, of course, choose to write fiction about war. Referring to Cru once again, it is worth mentioning his significant observation that "facts" (frequently imposed and composed by those who are high in the chain of command) are not always the real history: "If history, great history, deals with realities and not flights of fancy, it must take into account the troubles, the sufferings, the hatreds, the rages, the desires, the judgments, the war philosophy of the soldier; the part played, both mentally and physically, in the battle by the human machine and the instruments of warfare, not according to the chiefs but according to the man who was in this machine and handled these instruments" (14–15). This puts us, of course, on slippery ground again because the real emotions of a real soldier during real combat differ from those described in a docu-fictional account. Yet the proximity that a docu-fictional narrative tries to achieve is key in the attempt to demonstrate "how it was." Cru might have been too pessimistic, but, although limiting himself to World War I narratives, he turns out to have been sharply prophetic with regard to recent war stories, when he notes, "The criticism of war books has . . . been the work of literary critics who knew no more about war than everybody knows" (52).

Docu-fictions are unique sources that present a somewhat transformed sense of historical events that, despite the changes made to the events depicted, nonetheless contribute to the creation of a collective understanding of war. While telling their readers or viewers about the brutality, severity, and injustice of war in general, they also disclose the nature of the individual wars that are their particular subjects. The bulk of the novels and films analyzed in this work have been devoted to the examination of the post–Vietnam War period and to the investigation of a change in U.S. interventionism after the controversial involvement in Vietnam. Starting with the First Gulf War, moving to the Balkan War, and then to the recent interventions in the Middle East, this book has aimed to demonstrate a shift in the nature of U.S. interventionism. It is apparent that, after the experience in Vietnam, the U.S. was not willing to open itself to international criticism directed toward its military policies, nor was it ready to sacrifice any more American lives through military deployment. The main reason for military involvement that the U.S. has considered since 1990 has been humanitarianism—this is the issue that works, addressing these conflicts in both literature and film, have attempted, either explicitly or implicitly, to reveal.

The large body of docu-fictional narratives I have discussed shows that the cultural representation of U.S. interventions carried out since

1990 is not easy to deal with. Whatever the initial humanitarian aim of the interventions—whether to conquer tyranny, help the oppressed, stop genocide, or free the world from terrorism—the texts underline its equivocal nature, frequently foregrounding the economic or imperialist reasons behind U.S. deployment of troops to the areas that were (or would soon become) war zones. Yet under the crust of criticism, there is always reference to the initial goals and ultimate aims that the U.S. has been fighting for, and these are explicitly humanitarian. Attempting to display history in the docu-fictional mode they have adopted, these narratives turn the political atmosphere that surrounded these wars into stories, merging politics with cultural analysis to offer their audience a symbiosis of history, politics, and cultural interpretation. That aim is certainly a priority.

The salient questions in the overall analysis of the problem of U.S. interventionism in film and literature are these: What do these texts tell their audience, and what is their cultural contribution to war studies in general and studies of American culture in particular? These accounts undoubtedly mark a new epoch of U.S. interventionism, evincing a change in politics and in the nature of wars as they have been carried out in recent years. They overtly present the transformation of war as a cultural phenomenon whose changes have manifested in several trajectories, including time, geographical space, and the (recently booming) progress of technology. Yet these accounts not only provide a geography of recent U.S. interventions, marking the countries where the U.S. has carried out military actions, and not only tell their audience when and how those wars were conducted; most significant, they display the change in the attitudes of the soldiers who fought the wars, and they reveal the historical and political transformation that the United States has been undergoing, stressing the significance of the new period of U.S. interventionism that started with the country's involvement in the First Gulf War. The emancipation of these texts from the presiding norms that marks the body of work on wars that took place before 1990 is both striking and a sign of a gradual process. On the one hand, no work of film or literature of that period makes the claim that war as the apotheosis of man-made catastrophe has vanished. Every narrative focuses on the disastrous side of war, which exhibits itself in human losses, infrastructural disruption, and the moral degradation of those who, voluntarily or not, find themselves involved in armed conflict. These narratives continue the tradition of their predecessors, examining the rupture that every war forces on people, territories, and its time. Yet the examined docu-fictions combine this rupture with the representation of distinguishing qualities that have served to construct the period since 1990 as a new, distinct epoch of U.S. interventionism. Attempting to reflect the advantages of the interventions, these narratives do not seek only to justify the involvements; they unflinchingly mark this new period of U.S. interventionism as a time of humanitarianism, thus displaying as well as creating and generating a cultural change in the representation of U.S. interventions.

While these narratives culturally construct and define recent U.S. interventions, providing their own interpretations, they also have set the tone for newly emerging texts that continue to construe not only the recent American involvements but also the country's participation in other wars. It is apparent that while all four wars that this project draws on have been equally important in the creation of a new image of U.S. interventionism, the Afghanistan War and the Iraq War are freshest in the memory of the domestic and international public. Therefore the current cultural narratives of war are largely focused on the stories of Afghanistan and Iraq. U.S. involvement in these two countries has attracted much criticism, especially because its initially declared humanitarian goal—to stop terrorism—has not been fulfilled. So it is unsurprising that the interventions are still characterized as failures. Cultural artifacts like films and literary texts, although prolific, are weak at convincing the world of the positive nature of the recent wars. But they do not really *have to* persuade the audience, since if they had done so their documentary element would have turned into a biased form of speculation. What is important is that the idea of humanitarianism that was initiated and speedily developed with the narratives on the four wars stimulated the justification, purification, and promulgation of U.S. interventionism. In this connection, the return to the American participation in World War II—America's Good War—that has energetically been promoted in recent war films is particularly interesting. It is obvious that the recent involvements in the Middle East make up too shaky a ground on which to continue to build the humanitarian image of the U.S. at war. The solid image of the country's participation in World War II, which reflects a wide consensus about the conflict, is, on the contrary, the most effective way to reinforce the idea of U.S. interventionism as a mode of action initiated by good intentions, which the nation then fulfills through its military power and the competence of its representatives. Some of the most prominent cinematic examples that illustrate this turn are David Ayer's *Fury* (2014), Angelina Jolie's *Unbroken* (2014), Mario Van Peebles's uss *Indianapolis: Men of Courage* (2016), and Mel Gibson's *Hacksaw Ridge* (2016). These films tell the stories of brave American soldiers who fight, suffer, and die for freedom in Europe, the Pacific, and across the world, and their emergence in the twenty-first century is clearly purposeful. While by no means contributing to the collective forgetting of the wrong turns taken by the U.S. during its interventions in Afghanistan and Iraq, the films on World War II skillfully veil the negative side of the two wars that were largely supported and even boosted by various narratives, and keep promoting the humanitarian intentions of U.S. military involvements. The turn to World War II is therefore a dangerous move that might propagandize American military dominance and the country's eagerness to be involved in various conflicts simply because the U.S. can help win a war. Yet it is also an inevitable choice that sanitizes the image of the country after the public discontent with its actions in the Middle East. It is a form of moving on.

It is hard to predict how the military policy of the United States will develop in the future, especially after the election of President Trump and the changes to U.S. foreign policy that his presidency will bring. It is, however, apparent that works of film and literature will continue to shed light on U.S. war experiences, both current conflicts and those of the past. Creating new stories or resurrecting the old ones, both media will continue forming and transforming the cultural perspectives on U.S. interventionism, helping their audiences understand the reasons for U.S. involvement and the desire of the country (Trump's rhetoric notwithstanding) to remain the world's policeman, no matter how hard it tries to stay away from this task. The persistent reference to U.S. goals as humanitarian in these cultural narratives, however, leaves room for hope that future interventions will take place only when the initial and ultimate goals are exclusively humanitarian.

NOTES

INTRODUCTION

1. Along with the issue of truth, I will occasionally refer to the issue of reality in this introduction. While the issue of truth will be analyzed in greater detail in the following chapter, it is necessary to provide my understanding of reality now, since this work primarily employs such terms as "reality" and "fiction." Scholars interpret reality in multiple ways: as being "the real world," that is, everything that "exists" (Dawkins, *The Magic of Reality*, 13), as being "a canon of shared interpretation" (Vattimo, *Of Reality*, 87), and more. While not refuting these definitions, in this work I propose thinking of reality as a mode of existence that is distinctly valid and directly opposed to any imaginative or fictional form.

2. Haig, "Introduction," 7. Francesca Haig, for example, insists that in Holocaust studies the understanding of the difference between fiction and documentary is crucial (7).

3. Lee, "Defining the Genre."

4. Johnson, "Defining the Genre."

5. Walsh qtd. in Rodwell, *Whose History?*, 48.

6. Johnson, "Defining the Genre."

7. Rodwell, *Whose History?*, 54.

8. White, "The Burden of History," 27; italics in original.

9. White, "The Historical Text," 83; italics in original.

10. White, "Historical Emplotment," 39; White, "The Structure," 113; italics in original.
11. White, "Interpretation in History," 51.
12. White, "The Problem of Style," 170.
13. White, "Interpretation in History," 52.
14. White, *Metahistory*, 2.
15. White, "Interpretation in History," 52.
16. White, "Interpretation in History" 67.
17. Collingwood qtd. in White, "The Historical Text," 83.
18. White, "Historicism," 107.
19. White, "The Fictions," 121, 122.
20. Auerbach qtd. in White, "The Abiding Relevance," 50.
21. White, "The Fictions," 121–22.
22. Zelizer, "Every Once in a While," 27; italics in original.
23. Hirsch, *After Image*, 6–7.
24. Sobchack, "The Charge of the Real," 261, 284; italics in original.
25. White, "Historical Emplotment," 40.
26. White, "Historical Emplotment," 45.
27. LaCapra, "Representing the Holocaust," 112.
28. Lang, "Representations of Limits," 316; italics in original.
29. According to Deborah L. Madsen, exceptionalism "describes the perception of Massachusetts Bay colonists that as Puritans they were charged with a special spiritual and political destiny: to create in the New World a church and a society that would provide the model for all the nations of Europe as they struggled to reform themselves (a redeemer nation)" (*American Exceptionalism*, 1–2). The scholar continues, "Thus, America and Americans are special, exceptional, because they are charged with saving the world from itself and, at the same time, America and Americans must sustain a high level of spiritual, political and moral commitment to this exceptional destiny—America must be as 'a city upon a hill' exposed to the eyes of the world" (2).
30. Viotti, *American Foreign Policy*, 100.
31. Lowi et al., *American Government*, 449.
32. Fiske qtd. in May, *From Imperialism to Isolationism*, 12.
33. May, *From Imperialism to Isolationism*, 13.
34. Beveridge qtd. in May, *From Imperialism to Isolationism*, 15.
35. Trask, *The War with Spain*, 59; McKinley qtd. in Sewell, "Humanitarian Intervention," 303.
36. Viotti, *American Foreign Policy*, 77, 73.
37. May, *From Imperialism to Isolationism*, 27.

38. Beveridge qtd. in May, *From Imperialism to Isolationism*, 18.

39. Schurz qtd. in May, *From Imperialism to Isolationism*, 18.

40. U.S. Department of State, Office of the Historian, "American Isolationism."

41. Pease, *The New American Exceptionalism*, 162.

42. Pease, *The New American Exceptionalism*, 162, 165–66.

43. Hart, "Enlightened Engagement," 13.

44. Tillema, "The Meaning," 25, 27–28.

45. Simms and Trim, "Towards a History," 6.

46. Valentino, "The True Costs," 61.

47. Knott, "George H. W. Bush."

48. Pattison, *Humanitarian Intervention*, 2–3.

49. Simms and Trim, "Towards a History," 1, 4, 3.

50. Holzgrefe, "The Humanitarian Intervention Debate,"18.

51. Seybolt, *Humanitarian Military Intervention*, 7.

52. Hehir, *Humanitarian Intervention*, 12.

53. Chandler, *From Kosovo to Kabul*, 50; Seybolt, *Humanitarian Military Intervention*, 17; my italics.

54. Seybolt, *Humanitarian Military Intervention*, 17.

55. Lowi et al., *American Government*, 467.

56. Lowi et al., *American Government*, 470.

57. Bremmer, *Superpower*, 60.

58. LaRocca, "Introduction," 58.

59. LaRocca, "Introduction," 4.

60. LaRocca, "Introduction," 4; my italics.

61. LaRocca, "Introduction," 29.

62. Adhikari, "History and Story," 43.

63. Adhikari, "History and Story," 44.

64. For more on the influence of the military and the government on the production of films in the U.S. see Alford, *Reel Power*; Robb, *Operation Hollywood*.

1. CONCEPTUALIZING (WAR) DOCU-FICTIONS

1. Aristotle qtd. in Walker, "Spinoza," 4. Here and further in this chapter, for the reason that original sources (or their English translations) were not available, some of the quotes are borrowed from various other sources.

2. Plato qtd. in Lacey, *Image and Representation*, 230.

3. Augustine qtd. in Allen, *Truth in Philosophy*, 45.

4. Descartes qtd. in Lacey, *Image and Representation*, 230.

5. Walker, "Spinoza," 2.

6. Walker, "Spinoza," 4.

7. Spinoza qtd. in Walker, "Spinoza," 6.

8. Walker, "Spinoza," 5–6.

9. Spinoza, *On the Improvement*, n. p.

10. Walker, "Spinoza," 4.

11. Kant qtd. in Nesher, *On Truth*, 3–4.

12. Nesher, *On Truth*, 4; Kant qtd. in Nesher, *On Truth*, 4.

13. Nietzsche qtd. in Nola, "Nietzsche's Theory," 525, 526, 527, 547; italics in original.

14. Nietzsche qtd. in Nola, "Nietzsche's Theory," 549, 551.

15. Lacan, *Écrits*, 340, 341.

16. Lacan, *Écrits*, 212, 436, 739.

17. Lacan, *Écrits*, 7, 340.

18. Lewis, *Cultural Studies*, 340.

19. See Foucault, "Truth and Power."

20. Helsby, "Representation," 12.

21. Field, "Tarski's Theory," 370–71.

22. Foulkes, "Theories of Truth," 63.

23. Foulkes, "Theories of Truth," 71.

24. Lynch, "Realism," 9.

25. Allen, *Truth in Philosophy*, 61.

26. James, *Essays*.

27. Russell, "Truth and Falsehood," 17–18.

28. Ramsey, "The Nature of Truth," 433; italics in original.

29. Wittgenstein qtd. in Allen, *Truth in Philosophy*, 115.

30. Theodossopoulos, "Laying Claim," 339.

31. Hall, "The Work of Representation," 3, 4–5; italics in original.

32. Hall, "The Work of Representation," 10–11; italics in original.

33. Hall, "The Work of Representation," 27.

34. Helsby, "Representation," 2–3.

35. Helsby, "Representation," 3–4.

36. Foucault, "Truth and Power," 317.

37. Hall, "The Work of Representation," 31; italics in original.

38. Barthes, "Myth Today," 6, 7, 10, 16; my italics.

39. Baudrillard, *Simulacra and Simulation*, 1, 2.

40. Baudrillard, *Simulacra and Simulation*, 2, 3.

41. Baudrillard, *Simulacra and Simulation*, 6, 12–13, 19, 21; italics in original.

42. Trinh, "The Totalizing Quest," 90, 92; italics in original.

43. Helsby, "Representation," 6.

44. Trinh, "The Totalizing Quest," 94.

45. Sontag, *On Photography*, 4.

46. Derrida et al., "The Purveyor of Truth," 89.

47. Currie, "Unreliability Refigured," 19.

48. Platinga, "Moving Pictures," 310.

49. Ward, *Documentary*, 8.

50. Nichols qtd. in Godmilow and Shapiro, "How Real Is the Reality," 80.

51. Godmilow and Shapiro, "How Real Is the Reality," 80, 81.

52. Trinh, "The Totalizing Quest," 94; italics in original.

53. Jones, "Interpreting Reality," 22.

54. Chute, *Disaster Drawn*, 18.

55. Bonner, "Recording Reality," 62.

56. Grierson qtd. in Bonner, "Recording Reality," 62. John Grierson (1898–1972) was a Scottish film critic who founded the British documentary movement (Druick and Williams, introduction, 1). He proposed a theory of documentary film that, interestingly, "derived from an earlier theory of 'epic cinema,' which was primarily concerned with feature-length fiction films" (Aitken, *Film and Reform*, 59).

57. Winston, *Claiming the Real*, 11.

58. Bonner, "Recording Reality," 62, 64.

59. Godmilow and Shapiro, "How Real Is the Reality," 84.

60. Grierson qtd. in Trinh, "The Totalizing Quest," 96.

61. Macdonald and Cousins, *Imagining Reality*, 249–50.

62. Bonner, "Recording Reality," 75.

63. Ward, *Documentary*, 6, 8; italics in original.

64. Renov, "The Truth," 2, 3; italics in original.

65. Nichols qtd. in Ward, *Documentary*, 31.

66. Bonner, "Recording Reality," 75–76.

67. Bruzzi qtd. in Ward, *Documentary*, 10, 11.

68. Ward, *Documentary*, 24.

69. White, "The Value of Narrativity," 6–7, 9, 10; italics in original.

70. Nichols qtd. in Ward, *Documentary*, 31.

71. Trinh, "The Totalizing Quest," 90.

72. Kurowski qtd. in Ernst, "Distory," 400.

73. Trinh, "The Totalizing Quest," 96.

74. Trinh, "The Totalizing Quest," 96.

75. Georges Franju qtd. in Trinh, "The Totalizing Quest," 99.

76. Trinh, "The Totalizing Quest," 99.

77. Bruzzi, *New Documentary*, 121.

78. Henry James qtd. in Paris, "Form," 140.

79. Rosen, "Document and Documentary," 72).

80. Bruzzi, *New Documentary*, 122.

81. Wolper, "The Documentary," 285, 287.

82. Ferro, "The Fiction Film," 80.

83. John Searle qtd. in Bann, *The Inventions of History*, 65.

84. Ward, *Documentary*, 7.

85. Platinga, "I'll Believe It," 41.

86. Lacey, *Image and Representation*, 228.

87. Barthes, "Myth Today," 14.

88. Lacey, *Image and Representation*, 229.

89. Lacey, *Image and Representation*, 243.

90. Lacey, *Image and Representation*, 232.

91. Derrida et al., "The Purveyor of Truth," 32, 38–39, 46.

92. Lacan, *Écrits*, 7; Derrida et al., "The Purveyor of Truth," 46–47.

93. Derrida et al., "The Purveyor of Truth," 88.

94. Livingston, "Characterization," 154–55.

95. Lacan, *Écrits*, 340; my italics.

96. Livingston, "Characterization," 162.

97. Currie, "Unreliability Refigured," 20.

98. Livingston, "Characterization," 164.

99. While this work primarily focuses on fictional narratives that emerged during the past few decades and employs theories that were introduced in the twentieth and twenty-first centuries, it is apparent that fictional texts were written prior to that time too, and various scholars and writers attempted to interpret the nature of those writings. In the nineteenth century, Nathaniel Hawthorne and Marie-Henri Beyle (better known as Stendhal) discussed the peculiar nature of a novel, practically equating the novel to what is now commonly known as a documentary. Hawthorne, for example, proposes distinguishing between a romance and a novel. He writes that a romance, although it "sins unpardonably so far as it may swerve aside from the truth of the human heart," "has fairly a right to present that truth under circumstances . . . of the writer's own choosing or creating" (preface, 13). As for the readers of a romance, Hawthorne writes that they "may perhaps choose to assign an actual locality to the imaginary events of this narrative"; yet, the author, "if permitted by the historical connection," "would very willingly have avoided anything of this nature" (15). A novel, however, is "presumed to aim at a very minute fidelity, not merely to the possible, but to the probable and ordinary course of man's experience" (13). Thus Hawthorne draws a distinct line between a romance and a novel, claiming that, unlike a romance that reflects a writer's imagination, a novel is not

exactly a work of fiction as it presents everyday truth and cannot deviate from this canon. A somewhat similar understanding is provided by Stendhal, who, in his historical psychological novel *Le Rouge et le Noir* (*The Red and the Black*), published in 1830, claimed that "a novel is a mirror carried along a high road." For Stendhal, to write a novel is "to imitate nature as a mirror reflects what is before it" (Gershman and Whitworth, "Art," 188). In his prefaces to *Armance* (1827), *Lucien Leuwen* (1834), and *La Chartreuse de Parme* (*The Charterhouse of Parma*, 1839), Stendhal "acknowledges that he has held a mirror up to reality, not because he feels that this is the best way to achieve eternal glory, but because it seems to him the simplest way to write a novel" (Gershman and Whitworth, "Art," 189). He "rejects the temptation to utilize the novel for didactic purposes, preferring instead to remain an objective, accurate viewer of the real world about him" (189). And although there were other understandings of why to write a novel (consider, for example, Guy de Maupassant's interpretation: "The novel's function is not merely to be that of a mirror, passively registering everything that occurs; the artist must strive to present the illusion of truth" [Gershman and Whitworth, "Art," 192]), it is fascinating that already in the nineteenth century a novel was viewed by some as credible literature, whose aim was to tell its readers the truth that was not embellished by the imagination of the author. Despite the obvious fact that no novel has ever documented pure truth, the idea that a novel, that is, *fiction*, can contain *truth* clearly has a long history.

100. Brooke, *Jane Austen*, 9.
101. Ward, *Documentary*, 34.
102. Currie, "Film," 325, 326, 331.
103. Lipkin, Paget, and Roscoe, "Docudrama and Mock-Documentary," 13, 15, 18, 20.
104. Godmilow and Shapiro, "How Real Is the Reality," 85, 93.
105. Lipkin, Paget, and Roscoe, "Docudrama and Mock-Documentary," 23; italics in original.
106. Lipkin, Paget, and Roscoe, "Docudrama and Mock-Documentary," 23.
107. Ward, *Documentary*, 49.
108. Platinga, "I'll Believe It," 25.
109. Platinga, "Moving Pictures," 311.
110. Carroll, "Nonfiction Film," 287; italics in original.
111. Stoehr, *Words and Deeds*, 1, 2, 3.
112. Stoehr, *Words and Deeds*, 3.
113. Stoehr, *Words and Deeds*, 4–19.
114. Baudrillard, *Simulacra and Simulation*, 14.

115. Baudrillard, *Simulacra and Simulation*, 46. Baudrillard argues this in relation to film only. I expand his view to fiction in general, and literary and cinematic works in particular.
116. Trinh, "The Totalizing Quest," 99; Ward, *Documentary*, 7.
117. Barbara Webb qtd. in Williams, "Truth and Representation," 276.
118. White, "The Value of Narrativity," 8; italics in original.
119. Carroll, "Nonfiction Film," 288.
120. Ferro, "The Fiction Film," 80, 81.
121. Derrida and Prenowitz, "Archive Fever," 12; Orrells, "Derrida's Impression of *Gradiva*," 160.
122. Ferro, "The Fiction Film," 81; italics in original.
123. Lacey, *Image and Representation*, 269.
124. De Palma, *Redacted*, qtd. in Lacey, *Image and Representation*, 270.
125. Lacey, *Image and Representation*, 270.
126. Lacey, *Image and Representation*, 270; italics in original.

2. THE FIRST GULF WAR

1. Haass, *Intervention*, 31–35.
2. Hehir, "Strategy and Ethics," 119.
3. Gambone, *Small Wars*, 111.
4. Eckes and Zeiler, *Globalization*, 222.
5. Said, *Culture and Imperialism*, 292, 295. Such an interpretation and presentation of Arab culture influenced the strategies of the U.S. government and attitudes of U.S. citizens toward Arabs during the course of the First Gulf War and were manifested to the greatest degree in the twenty-first century during the War on Terror, which will be discussed in more detail later.
6. Said, *Culture and Imperialism*, 286, 290, 295.
7. Bush, "Address before a Joint Session," 74.
8. Bush, "Radio Address," 11.
9. Walker and Malici, *U.S. Presidents*, 66.
10. Jones, "America," 209–10.
11. Bacevich, *The New American Militarism*, 183.
12. Peterson, *American Foreign Policy*, 100.
13. Peterson, *American Foreign Policy*, 91.
14. Dodge, "US Foreign Policy," 233.
15. Thornton, "The US-Russian Struggle," 305.
16. Hehir, "Strategy and Ethics," 120; Gambone, *Small Wars*, 112.
17. McEvoy-Levy, *American Exceptionalism*, 77–78.
18. McEvoy-Levy, *American Exceptionalism*, 79.

19. McEvoy-Levy, *American Exceptionalism*, 81.

20. Bush, "Remarks at the Community Welcome," 280.

21. Brooks and Wohlforth, *World Out of Balance*, 186.

22. Kratochwil, "Leaving Sovereignty Behind?," 139–40.

23. Westwell, *War Cinema*, 85–86; my italics.

24. Ames, "Herzog," 49.

25. Murray and Heumann, "The First Eco-Disaster Film?," 50.

26. Herzog, "On the Absolute," 1.

27. Herzog, "On the Absolute," 2.

28. Bush, "Address before a Joint Session," 75.

29. Martinez, "The 1991 Iraq Invasion," 357.

30. Dickenson, *Hollywood's New Radicalism*, 199, 181.

31. Martinez, "The 1991 Iraq Invasion," 358.

32. Lacy, "War," 630.

33. Lacy, "War," 631.

34. Lacy, "War," 631.

35. Martinez, The 1991 Iraq Invasion," 358.

36. Baudrillard, *The Gulf War*, 64; LaRocca, "Introduction," 34; Harrison, *American Culture*, 102.

37. Harrison, *American Culture*, 102.

38. Horsley, *Dogville vs Hollywood*, 324; Lacy, "War," 631.

39. Martinez, "The 1991 Iraq Invasion," 349.

40. Mortensen, "The Camera at War," 53.

41. Westwell, *War Cinema*, 110.

42. Martinez, "The 1991 Iraq Invasion," 347, 349.

43. Martinez, "The 1991 Iraq Invasion," 355.

44. Martinez, "The 1991 Iraq Invasion," 351.

45. Martinez, "The 1991 Iraq Invasion," 355.

46. Martinez, "The 1991 Iraq Invasion," 356.

47. Martinez, "The 1991 Iraq Invasion," 356.

48. Martinez, "The 1991 Iraq Invasion," 357.

49. The role of the British military in the First Gulf War should not be underestimated because, to borrow from James W. Peterson, the U.S. government's "new multilateralism" presupposed having "the Royal Air Force (RAF) from the United Kingdom fly the first sorties in the war" (*American Foreign Policy*, 96).

50. Forsyth, *The Fist of God*, 63, 482, 281. Subsequent references are cited parenthetically in the text.

51. Hudson, *Dear Mr. President*, 4. Subsequent references are cited parenthetically in the text.

52. Arnold, "Reik's Theory," 759.

53. Having introduced President Bush as a character in his short-story cycle, the author changes the status of *Dear Mr. President* from a purely fictional narrative to a docu-fictional one. While it is apparent that none of the events described have ever happened to President Bush in real life, the presence of the character Bush legitimizes the endeavor of the author to tell about the real war in the genre of fiction and inevitably charges the narrative with truth.

54. Paine, *The Pearl of Kuwait*, 80, 299, 214. Subsequent references are cited parenthetically in the text.

3. THE BALKAN WAR

1. Haass, *Intervention*, 37–38.
2. Power, *"A Problem from Hell,"* 247–48, 249, 251, 283, 284.
3. Power, *"A Problem from Hell,"* 280; Holbrooke, *To End a War*, 42; italics in original.
4. Holbrooke, *To End a War*, 42.
5. Power, *"A Problem from Hell,"* 327.
6. Iordanova, *Cinema of Flames*, 50.
7. Haass, *Intervention*, 39.
8. Power, *"A Problem from Hell,"* 281.
9. Parish, *A Free City*, 4–5.
10. Power, *"A Problem from Hell,"* 327.
11. Allin, NATO's *Balkan Interventions*, 30.
12. Parish, *A Free City*, 5, 4–5.
13. Stokes, "Solving the Wars," 193.
14. Morris, "Humanitarian Intervention," 102.
15. Allin, NATO's *Balkan Interventions*, 32, 38.
16. Holbrooke qtd. in Allin, NATO's *Balkan Interventions*, 38.
17. Allin, NATO's *Balkan Interventions*, 38.
18. Bert, *American Military Intervention*, 106, 105, 117, 125.
19. Bert, *American Military Intervention*, 124, 112.
20. Morris, "Humanitarian Intervention," 100.
21. Bert, *American Military Intervention*, 115, 103.
22. Clinton qtd. in Power, *"A Problem from Hell,"* 374–75.
23. Power, *"A Problem from Hell,"* 285, 286.
24. Iordanova, *Cinema of Flames*, 46.
25. Weber, *Imagining America at War*, 59.
26. Weber, *Imagining America at War*, 59.
27. Weber, *Imagining America at War*, 63.

28. Bert, *American Military Intervention*, 115.

29. Roberts, *Humanitarian Action in War*, 79.

30. Haass, *Intervention*, 41.

31. Power, "*A Problem from Hell*," 274–75.

32. Corbin, "*No Man's Land*," 48.

33. Horton, "*No Man's Land*," 38.

34. Cavanaugh, *Into Hell's Fire*, 26. Subsequent references are cited parenthetically in the text.

35. Foley, *This Way to Heaven*, 88. Subsequent references are cited parenthetically in the text.

36. Kramer, "America's Lafayette," 230.

37. Bert, *American Military Intervention*, 103.

4. THE WAR ON TERROR: THE AFGHANISTAN WAR

1. Prince, *Firestorm*, 143; Merry, *Sands of Empire*, 195.

3. Carr, "Slouching towards Dystopia," 17.

3. Merry, *Sands of Empire*, 175.

4. Gambone, *Small Wars*, 229; Prince, *Firestorm*, 3.

5. Mendelsohn, *Combating Jihadism*, 189–90.

6. Bert, *American Military Intervention*, 130.

7. Gates qtd. in Bert, *American Military Intervention*, 131.

8. Kozol, *Distant Wars Visible*, 76.

9. Bert, *American Military Intervention*, 131.

10. Mendelsohn, *Combating Jihadism*, 188.

11. Mendelsohn, *Combating Jihadism*, 188.

12. Bert, *American Military Intervention*, 133.

13. Bert, *American Military Intervention*, 134.

14. Viotti, *American Foreign Policy*, 79.

15. Bert, *American Military Intervention*, 132–33.

16. Bert, *American Military Intervention*, 138; my italics.

17. Viotti, *American Foreign Policy*, 84.

18. Bert, *American Military Intervention*, 139.

19. Westcott, "Afghanistan."

20. Sarah Chayes qtd. in Bert, *American Military Intervention*, 147.

21. Bert, *American Military Intervention*, 147.

22. Altheide, *Media Edge*, 65, 64, 66.

23. Kozol, *Distant Wars Visible*, 69.

24. Viotti, *American Foreign Policy*, 92.

25. Burbank and Cooper, *Empires in World History*, 456.

26. Orford, "What Can We Do," 428.
27. Kozol, *Distant Wars Visible*, 70, 71.
28. Orford, "What Can We Do," 444.
29. Sklar, "*Charlie Wilson's War*," 48.
30. IMDb, "Synopsis for *Rambo III*."
31. Gooch, "Beyond Panopticism," 162.
32. Greenbaum, *The Tropes of War*, 37.
33. Luttrell qtd. in Blumenfeld, "The Sole Survivor."
34. Lee, "SWJ Film Review."
35. Luttrell qtd. in Blumenfeld, "The Sole Survivor."
36. Gwyn, *Wynne's War*, 53. Subsequent references are cited parenthetically in the text.
37. Although in this analysis only *Wynne's War* is considered a "cowboy story," the motif of westernization is entwined in practically all narratives on U.S. interventionism. *Wynne's War*—a story about good American soldiers and bad Afghan terrorists, with an evocative geographic location (mountains and deserts) and a strong focus on horses—is clearly the most illustrative example of a war western to be examined here. Narratives on U.S. involvements in the Middle East often vividly illustrate the dichotomy between "good guys" and "bad guys" through the lens of the western, with U.S. soldiers placed in a desert to fight evil. One such example—examined earlier in this project—is *Three Kings*, a film that, with its overt hints about America and globalization, presents an adventure story of U.S. soldiers who travel though the desert to hunt for gold (despite their ostensible purpose of being in Iraq). When analyzed deeply, the choice of portraying soldiers as cowboys does not necessarily create an image of U.S. soldiers who are purely a force for justice (they are, after all, intruders), but it helps the viewer to divide the characters into good and bad, thus clearly differentiating between Americans (whose mission is to fight the evil) and armed others (who pose a threat to American characters) or local terrorists (who are there to fight the good, kill the innocent, and spread hatred).
38. Creekmur, "The American Western Film," 397.
39. Creekmur 398; my italics.
40. Robert Warshow qtd. in Creekmur, "The American Western Film," 398.
41. Creekmur, "The American Western Film," 398.
42. Creekmur, "The American Western Film," 398.
43. Creekmur, "The American Western Film," 398. After Russell is back in the U.S., he finds Sara and tries to build a life with her. But the image of Russell's peaceful life switches to the description of riders who continue serving in Afghanistan. The author's decision to end with an image like that adds another

note of brutality to the novel, making it conventionally male-oriented. Yet this choice should not be considered a simple rejection of any "feminized" ending. Rather it unveils the complex problem of soldiers' addiction to war, which is to be dealt with in greater detail later in the analysis as well as in the section on the Iraq War, specifically in the examination of Kathryn Bigelow's film *The Hurt Locker*.

44. Creekmur, "The American Western Film," 399.
45. Däwes, *Ground Zero Fiction*, 86.
46. Goolsby, *I'd Walk with My Friends*, 56, 71, 183. Subsequent references are cited parenthetically in the text.
47. The passage is part of the speech delivered by Colin Powell to the United Nations on February 5, 2003, http://www.americanrhetoric.com/speeches /wariniraq/colinpowellunsecuritycouncil.htm.
48. This quote and others from Obama and McCain in this section are taken from their debate on September 26, 2008. See "Transcript of First Presidential Debate," CNN, updated October 14, 2008, http://edition.cnn.com/2008 /POLITICS/09/26/debate.mississippi.transcript/.

5. THE WAR ON TERROR: THE IRAQ WAR

1. Three generations of scholars have provided interpretations of anti-Americanism. The first defines it "in terms of actions or statements that involve sanctions or attacks against the policy, society, culture, and values of the United States." According to the second, anti-Americanism is "a prejudice, in which views toward the United States were seen as immutable, irrational, and even obsessive." The third generation construed anti-Americanism as "an *attitude*, based on how an individual identifies with the policies and values of the American people and US Government over time" (Datta, *Anti-Americanism*, 5; italics in original).
2. Bert, *American Military Intervention*, 162.
3. Richard Clarke qtd. in Bert, *American Military Intervention*, 163.
4. Paul Wolfowitz qtd. in Bert, *American Military Intervention*, 164.
5. Bâli, "Legality and Legitimacy," 301.
6. Mendelsohn, *Combating Jihadism*, 192–93.
7. Brooks and Wohlforth, *World Out of Balance*, 196.
8. Bush qtd. in Mendelsohn, *Combating Jihadism*, 192.
9. Bert, *American Military Intervention*, 171.
10. Bert, *American Military Intervention*, 172.
11. Bert, *American Military Intervention*, 168.
12. Bush qtd. in Bert, *American Military Intervention*, 166.

13. Bert, *American Military Intervention*, 166.

14. Brent Scowcroft qtd. in Bert, *American Military Intervention*, 159.

15. Bert, *American Military Intervention*, 180.

16. Ferguson, "The Gift of Freedom," 39–40.

17. Bert, *American Military Intervention*, 189.

18. Amy Zegat qtd. in Bert, *American Military Intervention*, 193.

19. Hehir, *Humanitarian Intervention*, 221.

20. Brooks and Wohlforth, *World Out of Balance*, 197.

21. Bellamy qtd. in Hehir, *Humanitarian Intervention*, 229.

22. Hehir, *Humanitarian Intervention*, 230.

23. Bert, *American Military Intervention*, 188.

24. *BBC News*, "Iraq Estimates," n.p.

25. Goodman, "4,486 American Soldiers," n.p.

26. McSweeney, *The "War on Terror*," 59; Zabel qtd. in McSweeney, *The "War on Terror*," 59.

27. McSweeney, *The "War on Terror*," 59.

28. A. O. Scott qtd. in Gooch, "Beyond Panopticism," 160.

29. Just as in the section on the Afghanistan War, here I examine documentaries to provide a broader overview of the existing cultural representations of U.S. intervention. Analyzing the goals of the military involvement, the role of U.S. soldiers, as well as the perspective of the locals—as these are portrayed in documentaries—I seek to demonstrate that fictional narratives present similar views on the war and thus help one understand the truths about the war. This ultimately turns them into docu-fictions.

30. LaRocca, "Introduction," 59.

31. Peebles, "Lenses into War," 140.

32. Benson-Allott, "Undoing Violence," 43.

33. Sklar, *"The Hurt Locker*," 56.

34. Naremore, "Films of the Year, 2009," 28.

35. Westwell, "In Country," 31.

36. Sklar, *"The Hurt Locker*," 56.

37. McSweeney, *The "War on Terror*," 69, 68, 69.

38. Sklar, *"The Hurt Locker*," 56.

39. Clover, "Allegory Bomb," 9.

40. As I argued in earlier chapters, the use of soldiers' video footages in a film serves to intensify the film's authenticity. This film-within-a-film technique is frequently applied to make the viewer believe that what is shown is true; that is, the soldiers are not fictional characters but are indeed witnesses of and participants in war, whose stories are therefore reliable. While the reliability

of dates, places, and events can be questioned in such docu-fictions, the contribution of these narratives to the construction of the cultural history of war remains valuable.

41. Gallagher, *Kaboom*, 372. Subsequent references are cited parenthetically in the text.

42. It is crucial that the novel deals with the events in Iraq in 2007–9, years after the first troops were brought to the country. This makes the frustration of the domestic (American) and international public with the intervention and its obscure goals understandable and hard to criticize.

43. Klay, *Redeployment*, 42–43; my italics. Subsequent references are cited parenthetically in the text.

44. Powers, *The Yellow Birds*, 125. Subsequent references are cited parenthetically in the text.

CONCLUSION

1. Cru, *War Books*, 6. Subsequent references are cited parenthetically in the text.

BIBLIOGRAPHY

Adhikari, Madhumalati. "History and Story: Unconventional History in Michael Ondaatje's *The English Patient* and James A. Michener's *Tales of the South Pacific.*" *History and Theory* 41 (2002): 43–55.

Aitken, Ian. *Film and Reform: John Grierson and the Documentary Film Movement.* London: Routledge, 1990.

Alford, Matthew. *Reel Power: Hollywood Cinema and American Supremacy.* London: Pluto Press, 2010.

Allen, Barry. *Truth in Philosophy.* Cambridge MA: Harvard University Press, 1993.

Allin, Dana H. *NATO's Balkan Interventions.* Adelphi Paper 347. Oxford: Oxford University Press, 2002.

Altheide, David. L. *Media Edge: Media Logic and Social Reality.* New York: Peter Lang, 2014.

Ames, Eric. "Herzog, Landscape, and Documentary." *Cinema Journal* 48, no. 2 (2009): 49–69. http://www.jstor.org/stable/20484448.

Antonijević, Predrag, dir. *Savior.* Santa Monica CA: Lionsgate, 1998.

Arnold, Kyle. "Reik's Theory of Psychoanalytic Listening." *Psychoanalytic Psychology* 23, no. 4 (2000): 754–65.

Ayer, David, dir. *Fury.* Culver City CA: Columbia Pictures, 2014.

Bacevich, Andrew J. *The New American Militarism: How Americans Are Seduced by War.* Updated edition. Oxford: Oxford University Press, 2013.

Bann, Stephen. *The Inventions of History: Essays on the Representation of the Past.* Manchester, UK: Manchester University Press, 1990.

Barthes, Roland. "Myth Today." In *Mythologies.* Translated by Annette Lavers. New York: Hill and Wang, 1984. http://www.turksheadreview.com/library/barthes -mythtoday.pdf.

Baudrillard, Jean. *The Gulf War Did Not Take Place.* Translated by Paul Patton. Bloomington: Indiana University Press, 1995.

———. *Simulacra and Simulation.* Translated by Sheila Faria Glaser. Ann Arbor: University of Michigan Press, 1999.

Bâli, Aslı Ü. "Legality and Legitimacy in the Global Order: The Changing Landscape of Nuclear Non-Proliferation." In *Legality and Legitimacy in Global Affairs,* edited by Richard Falk, Mark Juergensmeyer, and Vesselin Popovski, 291–362. Oxford: Oxford University Press, 2012.

BBC News. "Iraq Estimates War-Related Deaths at 461,000." October 16, 2013. http:// www.bbc.com/news/world-middle-east-24547256.

Benson-Allott, Caetlin. "Undoing Violence: Politics, Genre, and Duration in Kathryn Bigelow's Cinema." *Film Quarterly* 64, no. 2 (2010): 33–43. http://www.jstor .org/stable/10.1525/fq.2010.64.2.33.

Berg, Peter, dir. *Lone Survivor.* Universal City CA: Universal Pictures, 2013.

———, dir. *The Kingdom.* Universal City CA: Universal Pictures, 2007.

Bert, Wayne. *American Military Intervention in Unconventional War: From the Philippines to Iraq.* New York: Palgrave Macmillan, 2011.

Bigelow, Kathryn, dir. *The Hurt Locker.* Santa Monica CA: Summit Entertainment, 2008.

———, dir. *Zero Dark Thirty.* Culver City CA: Columbia Pictures, 2012.

Blumenfeld, Laura. "The Sole Survivor." *Washington Post.* June 11, 2007. http://www .washingtonpost.com/wp-dyn/content/article/2007/06/10/AR2007061001492 .html.

Bonner, Frances. "Recording Reality: Documentary Film and Television." In *Representation,* 2nd edition, edited by Stuart Hall, Jessica Evans, and Sean Nixon, 60–119. London: Sage, 2013.

Bremmer, Ian. *Superpower: Three Choices for America's Role in the World.* London: Portfolio Penguin, 2015.

Brooke, Christopher. *Jane Austen: Illusion and Reality.* Cambridge, UK: D. S. Brewer, 1999.

Brooks, Stephen G., and William C. Wohlforth. *World Out of Balance: International Relations and the Challenge of American Primacy.* Princeton NJ: Princeton University Press, 2008.

Bruzzi, Stella. *New Documentary.* 2nd edition. London: Routledge, 2006.

Burbank, Jane, and Frederick Cooper. *Empires in World History: Power and the Politics of Difference*. Princeton NJ: Princeton University Press, 2010. Print.

Bush, George H. W. "Address before a Joint Session of the Congress on the State of the Union." January 29, 1991. In *Public Papers of the Presidents of the United States*, 74–80. Washington DC: U.S. Government Publishing Office, 1991. https://www.gpo.gov/fdsys/pkg/PPP-1991-book1/pdf/PPP-1991-book1-doc-pg74.pdf.

———. "Radio Address to the Nation on the Persian Gulf Crisis." January 5, 1991. In *Public Papers of the Presidents of the United States*, 10–11. Washington DC: U.S. Government Publishing Office, 1991. https://www.gpo.gov/fdsys/pkg/PPP -1991-book1/pdf/PPP-1991-book1-doc-pg10.pdf.

———. "Remarks at the Community Welcome for Returning Troops in Sumter, South Carolina." March 17, 1991. In *Public Papers of the Presidents of the United States*, 279–81. Washington DC: U.S. Government Publishing Office, 1991. https://www.gpo.gov/fdsys/pkg/PPP-1991-book1/pdf/PPP-1991-book1 -doc-pg279.pdf.

Carr, Matt. "Slouching towards Dystopia: The New Military Futurism." *Race & Class* 51, no. 3 (2010): 13–32.

Carroll, Noël. "Nonfiction Film and Postmodernist Skepticism." In *Post-Theory: Reconstructing Film Studies*, edited by David Bordwell and Noël Carroll, 283–306. Madison: University of Wisconsin Press, 1996.

Cavanaugh, Douglas. *Into Hell's Fire*. Davenport IA: Kirostar, 2007.

Chandler, David. *From Kosovo to Kabul and Beyond: Human Rights and International Intervention*. 2nd edition. London: Pluto Press, 2006.

Chute, Hillary L. *Disaster Drawn: Visual Witness, Comics, and Documentary Form*. Cambridge MA: Belknap Press of Harvard University Press, 2016.

Clover, Joshua. "Allegory Bomb." *Film Quarterly* 63, no. 2 (2009): 8–9. http://www.jstor.org/stable/10.1525/fq.2009.63.2.8.

Coixet, Isabel, dir. *The Secret Life of Words*. Zurich: Monopole Pathé, 2005.

Corbin, Amy. "*No Man's Land (Nikogaršnja zemlja)*." *Film Quarterly* 60, no. 1 (2006): 46–50. http://www.jstor.org/stable/10.1525/fq.2006.60.1.46.

Creekmur, Corey K. "The American Western Film." In *A Companion to the Literature and Culture of the American West*, edited by Nicolas S. Witschi, 395–408. Malden MA: Wiley-Blackwell, 2011.

Cru, Jean Norton. *War Books: A Study in Historical Criticism*. Edited and translated by Stanley J. Pincetl Jr. and Ernest Marchand. San Diego CA: San Diego State University Press, 1976.

Currie, Gregory. "Film, Reality, and Illusion." In *Post-Theory: Reconstructing Film Studies*, edited by David Bordwell and Noël Carroll, 325–44. Madison: University of Wisconsin Press, 1996.

———. "Unreliability Refigured: Narrative in Literature and Film." *Journal of Aesthetics and Art Criticism* 53, no. 1 (1995): 19–29. http://www.jstor.org/stable /431733.

Datta, Monti Narayan. *Anti-Americanism and the Rise of World Opinion: Consequences for the US National Interest*. New York: Cambridge University Press, 2014.

Däwes, Birgit. *Ground Zero Fiction: History, Memory, and Representation in the American 9/11 Novel*. Heidelberg: Winter, 2011.

Dawkins, Richard. *The Magic of Reality: How We Know What's Really True*. New York: Free Press, 2011.

De Palma, Brian, dir. *Redacted*. Dallas TX: Magnolia Pictures, 2007.

Dennis, Danfung, dir. *Hell and Back Again*. New York: New Video, 2011.

Derrida, Jacques, Willis Domingo, James Hulbert, Moshe Ron, and M.-R. L. "The Purveyor of Truth." In "Graphesis: Perspectives in Literature and Philosophy." Special issue, *Yale French Studies* 52 (1975): 31–113. http://www.jstor .org/stable/2929747.

Derrida, Jacques, and Eric Prenowitz. "Archive Fever: A Freudian Impression." *Diacritics* 25, no. 2 (1995): 9–63. http://www.jstor.org/stable/465144.

Dickenson, Ben. *Hollywood's New Radicalism: War, Globalisation and the Movies from Reagan to George W. Bush*. London: I. B. Tauris, 2006.

Dodge, Toby. "US Foreign Policy in the Middle East." In *US Foreign Policy*, edited by Michael Cox and Doug Stokes, 213–35. Oxford: Oxford University Press, 2008.

Druick, Zoë, and Deane Williams. Introduction to *The Grierson Effect: Tracing Documentary's International Movement*, edited by Zoë Druick and Deane Williams, 1–11. London: Palgrave Macmillan, 2014.

Eckes, Alfred E., Jr., and Thomas W. Zeiler. *Globalization and the American Century*. New York: Cambridge University Press, 2003.

Eastwood, Clint, dir. *American Sniper*. Burbank CA: Warner Bros., 2014.

Ernst, Wolfgang. "Distory: Cinema and Historical Discourse." In "Historians and Movies: The State of the Art: Part 1." Special issue, *Journal of Contemporary History* 18, no. 3 (1983): 397–409. http://www.jstor.org/stable/260544.

Ferguson, Kennan. "The Gift of Freedom." In "The Ends of War." Special issue, *Social Text* 91 25, no. 2 (2007): 39–52.

Ferro, Marc. "The Fiction Film and Historical Analysis." In *The Historian and Film*, edited by Paul Smith, 80–94. Cambridge, UK: Cambridge University Press, 1976.

Field, Hartry. "Tarski's Theory of Truth." *Journal of Philosophy* 69, no. 13 (1972): 347–75. http://www.jstor.org/stable/2024879.

Foley, Tom. *This Way to Heaven*. New York: Forge, 2000.

Forsyth, Frederick. *The Fist of God*. New York: Bantam Books, 1994.

Foucault, Michel. "Truth and Power." In *The Nature of Truth: Classic and Contemporary Perspectives*, edited by Michael P. Lynch, 317–30. Cambridge: Massachusetts Institute of Technology Press, 2001.

Foulkes, Paul. "Theories of Truth." *Proceedings of the Aristotelian Society*, "New Series" 77 (1976–77): 63–72. http://www.jstor.org/stable/4544899.

Gallagher, Matt. *Kaboom: Embracing the Suck in a Savage Little War*. London: Gorgi Books, 2011.

Gambone, Michael D. *Small Wars: Low-Intensity Threats and the American Response since Vietnam*. Knoxville: University of Tennessee Press, 2012.

Gershman, Herbert S., and Kernan B. Whitworth. "Art, Truth, Morality and the Nineteenth-Century French Novel." *Modern Language Journal* 43, no. 4 (1959): 188–93. http://www.jstor.org/stable/320456.

Gibson, Mel, dir. *Hacksaw Ridge*. Santa Monica CA: Summit Entertainment, 2017.

Glatter, Lesli Linka, et al., dirs. *Homeland*. Los Angeles: 20th Century Television, 2011–.

Godmilow, Jill, and Ann-Louise Shapiro. "How Real Is the Reality in Documentary Film." In "Producing the Past: Making Histories inside and outside the Academy." Special issue, *History and Theory* 36, no. 4 (1997): 80–101. http://www.jstor.org/stable/2505576.

Gooch, Joshua. "Beyond Panopticism: The Biopolitical Labor of Surveillance and War in Contemporary Film." In *The Philosophy of War Films*, edited by David LaRocca, 155–78. Lexington: University Press of Kentucky, 2014.

Goodman, H. A. "4,486 American Soldiers Have Died in Iraq. President Obama Is Continuing a Pointless and Deadly Quagmire." *Huffington Post*, November 17, 2014. http://www.huffingtonpost.com/h-a-goodman/4486-american-soldiers-ha_b_5834592.html.

Goolsby, Jesse. *I'd Walk with My Friends If I Could Find Them*. Boston: Houghton Mifflin Harcourt, 2015.

Greenbaum, Andrea. *The Tropes of War: Visual Hyperbole and Spectacular Culture*. New York: Palgrave Macmillan, 2015.

Gwyn, Aaron. *Wynne's War*. Boston: Mariner Books, 2014.

Haass, Richard N. *Intervention: The Use of American Military Force in the Post–Cold War World*. Washington DC: Brookings Institution Press, 1999.

Haggis, Paul, dir. *In the Valley of Elah*. Burbank CA: Warner Bros., 2007.

Haig, Francesca. "Introduction: Holocaust Representations since 1975." *Modernism/Modernity* 20, no. 1 (2013): 1–13. https://muse.jhu.edu/article/508638.

Hall, Stuart. "The Work of Representation." In *Representation*, 2nd edition, edited by Stuart Hall, Jessica Evans, and Sean Nixon, 1–59. London: Sage, 2013.

Harrison, Colin. *American Culture in the 1990s*. Edinburgh: Edinburgh University Press, 2010.

Hart, Gary. "Enlightened Engagement in American Foreign Policy." In *American and Soviet Intervention: Effects on World Stability*, edited by Karen A. Feste, 11–16. New York: Crane Russak, 1990.

Hawthorne, Nathaniel. Preface to *The House of the Seven Gables* (1851), 13–16. Boston: Riverside Press Cambridge, 1913.

Hehir, Aidan. *Humanitarian Intervention: An Introduction*. Basingstoke, UK: Palgrave Macmillan, 2010.

Hehir, J. Bryan. "Strategy and Ethics in World Politics." In *At the End of the American Century: America's Role in the Post–Cold War World*, edited by Robert L. Hutchings, 110–28. Washington DC: Woodrow Wilson Center Press, 1998.

Helsby, Wendy. "Representation and Theories." In *Understanding Representation*, edited by Wendy Helsby, 3–25. London: British Film Institute, 2005.

Herzog, Werner, dir. *Lessons of Darkness*. Munich: Werner Herzog Filmproduktion, 1992.

———. "On the Absolute, the Sublime, and Ecstatic Truth." Milano, Italy. Speech before screening *Lessons of Darkness*. Translated by Moira Weigel. *Arion*, 3rd series, 17, no. 3 (2010): 1–12. http://www.jstor.org/stable/40645998.

Hetherington, Tim, and Sebastian Junger, dirs. *Restrepo*. Washington DC: National Geographic Entertainment, 2010.

Hirsch, Joshua. *After Image: Film, Trauma, and the Holocaust*. Philadelphia: Temple University Press, 2004.

Holbrooke, Richard. *To End a War*. New York: Modern Library, 1999.

Holzgrefe, J. L. "The Humanitarian Intervention Debate." In *Humanitarian Intervention: Ethical, Legal, and Political Dilemmas*, edited by J. L. Holzgrefe and Robert O. Keohane, 15–53. Cambridge, UK: Cambridge University Press, 2003.

Horsley, Jake. *Dogville vs. Hollywood*. London: Marion Boyars, 2005.

Horton, Andrew. "*No Man's Land* by Marc Baschet; Danis Tanovic." *Cinéaste* 27, no. 2 (2002): 38–39. http://www.jstor.org/stable/41690133.

Hudson, Gabe. *Dear Mr. President*. New York: Vintage Books, 2003.

IMDb. Synopsis for *Rambo III* (1988). http://www.imdb.com/title/tt0095956/plotsummary#synopsis.

Iordanova, Dina. *Cinema of Flames: Balkan Film, Culture and the Media*. London: British Film Institute, 2001.

James, William. *Essays and Lectures*. New York: Routledge, 2007.

Johnson, Sarah. "Defining the Genre: What Are the Rules for Historical Fiction?" *Historical Novel Society*. Accessed April 30, 2017. https://historicalnovelsociety

.org/guides/defining-the-genre/defining-the-genre-what-are-the-rules-for
-historical-fiction/.

Jolie, Angelina, dir. *Unbroken*. Universal City CA: Universal Pictures, 2014.

Jones, Julie. "Interpreting Reality: *Los olvidados* and the Documentary Mode."
Journal of Film and Video 57, no. 4 (2005): 18–31. http://www.jstor.org/stable
/20688502.

Jones, Toby Craig. "America, Oil, and War in the Middle East." *Journal of American
History* 99, no. 1 (2012): 208–18. https://mereliberty.com/wp-content/uploads
/2015/11/Journal-of-American-History-2012-Jones-208-18.pdf.

Klay, Phil. *Redeployment*. New York: Penguin Books, 2014.

Knott, Stephen. "George H. W. Bush: Foreign Affairs." *U.S. Presidents: George H. W.
Bush*. Miller Center, University of Virginia. Accessed April 30, 2017. https://
millercenter.org/president/bush/foreign-affairs.

Kondracki, Larysa, dir. *The Whistleblower*. Culver City CA: Samuel Goldwyn, 2010.

Kozol, Wendy. *Distant Wars Visible: The Ambivalence of Witnessing*. Minneapolis:
University of Minnesota Press, 2014.

Kramer, Lloyd S. "America's Lafayette and Lafayette's America: A European and
the American Revolution." *William and Mary Quarterly* 38, no. 2 (1981): 228–
41. http://www.jstor.org/stable/1918776.

Kratochwil, Friedrich. "Leaving Sovereignty Behind? An Inquiry into the Politics
of Post-modernity." In *Legality and Legitimacy in Global Affairs*, edited by
Richard Falk, Mark Juergensmeyer, and Vesselin Popovski, 127–48. Oxford:
Oxford University Press, 2012.

Lacan, Jacques. *Écrits*. Translated by Bruce Fink. New York: Norton, 2006.

LaCapra, Dominick. "Representing the Holocaust: Reflections on the Historian's
Debate." In *Probing the Limits of Representation: Nazism and the "Final Solu-
tion,"* edited by Saul Friedlander, 108–27. Cambridge MA: Harvard University
Press, 1992.

Lacey, Nick. *Image and Representation: Key Concepts in Media Studies*. 2nd edition.
Basingstoke, UK: Palgrave Macmillan, 2009.

Lacy, Mark J. "War, Cinema, and Moral Anxiety." *Alternatives: Global, Local, Political* 28, no. 5 (2003): 611–36. http://journals.sagepub.com/doi/pdf/10.1177
/030437540302800504.

Lang, Berel. "Representations of Limits." In *Probing the Limits of Representation:
Nazism and the "Final Solution,"* edited by Saul Friedlander, 300–317. Cambridge MA: Harvard University Press, 1992.

LaRocca, David. "Introduction: War Films and the Ineffability of War." In *The Philosophy of War Films*, edited by David LaRocca, 1–77. Lexington: University
Press of Kentucky, 2014.

Leder, Mimi, dir. *The Peacemaker*. Universal City CA: DreamWorks Pictures, 1997.

Lee, Jeong. "SWJ Film Review: *Lone Survivor*." *Small Wars Journal*, January 6, 2014. http://smallwarsjournal.com/jrnl/art/swj-film-review-lone-survivor.

Lee, Richard. "Defining the Genre." *Historical Novel Society*. Accessed April 30, 2017. https://historicalnovelsociety.org/guides/defining-the-genre/.

Levinson, Barry, dir. *Wag the Dog*. Burbank CA: New Line Cinema, 1997.

Lewis, Jeff. *Cultural Studies: The Basics*. 2nd edition. London: Sage, 2008.

Lipkin, Steven N., Derek Paget, and Jane Roscoe. "Docudrama and Mock-Documentary: Defining Terms, Proposing Canons." In *Docufictions: Essays on the Intersection of Documentary and Fictional Filmmaking*, edited by Gary D. Rhodes and John Parris Springer, 11–26. Jefferson NC: McFarland, 2006.

Livingston, Paisley. "Characterization and Fictional Truth in the Cinema." In *Post-Theory: Reconstructing Film Studies*, edited by David Bordwell and Noël Carroll, 149–74. Madison: University of Wisconsin Press, 1996.

Longley, James, dir. *Iraq in Fragments*. New York: HBO Documentary Films, 2006.

Lowi, Theodore J., Benjamin Ginsberg, Kenneth A. Shepsle, and Stephen Ansolabehere. *American Government: Power and Purpose*. Brief 12th edition. New York: Norton, 2012.

Lynch, Michael P. "Realism and the Correspondence Theory: Introduction." In *The Nature of Truth: Classic and Contemporary Perspectives*, edited by Michael P. Lynch, 9–15. Cambridge MA: MIT Press, 2001.

Macdonald, Kevin, and Mark Cousins. *Imagining Reality: The Faber Book of the Documentary*. London: Faber and Faber, 1996.

MacDonald, Peter, dir. *Rambo III*. Culver City CA: TriStar Pictures, 1988.

Madsen, Deborah L. *American Exceptionalism*. Jackson: University Press of Mississippi, 1998.

Malagurski, Boris, dir. *The Weight of Chains*. New York: Journeyman Pictures, 2010.

Markle, Peter, dir. *Saving Jessica Lynch*. 2003. NBC.

Martinez, Elizabeth E. "The 1991 Iraq Invasion in Cinematic Perspective: *Jarhead* and *Three Kings*." In *Cinematic Sociology: Social Life in Film*, edited by Jean-Anne Sutherland and Kathryn Feltey, 347–61. 2nd edition. Los Angeles: Sage, 2013.

May, Earnest R. *From Imperialism to Isolationism, 1898–1919*. New York: Macmillan, 1964.

McEvoy-Levy, Siobhán. *American Exceptionalism and US Foreign Policy: Public Diplomacy at the End of the Cold War*. Basingstoke, UK: Palgrave, 2001.

McSweeney, Terence. *The "War on Terror" and American Film: 9/11 Frames per Second*. Edinburgh: Edinburgh University Press, 2014.

Mendelsohn, Barak. *Combating Jihadism: American Hegemony and Interstate Cooperation in the War on Terrorism*. Chicago: University of Chicago Press, 2009.

Mendes, Sam, dir. *Jarhead*. Universal City CA: Universal Pictures, 2005.

Merry, Robert W. *Sands of Empire: Missionary Zeal, American Foreign Policy, and the Hazards of Global Ambition*. New York: Simon & Schuster, 2005.

Moore, John, dir. *Behind Enemy Lines*. Los Angeles: 20th Century Fox, 2001.

Moran, Luke, dir. *Boys of Abu Ghraib*. Santa Monica CA: Vertical Entertainment, 2014.

Morris, Nicholas. "Humanitarian Intervention in the Balkans." In *Humanitarian Intervention and International Relations*, edited by Jennifer M. Welsh, 98–119. Oxford: Oxford University Press, 2004.

Mortensen, Mette. "The Camera at War: When Soldiers Become War Photographers." In *War Isn't Hell, It's Entertainment: Essays on Visual Media and the Representation of Conflict*, edited by Rikke Schubart, Fabian Virchow, Debra White-Stanley, and Tanja Thomas, 44–60. Jefferson NC: McFarland, 2009.

Murray, Robin L., and Joseph K. Heumann. "The First Eco-Disaster Film?" *Film Quarterly* 59, no. 3 (2006): 44–51. http://www.jstor.org/stable/10.1525/fq.2006.59.3.44.

Naremore, James. "Films of the Year, 2009." *Film Quarterly* 63, no. 4 (2010): 18–32. http://www.jstor.org/stable/10.1525/fq.2010.63.4.18.

Nesher, Dan. *On Truth and the Representation of Reality: A Collection of Inquiries from a Pragmatist Point of View*. Lanham MD: University Press of America, 2002.

Nichols, Mike, dir. *Charlie Wilson's War*. Universal City CA: Universal Pictures, 2007.

Nola, Robert. "Nietzsche's Theory of Truth and Belief." *Philosophy and Phenomenological Research* 47, no. 4 (1987): 525–62. http://www.jstor.org/stable/2107228.

Orford, Anne. "What Can We Do to Stop People Harming Others?" In *Global Politics: A New Introduction*, edited by Jenny Edkins and Maja Zehfuss, 427–53. London: Routledge, 2009.

Orrells, Daniel. "Derrida's Impression of *Gradiva*: Archive Fever and Antiquity." In *Derrida and Antiquity*, edited by Miriam Leonard, 159–84. Oxford: Oxford University Press, 2010.

Paine, Tom. *The Pearl of Kuwait*. Orlando FL: Harcourt, 2003.

Paris, Bernard J. "Form, Theme, and Imitation in Realistic Fiction." *Novel: A Forum on Fiction* 1, no. 2 (1968): 140–49. http://www.jstor.org/stable/1345264.

Parish, Matthew. *A Free City in the Balkans: Reconstructing a Divided Society in Bosnia*. London: I. B. Tauris, 2010.

Pattison, James. *Humanitarian Intervention and the Responsibility to Protect: Who Should Intervene?* New York: Oxford University Press, 2010.

Pease, Donald E. *The New American Exceptionalism*. Minneapolis: University of Minnesota Press, 2009.

Peebles, Stacey. "Lenses into War: Digital Vérité in Iraq War Films." In *The Philosophy of War Films*, edited by David LaRocca, 133–54. Lexington: University Press of Kentucky, 2014.

Peirce, Kimberly, dir. *Stop-Loss*. Hollywood CA: Paramount Pictures, 2008.

Peterson, James W. *American Foreign Policy: Alliance Politics in a Century of War, 1914–2014*. London: Bloomsbury, 2014.

Platinga, Carl. "'I'll Believe It When I Trust the Source': Documentary Images and Visual Evidence." In *The Documentary Film Book*, edited by Brian Winston, 40–47. London: Palgrave Macmillan, 2013.

———. "Moving Pictures and the Rhetoric of Nonfiction: Two Approaches." In *Post-Theory: Reconstructing Film Studies*, edited by David Bordwell and Noël Carroll, 307–24. Madison: University of Wisconsin Press, 1996.

Power, Samantha. *"A Problem from Hell": America and the Age of Genocide*. New York: HarperCollins, 2002.

Powers, Kevin. *The Yellow Birds*. London: Sceptre, 2012.

Prince, Stephen. *Firestorm: American Film in the Age of Terrorism*. New York: Columbia University Press, 2009.

Ramsey, Frank Plumpton. "The Nature of Truth." In *The Nature of Truth: Classic and Contemporary Perspectives*, edited by Michael P. Lynch, 433–45. Cambridge MA: MIT Press, 2001.

Redford, Robert, dir. *Lions for Lambs*. Beverly Hills CA: Metro-Goldwyn-Mayer, 2007.

Renov, Michael. "The Truth about Non-Fiction." In *Theorizing Documentary*, edited by Michael Renov, 1–11. New York: Routledge, 1993.

Robb, David L. *Operation Hollywood: How the Pentagon Shapes and Censors the Movies*. Amherst NY: Prometheus Books, 2004.

Roberts, Adam. *Humanitarian Action in War: Aid, Protection and Impartiality in a Policy Vacuum*. New York: Oxford University Press, 1996.

Rodwell, Grant. *Whose History? Engaging History Students through Historical Fiction*. Adelaide: University of Adelaide Press, 2013.

Rosen, Philip. "Document and Documentary: On the Persistence of Historical Concepts." In *Theorizing Documentary*, edited by Michael Renov, 58–89. New York: Routledge, 1993.

Russell, Bertrand. "Truth and Falsehood." In *The Nature of Truth: Classic and Contemporary Perspectives*, edited by Michael P. Lynch, 17–24. Cambridge MA: MIT Press, 2001.

Russell, David O., dir. *Three Kings*. Burbank CA: Warner Bros. Pictures and Village Roadshow Pictures, 1999.

Said, Edward W. *Culture and Imperialism*. New York: Knopf, 1993.

Scott, Ridley, dir. *Body of Lies*. Burbank CA: Warner Bros., 2008.

Scranton, Deborah, dir. *The War Tapes*. 2006.

Sewell, Mike. "Humanitarian Intervention, Democracy, and Imperialism: The American War with Spain 1898, and After." In *Humanitarian Intervention:*

A History, edited by Brendan Simms and D. J. B. Trim, 303–22. Cambridge, UK: Cambridge University Press, 2011.

Seybolt, Taylor B. *Humanitarian Military Intervention: The Conditions for Success and Failure*. New York: Oxford University Press, 2007.

Sheridan, Jim, dir. *Brothers*. Santa Monica CA: Lionsgate and Relativity Media, 2009.

Simms, Brendan, and D. J. B. Trim. "Towards a History of Humanitarian Intervention." In *Humanitarian Intervention: A History*, edited by Brendan Simms and D. J. B. Trim, 1–24. New York: Cambridge University Press, 2011.

Sklar, Robert. "*Charlie Wilson's War* by Gary Goetzman; Tom Hanks; Mike Nichols; Aaron Sorkin." *Cinéaste* 33, no. 2 (2008): 48–49. http://www.jstor.org/stable /41690631.

———. "*The Hurt Locker* by Kathryn Bigelow; Mark Boal; Nicolas Chartier; Greg Shapiro." *Cinéaste* 35, no. 1 (2009): 55–56. http://www.jstor.org/stable/41690856.

Sobchack, Vivian. "The Charge of the Real: Embodied Knowledge and Cinematic Consciousness." In *Carnal Thoughts: Embodiment and Moving Image Culture*, 258–85. Berkeley: University of California Press, 2004.

Sontag, Susan. *On Photography*. 1973. New York: Rosetta Books, 2005. http://www .lab404.com/3741/readings/sontag.pdf.

Spinoza, Benedict de. *On the Improvement of Understanding*. Translated by R. H. M. Elwes. Adelaide: eBooks@Adelaide, University of Adelaide Library, last updated December 17, 2014. https://ebooks.adelaide.edu.au/s/spinoza/benedict /understanding/complete.html.

Stendhal. *The Red and the Black*. 1830. Translated by C. K. Scott Moncrieff. eBooks@ Adelaide, University of Adelaide Library. Last updated December 17, 2014, https://ebooks.adelaide.edu.au/s/stendhal/red/complete.html.

Stoehr, Taylor. *Words and Deeds: Essays on the Realistic Imagination*. New York: AMS Press, 1986.

Stokes, Gale. "Solving the Wars of Yugoslav Succession." In *Yugoslavia and Its Historians: Understanding the Balkan Wars of the 1990s*, edited by Norman M. Naimark and Holly Case, 193–207. Stanford CA: Stanford University Press, 2003.

Strouse, James C., dir. *Grace Is Gone*. New York: Weinstein Company, 2007.

Tanović, Danis, dir. *No Man's Land*. Asnières-sur-Seine, France: Océan Films, Rai Cinema, and United Artists, 2001.

Theodossopoulos, Dimitrios. "Laying Claim to Authenticity: Five Anthropological Dilemmas." *Anthropological Quarterly* 86, no. 2 (2013): 337–60. https://muse .jhu.edu/article/508135.

Thornton, Richard C. "The US-Russian Struggle for World Oil 1979–2010." In *Le Pétrole et la Guerre/Oil and War*, edited by Alain Beltran, 299–311. Brussels: Peter Lang, 2012.

Tillema, Herbert. "The Meaning and Restraint of Superpower Intervention." In *American and Soviet Intervention: Effects on World Stability*, edited by Karen A. Feste, 23–28. New York: Crane Russak, 1990.

Trask, David F. *The War with Spain in 1898*. New York: Macmillan, 1981.

Trinh T. Minh-ha. "The Totalizing Quest of Meaning." In *Theorizing Documentary*, edited by Michael Renov, 90–107. New York: Routledge, 1993.

U.S. Department of State, Office of the Historian. "American Isolationism in the 1930s." https://history.state.gov/milestones/1937-1945/american-isolationism.

Valentino, Benjamin A. "The True Costs of Humanitarian Intervention: The Hard Truth about a Noble Notion." *Foreign Affairs* 90, no. 6 (2011): 60–73.

Van Peebles, Mario, dir. *USS Indianapolis: Men of Courage*. Los Angeles: Saban Films, 2016.

Vattimo, Gianni. *Of Reality: The Purposes of Philosophy*. New York: Columbia University Press, 2012.

Viotti, Paul R. *American Foreign Policy*. Cambridge, UK: Polity, 2010.

Walker, Ralph S. "Spinoza and the Coherence Theory of Truth." *Mind*, new series, 94, no. 373 (1985): 1–18. http://www.jstor.org/stable/2254694.

Walker, Stephen G., and Akan Malici. *U.S. Presidents and Foreign Policy Mistakes*. Stanford CA: Stanford University Press, 2011.

Ward, Paul. *Documentary: The Margins of Reality*. London: Wallflower, 2005.

Weber, Cynthia. *Imagining America at War: Morality, Politics, and Film*. London: Routledge, 2006.

Westcott, Ben. "Afghanistan: 16 Years, Thousands Dead and No Clear End in Sight." CNN, November 1, 2017. https://edition.cnn.com/2017/08/21/asia/afghanistan-war-explainer/index.html.

Westwell, Guy. "In Country: Mapping the Iraq War in Recent Hollywood Combat Movies." In *Screens of Terror: Representations of War and Terrorism in Film and Television since 9/11*, edited by Philip Hammond, 19–35. Suffolk, UK: Abramis Academic, Arima, 2011.

——— . *War Cinema: Hollywood on the Front Line*. London: Wallflower, 2006.

White, Hayden. "The Abiding Relevance of Croce's Idea of History." In *The Fiction of Narrative: Essays on History, Literature, and Theory, 1957–2007*, edited by Robert Doran, 50–67. Baltimore: Johns Hopkins University Press, 2010.

——— . "The Burden of History." In *Tropics of Discourse: Essays in Cultural Criticism*, 27–50. Baltimore: Johns Hopkins University Press, 1978.

——— . "The Fictions of Factual Representation." In *Tropics of Discourse: Essays in Cultural Criticism*, 121–34. Baltimore: Johns Hopkins University Press, 1978.

————. "Historical Emplotment and the Problem of Truth." In *Probing the Limits of Representation: Nazism and the "Final Solution,"* edited by Saul Friedlander, 37–53. Cambridge MA: Harvard University Press, 1992.

————. "The Historical Text as Literary Artifact." In *Tropics of Discourse: Essays in Cultural Criticism*, 81–100. Baltimore: Johns Hopkins University Press, 1978.

————. "Historicism, History, and the Figurative Imagination." In *Tropics of Discourse: Essays in Cultural Criticism*, 101–20. Baltimore: Johns Hopkins University Press, 1978.

————. "Interpretation in History." In *Tropics of Discourse: Essays in Cultural Criticism*, 51–80. Baltimore: Johns Hopkins University Press, 1978.

————. *Metahistory: The Historical Imagination in Nineteenth-Century Europe.* Baltimore: Johns Hopkins University Press, 1973.

————. "The Problem of Style in Realistic Representation: Marx and Flaubert." In *The Fiction of Narrative: Essays on History, Literature, and Theory, 1957–2007,* edited by Robert Doran, 167–86. Baltimore: Johns Hopkins University Press, 2010.

————. "The Structure of Historical Narrative." In *The Fiction of Narrative: Essays on History, Literature, and Theory, 1957–2007,* edited by Robert Doran, 112–25. Baltimore: Johns Hopkins University Press, 2010.

————. "The Value of Narrativity in the Representation of Reality." In "On Narrative." Special issue, *Critical Inquiry* 7, no. 1 (1980): 5–27. http://www.jstor.org/stable/1343174.

White, Susanna, and Simon Cellan Jones, dirs. *Generation Kill.* 7 episodes. New York: HBO, 2008.

Williams, Ted. "Truth and Representation: The Confrontation of History and Mythology in 'Omeros.'" *Callaloo* 24, no. 1 (2001): 276–86. http://www.jstor.org/stable/3300500.

Winston, Brian. *Claiming the Real: The Griersonian Documentary and Its Legitimations.* London: British Film Institute, 1995.

Wolper, David L. "The Documentary: Entertain and Inform, Not Just Inform." In *The Search for "Reality": The Art of Documentary Filmmaking,* edited by Michael Tobias, 285–87. Ann Arbor MI: Braun-Brumfield, 1998.

Zelizer, Barbie. "Every Once in a While: *Schindler's List* and the Shaping of History." In *Spielberg's Holocaust: Critical Perspectives on* Schindler's List, edited by Yosefa Loshitzky, 18–39. Bloomington: Indiana University Press, 1997.

CPSIA information can be obtained
at www.ICGtesting.com
Printed in the USA
LVHW092045150319
610813LV00005B/144/P